D0463412

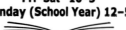
94

Bulbs for the
Rock Garden

Jack Elliott

Timber Press · Portland, Oregon

Acknowledgements

I am most indebted to Brian Mathew, whose books have been invaluable in my researches, and who has given me much-needed advice on the present status of *Chionodoxa*, and on some apparent incongruities in the naming of some irises; and to Geoffrey Charlesworth and Norman Singer, who have helped me to assess the the hardiness of bulbs in North America, by passing on their experiences with them in Zone 5 in Massachusetts.

First and foremost I am grateful to my wife Jean, who has always been encouraging during a lengthy period of 'computer-widowhood', and has very carefully proof-read the manuscript for non-botanical errors.

The cover photograph shows *Tulipa aucheriana*.

First published in North America in 1996 by Timber Press, Inc., The Haseltine Building, 133 S.W. Second Avenue, Suite 450, Portland, Oregon 97204, U.S.A.

Typeset by David Seabourne
and printed in China

ISBN 0-88192-346-X

CONTENTS

When it was suggested that there was a need for a book on bulbs in *The Rock Gardener's Library*, I had misgivings about the plethora of excellent books on dwarf bulbs available at the present time. In fact, many of these are specialist books on individual genera, which are invaluable to the enthusiast, and I hope that there is a place for a more general book on the use of bulbs in the garden, based as far as possible on my own experience, with the accent on cultivation rather than on botanical detail.

My choice of bulbs to describe has been based on availability as the first criterion, and I have endeavoured to cover as many as possible of those obtainable from trade sources, including cultivars which appear in catalogues but are generally ignored in the bulb literature. In some of the more difficult genera I have mentioned a few other plants which seem to be exchanged regularly between amateur enthusiasts and may become more freely obtainable in future. In some countries the number of bulbs obtainable from nurseries may be considerably less than in Britain, but the scope can be widened everywhere by growing bulbs from seed. Further details of this vital aspect of bulb growing are given in Chapter 3. *The Bernard E. Harkness Seedlist Handbook* is a useful guide to seed sources, including the specialist societies, in North America and elsewhere, and I have found *The Plantfinder* an invaluable guide to availability in Britain.

The term 'bulb' in the title is used very loosely and I have included corms and tubers, but in general I have omitted rhizomes, particularly in the genus *Iris*.

Whenever possible I have based my descriptions and suggestions on personal experience, but when I have considered a plant to be of importance but have lacked experience of it, I have sought guidance in the writings of experts in their fields, notably Brian Mathew, Martin Rix, and numerous contributors to the Bulletins of the Alpine Garden Society, which are an invaluable source of information based on personal experience.

My greatest indebtedness is to the late Paul Furse – bulb collector *extraordinaire* – who, through his trips to Turkey, Iran, and Afghanistan, and his writings about them, initiated the tremendous enthusiasm for growing the rarer bulbs that has blossomed during the last twenty years. He was a near neighbour who used me as his nearest 'grower', making sure that I had a generous share in all his collections so that he could study them in my garden. With his encouragement I also grew bulbs collected by those who enjoyed the benefit of his advice and followed him to the Middle East in subsequent years, Brian Mathew, Christopher Grey-Wilson, John Watson, Jim Archibald, and others, who added to and consolidated his rich collections.

Many of the areas in which these collectors worked are sadly now inaccessible, and some species have been lost after introduction, but many others are now well established or at least 'hanging on' in the collections of skilful amateurs and some botanic gardens, who make every effort to increase and distribute them. Also, amid an unceasing stream of 'new' plants, more bulbs are appearing, grown from seed from collecting expeditions to China and the Himalayas, to Russia, South America, and to the USA. Even the enthusiastic amateur has access to much of this exciting material, through shares in expeditions and especially from the remarkable seed lists of the specialist Societies (see Sources).

I have periodically referred to my own garden in Kent, when describing my experiences, and a word of explanation may be helpful. Kent is a dry county of England, the average rainfall being around 22–25 in (55–62 mm), and for four of the last six years it has been considerably lower. This has probably been good for the Mediterranean bulbs, but disastrous for the moisture lovers. Recent winter temperatures have been high, only occasionally dropping below -5°C (23°F), but in 'normal' years it reaches -12°C (10°F) and has only once been as low as -18°C (0°F). Bulbs are grown in all parts of the garden, which has a neutral loam, heavier in some parts than others but never excessively so. Those which definitely demand good drainage are grown in a rock garden or several raised beds, but other less demanding species are grown around the garden with the local drainage improved by digging in coarse grit.

I have tried, in the context of the various genera, to give some guidance on the vexed question of hardiness. In North America gardeners make use of Hardiness Zones, whereas British gardeners are virtually unaware of their existence, and would be umimpressed by the fact that there are only three zones (occasionally two are shown) to cover the British Isles. Most bulbs are hardy in Britain (Zones 7, 8, and 9) as far as temperature is concerned, but other factors, especially summer and winter rainfall, and the effectiveness of the drainage in the soil, are of far greater importance; hence the lack of interest in Hardiness Zones. In North America and elsewhere, the same factors must come into play, and I suspect that where they are favourable the Zones may be unduly pessimistic. On the other hand in Zones 5 and lower, the number of genuinely tender bulbs increases, but in the garden they can be protected to a considerable extent by suitable mulching.

I have grouped the plants according to season, but I have deliberately been imprecise about flowering times, so that the information will have some meaning to growers in countries with very different climates, and in different hemispheres. Although I have concentrated on bulbous plants hardy in Britain, I have included some which need a little protection from frost here, but will grow well outside in warmer climates.

CHAPTER 1

General information

BULBS, CORMS, AND TUBERS

In considering the genera included in this book I have to a large extent ignored the distinction between bulbs, corms, and tubers, but it may be helpful to outline the differences between them here, especially in so far as their structure is an adaptation to their habitat, and influences their behaviour in the garden.

The main characteristic of any bulbous plant is that it has a swollen underground storage organ, which makes it possible for the plant to survive conditions which are inimical to normal plant life – in particular hot, rainless conditions in summer – in a dormant state. In addition, the stored nourishment enables it to grow, to flower, and to set seed rapidly when conditions are suitable.

In true bulbs this storage organ has arisen from swelling of the leaf bases, the original bases forming the bulb scales, the outermost of which usually become the bulb tunic. The basal plate of the bulb, to which all the scales are attached, is all that remains of the original stem, and the new young leaves appear in the centre of the bulb. *Narcissus* species have bulbs of this type, with a large number of scales, and a tunic, which varies greatly in thickness. In the bulbs of *Tulipa* species, there are fewer scales, but the tunics are much thicker, and in some species they develop a woolly layer. The tunic protects the bulbs from excessive drought or frost, and is much more developed in plants from areas with extreme temperatures in summer and winter. In the bulbous irises, for example *Iris reticulata*, the scales are fewer but they are more swollen, and a thick reticulate tunic develops from the previous year's leaf bases.

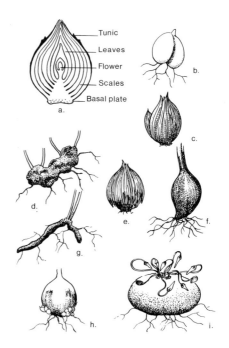

a. Tulip bulb
b. *Fritillaria meleagris* bulb
c. *Iris reticulata* bulb
d. *Anemone blanda* tuber
e. Crocus corm with fibrous tunic
f. Colchicum corm
g. *Anemone nemorosa* tuber
h. *Fritillaria* tuber with 'rice'
i. Cyclamen tuber

Lilies have a different type of true bulb, with the scales remaining separate and detachable rather than packed concentrically around the bulb, and there is no tunic. A similar bulb is seen in many *Fritillaria* species, but the scales are often much fewer, for example in *F. meleagris*, which usually has only two or three. Some *Fritillaria* species, for example *F. affinis* and many other American species, make large numbers of tiny bulbils ('rice-grains') around a bulb of many scales. The absence of a bulb tunic can be correlated to some extent with a difference in habitat. Most lilies grow in woodland or in areas with a considerable summer rainfall, whereas a large proportion of the bulbous plants with thick tunics come from areas with no summer rainfall. It must be said however that many *Fritillaria* species grow in the same habitat as the tulips with the thickest tunics!

Many of the 'bulbs' we grow are in fact corms and, although they behave in the same way and have the same requirements from the gardener's viewpoint, they have a structure very different from that of true bulbs. They are formed from the bases of stems, which swell into a round or flattened organ which is replaced every year. In many genera the previous year's corm disappears but in some, for example *Crocosmia*, they may survive for several years on top of each other. Many corms develop a tunic in the same way as bulbs, from the leaf bases. This is particularly noticeable in *Crocus*, in which the various types of tunic, reticulate, fibrous, papery, or smooth, protect the plant in the same way as bulb tunics, and incidentally are a diagnostic feature important to botanists.

None of the the Amaryllidaceae have corms, but corms are found in the other two main families associated with bulbous plants, *Crocus, Romulea,* and *Moraea,* in the Iridaceae, and *Colchicum, Erythronium, Bro-*

diaea, and *Tecophilea,* in the Liliaceae.

Tubers are swollen portions of underground stems or of roots, and there is not always a clear distinction between a rhizome and a tuber developed from it, or between a swollen root and a root tuber. This makes the decision whether to include certain species as 'bulbs' difficult. I intended to exclude typical rhizomes, and I have excluded rhizomatous irises, but I have included *Anemone nemorosa* with its thin rhizomes, with little justification except that it is so conveniently grouped with other early-flowering woodland bulbs, and perhaps because it is a personal favourite. With these exceptions, most of the tubers I have included are definitely 'bulbous', for example the Araceae, many anemones, *Eranthis,* and the fascinating members of the Berberidaceae, *Bongardia* and *Leontice.*

Root tubers are found in such definitely 'bulbous' genera as *Cyclamen,* and many *Corydalis* species, which I have included, but in many other plants they take the form of a cluster of swollen roots, as in *Dahlia, Eremurus,* and *Ranunculus ficaria,* and these I have passed over. The Juno irises are unusual in having both bulbs and swollen storage roots, and I have described their structure in Chapter 5.

CLIMATE AND HABITAT

The bulbous plants that we grow in our gardens come from a remarkably wide range of habitats around the world, and consideration of these habitats may give useful guidance to their requirements in cultivation.

Many of our least-demanding bulbs grow in areas of Europe where there is some summer rainfall, so that they are well-suited to the climate of Britain or the more temperate areas of the USA and elsewhere, with a moderate summer rainfall. They include, for example, the narcissi of Portugal and northern Spain, and the *Fritillaria, Crocus,* and *Colchicum* species of the European Alps and the mountains of Greece and the Balkans, which can generally be grown without any dry period in summer. Some grow at low levels around the Mediterranean, and one might expect that their hardiness would be in doubt. Experience suggests that in well-drained soil most will survive any but the most exceptional winters in Britain, but that problems may arise with them in Zone 5 or lower in North America or elsewhere.

The Mediterranean areas of Greece, southern Spain and North Africa are hotter and drier, and their bulbs have similar requirements to those from the Middle East. Most of this region, including Turkey, Iran, and Iraq, has hot dry summers, and extremely cold winters, tempered by a heavy snow cover. It supports the greatest population of bulbous plants in the world, especially of irises, tulips, cyclamen, and fritillaries, and hybridization and development of these species in the past has led to the present enormous trade in 'popular' bulbs. In theory these bulbs need to be kept dry in summer except in countries or areas that have a similar rainfall pattern. In reality many of them can be grown without difficulty, and if new and untried plants are first treated 'according to theory', it is usually possible to build up a stock, which can then be tried under normal garden conditions. It does seem that some of them at least become better adapted to garden conditions as they are grown and propagated over the years.

In such an enormous tract of country habitats must vary; there are places where, for example, woodland predominates and typical woodland bulbs thrive, and immediately around the Mediterranean the climate is similar to that of southern Europe, and the same doubts about hardiness may arise.

Further East into Russia and Afghanistan, the climate varies between hot and dry conditions similar to those of Turkey, and high mountain conditions resembling those of montane areas of Europe, where there is some summer rainfall. The extreme is reached in the Himalayas, and China, where the summer rainfall is high, and winters vary but are generally cold. Many of the bulbs from this part of the world can be treated as woodlanders, and difficulties are more likely to arise from summer drought than excessive rainfall. They include many lilies, some *Fritillaria* species, and other woodlanders.

North America has a range of different climates, and a vast number of different habitats, and the native bulbs differ greatly in their requirements accordingly. The cool northern woodlands support many bulbs, including *Erythronium* and *Trillium,* which are hardy and enjoy the British or similar climate. Most of the other bulbous plants are native to the western States, where the climate varies greatly, from the seaboard, to the woods and mountains of the Sierra Nevada and the Rockies, with some summer rain, to the inland plains of California, the Great Basin, and Mexico, with a climate approximating more to that of the Middle East. Several genera of bulbs are widely distributed throughout these areas, notably *Fritillaria, Calochortus,* and *Brodiaea* and its allies, and therefore their needs vary greatly between individual species. I have discussed these in more detail under the individual genera.

During recent years an increasing number of bulbous plants have been introduced from the Southern Hemisphere, notably from South America, and South Africa. They grow in a wide range of habitats, but are generally on the borderline of hardiness, needing an unheated or slightly heated greenhouse in cold countries. Like other bulbs they have a dormant period during which they may need to be kept dry or at least less wet. This period is most commonly in summer, but it must be remembered that in South Africa the bulbs fall into two different groups, those which grow mainly in winter and need to be dry in summer, and those which grow in summer and need to be dry in winter. The subject is complicated by the fact that some of the more important wide-ranging genera, like *Gladiolus* and *Moraea*, are distributed between the two groups, so that their requirements may differ completely; whereas *Rhodohypoxis,* for example, are native to a limited area, and can be relied upon to be winter-dormant. I have described briefly some of the hardier plants from these areas, but for details of the requirements of some of the trickier species I would recommend growers to consult more specialist books.

PESTS AND DISEASES

Amateur bulb enthusiasts are fortunate in that pests and diseases are rarely a great problem, except possibly where large collections of one species are grown in close proximity. For that reason I do not propose to go into great detail about the less common diseases, and I recommend that growers faced with unexpected problems should consult more comprehensive works. It must be said that the most important defence against diseases is to grow the plants well, in good conditions. Healthy bulbous plants rarely suffer from disease; lack of good drainage, and poor ventilation in a greenhouse, are more likely to cause trouble than any specific disease.

Pests

Birds and animals: The importance of birds seems to vary from garden to garden, and even from season to season. Attacks on yellow crocuses are notorious,

the birds nipping off the flowers at the base, and they may extend their attentions to other colours, and to other genera. I have frequently had blue reticulata iris flowers destroyed in the same way, and during one spring had every erythronium flower similarly nipped off, probably by pheasants. Control is only possible by some sort of netting – very unsightly – or by 'cottoning' with black thread on short sticks among the blooms, but in a few gardens yellow crocus, like polyanthus, cease to be worth growing. Squirrels can be a major pest, especially devouring crocuses, if they are given the opportunity. Mice are a more difficult problem, also eating crocus bulbs in the garden and under glass at every opportunity, and they can only satisfactorily be controlled by trapping or by keeping cats. It may be possible to prevent their attentions in a bulb-frame by putting wire netting just below the soil surface, but this makes it difficult to recover the bulbs when necessary.

Aphids, mites, etc.: These can affect bulbs but are generally less of a problem than for other alpine plants. Aphids are most important as potential vectors of virus diseases, and should always be treated as soon as they appear, with a suitable systemic or contact insecticide. In very small quantities it may be possible to 'squash' them by hand, but careful watch is necessary for any recurrence. Under glass, bulbs may be attacked by white fly or by red spider mite while they are in leaf, but these do not usually affect bulbs in the garden or in pots in the open. White fly are difficult to eradicate with insecticides, which will need repeated applications, but they are very susceptible to a predator, which may be obtained from specialist sources. The same applies to red spider mite, which often flourishes in the dry conditions favoured by bulbs.

Perhaps the most serious pest of bulbs is the vine weevil, which is especially likely to attack cyclamen and lilies, the grub being the damaging agent. The first symptom is frequently the sudden demise of a plant, which is found to have had its roots, and in bulbous plants the bulb itself, destroyed by the grubs, which are curved, white, with brown heads. If any plants are found to be affected the compost should be removed from the roots, any grubs destroyed, and the plants repotted into compost in which a suitable insecticide has been incorporated. If there is any doubt about the health of any other plants of susceptible genera, for example *Primula*, it is best to repot them all in this way. Some work is in progress on suitable soil insecticides, and also on a weevil predator, so up-to-date information should be sought.

The lily beetle is becoming a major pest in parts of southern England, spreading gradually towards my own area, having come from continental Europe. The beetle is an attractive bright red, and has very unattractive larvae, covered in their own excrement. Both beetles and larvae attack lilies and fritillaries, eating the leaves and the buds. The simplest control is to kill the conspicuous beetles as soon as they are seen, but they are also susceptible to insecticides.

Diseases

Virus diseases and fungus diseases both affect bulbous plants, but they are rarely serious in small amateur collections which are healthy and well-maintained. Symptoms vary and may start only with an unexplained loss of vigour, but there are often some signs of streaking or discoloration of the leaves, and plants definitely affected should be burnt. Viruses are spread by aphids, and are not transmitted through seeds, so that some control can be achieved by attacking aphids vigor-

ously, and by growing bulbs from seed whenever possible, including those which are easily propagated vegetatively. A further measure is to keep new acquisitions well away from established bulbs, until they are found to be healthy; and ideally one should avoid growing any plants known frequently to be virused in the garden, for example 'broken' tulips, *Lilium candidum*, unless grown from seed, many long-established cultivars of *Iris unguicularis*, etc. It is now possible to produce virus-free stocks of such plants by tissue culture, so one hopes that this problem will soon be solved.

Among the worst diseases are botrytis moulds, which are particularly likely to occur in excessively damp humid conditions. They usually start by producing brownish patches on the leaves, and eventually affect the whole plant. The dead flower may be the initial source, especially in Juno irises. Any infection should be treated immediately with a suitable fungicide, and soaking dormant bulbs in a fungicide may help to prevent attacks.

'Ink spot' disease affects irises of the Reticulata section, and has been responsible for the loss of many commercial stocks, as it becomes a problem when large numbers of bulbs are grown close together. Black stains appear on affected bulbs and eventually the whole plant is affected and dies. Although treatment by soaking the bulbs in a fungicide may be effective in the early stages, it is probably advisable to burn them, and treat any neighbouring bulbs with fungicide.

Garden chemicals are being developed constantly, and for that reason I have not given commercial names of suitable products. Many gardeners will have their own favourites, and advice can be obtained from stockists. Suppliers of predators for white fly, red spider, and vine weevil advertise their wares in the horticultural press.

CHAPTER 2

Bulbs in the garden

There must be few gardeners who do not appreciate the importance of bulbs in providing colour in the garden during the spring, before perennials and shrubs come into their own, but many look upon spring as the 'bulb season' and ignore their value during autumn and winter. The garden may not be very tempting during the winter months, but there are occasional dry and sunny spells when the flowers of bulbs can be appreciated even in the open, and the use of a cold greenhouse for them can add a new dimension to gardening, protecting the blooms and keeping the gardener comfortable while enjoying them.

The placing of bulbous plants in the garden needs careful thought. The size and impact of the flowers and leaves in relation to surrounding plants, the time taken for the leaves to die down, and the extent of the gap that they leave in a border, are all factors which need some consideration. Gaps in a border or in the rock garden are undesirable, so that one might consider planting the bulbs beneath other plants which will hide them completely when their season is over. This sounds an ideal arrangement, and is often recommended. It is certainly feasible for the stronger bulbs, and I am often pleasantly surprised by the blooming of autumn-flowering crocuses, dwarf narcissi etc., in the middle of other plants which have enveloped them over the years but have not prevented them flowering.

In choosing 'bulb cover' care is needed to avoid very vigorous plants which root down as they spread sideways, as many bulbs resent excessive root competition – better to use the many suitable low-growing plants which cover quite a large area in the course of a growing season and then die back to a central rootstock during the winter, or can be cut back to make way for the bulbs between them, without any permanent ill-effects. In addition to plants of borderline hardiness which lend themselves to this sort of treatment, such as osteospermums, verbenas, sphaeralceas and *Callirhoe involucrata*, other hardier plants can be used in the same way. Some longer-lived violas like the forms of *Viola cornuta* can have most of their growth pulled off in autumn and will soon fill their allotted space again after the bulbs have died down. Some of the diascias, for example *D. rigescens* in the larger garden, can be treated in the same way but many of them root down too much. Spreading dwarf origanums like 'Kent Beauty' and 'Barbara Tingey' can have most of their growth cut back after flowering, as can *Silene schafta*, *Saponaria ocymoides*, *Arenaria montana*, and some of the shade-loving phlox species.

THE ROCK GARDEN AND RAISED BEDS

Although this book is intended to be read primarily by rock gardeners and therefore it is appropriate to start discussing cultivation with the rock garden, it is important to realize that a rock garden is not a necessity for these plants, its only advantage being that it has excellent drainage, the first prerequisite for the more difficult species, and it is full of small plants which are the ideal companions to the smaller bulbs. Many gardeners today dispense with rocks or use very few, and grow their rock plants in raised beds, incorporating plenty of grit in the soil for drainage. When I have used the terms 'rock garden' and 'raised bed' in describing the cultivation of bulbs, the reader can take them as interchangeable.

To be suitable for a good collection of bulbs the rock garden should be in an open sunny position, and the first consideration should be the provision of adequate drainage. The fact that the beds or rock garden pockets are raised above the surrounding garden improves the drainage, but incorporation of coarse grit into the soil is necessary unless the normal soil is exceptionally light. The grit available varies in different parts of the world and even in different parts of a country, so it is impossible to make precise recommendations. Ideally it should be sharp rather than rounded and should be of varying size, with the minimum of dust. In my own garden we have a source of supply of 'crushed beach', which resembles shingle from a beach but is free from salt. It has been crushed and then graded, the grade used for the garden being ³⁄₁₆ in (5 mm) downwards. 'Cornish grit', which is often available in small quantities for horticultural use, can be obtained in a similar size range, but a local source of a suitable grit of some sort can usually be found and purchased in bulk.

A surfacing of clean grit, which can be granite or limestone chippings or 'beach' without the smaller particles, improves the appearance and is valuable in retaining moisture in dry spells and in keeping splashes of earth off the plants in heavy rain. Ideally it should be at least 2–3 cm (1 in) deep and should be replenished after it has been disturbed by a planting session.

The ideal time for planting bulbs is at the end of their summer dormancy. This is when they begin to make new roots, and the optimum time varies between genera and sometimes between species. Narcissi, for example, are notorious for starting into growth early, often during August in Britain, so that this is the ideal time to plant them. However, unless you are planting your own bulbs grown from seed or from splitting up established clumps, you are dependent on your source of supply, and nurseries frequently send out their bulbs later in the season than one would wish. Fortunately bulbs are remarkably tolerant and they will eventually recover, even from planting long after they should be in growth.

Spacing and depth of planting clearly depends on the size and requirements of individual bulbs, but a general guide is to plant at three times the depth of the bulb, and to space them sufficiently for the flowers to be enjoyed individually without touching. Special requirements will be indicated later in the book under the individual genera or species. Spacing of groups of bulbs relative to other plants is important, and has been discussed previously in general terms. In the rock garden care must be taken to leave enough space round the other plants for them to develop fully without encroaching too much on the bulbs. This applies especially to any precious plants that cannot be cut back hard when the bulbs come into growth. The alternative described above is deliberately to use plants which can become 'bulb cover' as they spread sideways, and then can be cut back for the bulb season without causing their owner or themselves too much grief.

The planning of colour schemes has become an important feature of the modern garden, but it is rarely a prime consideration among rock gardeners, who are content to enjoy their plants as a 'collection'. Even if you are a collector by nature it is worthwhile, when planting a group of bulbs, to give some thought to the colours of surrounding plants and of other bulbs to be planted. There is a common view, difficult to maintain when you see some of the results, that plants do not or cannot clash, but one look at a good patch of the scarlet *Zauschneria* 'Dublin' planted next to a group of the soft lavender *Crocus goulimyi* in my garden would suggest otherwise. This disaster could have been avoided with a little thought at planting time. One of the white crocus species would have made an exciting combination with the zauschneria. In general, bulbs flower at a time when few perennials are blooming so that avoiding clashes should not be too difficult.

It is advisable to avoid the use of larger bulbs in the rock garden, especially those with big leaves that remain in growth for a long time, even if their flowers are comparatively small. Colchicums would be fine if only their leaves were in proportion to their flowers, but sadly only the small-leaved, mainly spring-flowering, species are suitable. The same considerations apply to some of the narcissi and even the reticulata irises, whose leaves after flowering can be too large for the company of small plants, so that some care is needed in their placing, which should be with larger plants.

MIXED BORDERS

The rock garden or raised bed may be the ideal position for small and delicate bulbs, but the majority can be grown elsewhere in the garden, among shrubs or perennials, or in grass, bearing in mind their height in flower when choosing whether to plant them in front of a bed or further back. If the natural soil is light and soil fertility is good, a great range of bulbs can be grown without any special attention. In heavier soils many of the more robust bulbs will grow and increase, but the number can be extended by improving the drainage as described above. For a small group of bulbs a shovelful of coarse grit forked into the planting area will improve their prospects greatly.

Bulbs generally are not gross feeders but they will do better in soils of good fertility. They can suffer ill-effects from fresh manure in contact with the bulbs, and the ground should preferably be prepared with manure or compost well in advance of planting. Bone meal seems to suit most bulbs and this can be incorporated at the time of planting with no ill-effects, or used as a top dressing at a rate of 40–60 grammes to the square metre (2–3 ounces to the square yard). A disadvantage of its use on the surface of some gardens is that blackbirds and dogs are liable to scatter the bone meal, together with any top dressing of grit, in all directions including onto lawns and paths!

BULBS IN GRASS

Although the subject of growing bulbs in grass may not at first sight be of interest to the rock gardener, one has only to visit the Alpine Meadows at Wisley or the Savill Gardens at Windsor, with their superb plantings of dwarf narcissi, fritillarias, and erythroniums, to appreciate that this can be a successful method of cultivation for dwarf bulbs as well as for the usual large narcissi, fat 'Dutch' crocuses, and other robust growers, for which in many ways it is the ideal method, as it solves the problem of excessively large leaves overlying other plants in beds.

The most important consideration in

growing bulbs in grass is that the grass must be left uncut until the leaves of the bulbs are beginning to turn brown. Research at Wisley suggested that six weeks after flowering was usually the earliest time at which the leaves of narcissi could be cut without influencing later increase and flowering, and this can probably be taken as a good general rule. If it is hoped or intended that the bulbs should self-seed in the grass it will be necessary to leave mowing for longer, as the seed of many plants, for example *Fritillaria meleagris* which is one of the best plants for grass, is not shed for two or three weeks after the leaves begin to brown. There is at present an enthusiastic cult for 'meadow gardening', which carries the idea of growing plants in grass to its extreme, as it includes later-flowering bulbs such as terrestrial orchids, especially the dactylorhizas, as well as meadow perennials which are encouraged to sow their seed. Such a meadow looks very fine for the period during which the bulbs and later perennials are in flower, but the grass is becoming very long by that time and looks decidedly unattractive while in its 'uncut field' state, which lasts for several weeks – fine for a large garden in which visitors can be steered elsewhere during this crucial phase!

There are various techniques of planting bulbs in grass. The simplest for large bulbs such as narcissi is to use a bulb planter, which cuts a ring out of the turf to the required depth. A little of the earth plug removed can be broken into the hole, the bulb planted, and the remaining earth and portion of turf replaced. A long-handled planter which can be pushed down with the foot is very much better than the short hand planter which is very difficult to use unless the ground is unusually soft. An alternative, suitable for large or small bulbs, is to remove a square of turf with a spade or a turf remover, to break up the soil with a fork, and to plant the bulbs at the correct depth. Another good method which I use for small bulbs is to use a fork with reasonably wide tines, which can be pushed into the ground, and pushed backwards and forwards to widen the holes; the bulbs are then planted into them, and the holes filled with compost. If the fork is inserted in a different direction each time, the straight lines of the tines will be lost and a suitably random effect obtained. It is very important, whatever the method used, not to plant in rows or in any regular patterns. If a bulb planter is used the bulbs can be thrown onto the ground and then planted where they fall.

BULBS IN SHADE

Many of the most beautiful bulbs are shade-lovers. These will thrive in any part of the garden which is shaded for the major part of the day and remains reasonably moist at all times. Some are more demanding and will only flourish in a well-prepared position with abundant peat and leaf-mould incorporated in the soil. For these the ideal situation is provided by a peat bed, in which the soil is composed almost entirely of peat, leaf-mould, and grit.

WOODLAND

Natural woodland, in which the shade is provided by tall trees and the soil is composed of leaf-mould, is a wonderful place for suitable bulbs, but is only available to the fortunate few. Most gardeners must be content with an area of 'imitation' woodland, from the small area shaded by a solitary tree or large shrub, to a long bed shaded by a wall or by a fence. The most important factor governing the success of such an area is the presence or absence of tree roots. Unfortunately the area shaded by trees is often full of the trees' roots which keep the soil too dry and take away the major part of its nutrients. Deep-rooting trees like oaks are much better in this respect than shallow-rooting beech or ash, under which it is often impossible to garden. Tall trees will usually provide a shady area sufficiently far from the encroachment of their roots to enable bulbs to be grown. The shade of a fence or wall has the advantage of being free from roots, but it should be borne in mind that the bottom of a wall can become very dry, especially when the shady side is sheltered from the prevailing rain-carrying wind.

In preparing a shady area for bulb planting thorough soil preparation is essential for the best results. Most 'woodland' bulbs need a soil which contains abundant humus and retains moisture. In poor soils as much compost or manure as possible should be incorporated in the lower layers, at a depth which will be below the bulbs when they are newly planted, but will be within reach of their roots as they grow. Special care is needed if fresh farmyard manure is used shortly before planting that it is not in contact with the bulbs. The upper part of the soil, in which the bulbs are planted, should have plenty of leaf-mould – the ideal material – or peat or peat-substitute forked in. Many of these bulbs need an acid soil, and if an artificial fertilizer is used in poor soils, John Innes Base Fertilizer, or a lime-free general fertilizer, at a rate of 2–3 oz to the square yard (60–90 gm to the square metre), is more suitable than the bone meal suggested for general use, which is too alkaline. See page 17.

THE PEAT GARDEN

This is ideal for the smaller and more demanding woodland bulbs, for example the less robust trilliums, erythroniums, and terrestrial orchids. The classic peat garden consists of raised beds with peat blocks taking the place of rocks, and the pockets made up of a mixture of peat and leaf-mould, with sufficient grit to ensure good drainage. In many parts of Great Britain and elsewhere peat blocks are difficult or impossible to obtain, and very similar results can be obtained by using rockery stone for the walls and a similar compost for the pockets. The only real difference is that small plants in the interstices of the rocks may not flourish as they do when they can root into the blocks themselves.

DRY SHADE

I have described the ideal conditions for woodland bulbs, but in many parts of a garden there are likely to be difficult areas of dry shade, often full of roots to a greater or lesser degree, or overhung by dense foliage. The scope for growing bulbs in such areas is limited and largely dependent on the degree to which the soil can be improved, but certain bulbs will tolerate such conditions better than others and I will make some suggestions later when dealing with specific plants, notably among scillas, chionodoxas, anemones, and cyclamen.

BULBS UNDER GLASS

Most gardeners like to grow their bulbs in the open garden, where they hope they will flower well, and grow and increase over the years. The catalogues of the major bulb-growing firms are full of plants which will do this to perfection, but the bulb enthusiast will probably eventually want to include some (or all!) of the smaller and trickier species obtainable from specialist nurseries, or offered in seed lists of collectors or societies specializing in alpine plants. Growing bulbs from seed is one of the most rewarding branches of gardening, enabling the grower to acquire reasonable stocks of plants which are considered rare or difficult, with which to experiment under glass and in the garden.

A large proportion of the bulbs in cultivation occur naturally in areas with a very different climate from that in the British Isles or the wetter areas of America. This climate is characterized by a long dry summer resting period and a wet autumn and spring, in some areas with a dry winter of snow cover, in others with a wetter winter. The most important feature is undoubtedly the dry summer, and it is this which the bulb grower is trying to emulate when growing bulbs under glass. To a lesser extent the use of glass enables the grower to maintain bulbs which are on the borderline of frost-hardiness from warmer areas. It is probably true to say that all bulbs can be grown under glass and enjoyed under those slightly unnatural conditions, but increasing experience and experimentation suggests that many more can be grown in the open than a study of their natural growing conditions would suggest.

This knowledge of a plant's habitat is very helpful as you come to a decision regarding the conditions needed for a 'new' plant, and should make it possible for the grower to build up a stock, probably in the first instance under glass. Once sufficient bulbs are available for experiment one can forget the natural growing conditions and try them in a very well-drained soil in the garden. The results will often be unexpected. I have been pleasantly surprised by the number of *Fritillaria* species from dry areas of the Middle East that will thrive in the open in my garden.

There are basically two methods of growing bulbs under glass: in pots, and planted in beds with a 'frame' overhead. Both methods have their advantages and disadvantages. Bulb frames give the bulbs the maximum possible root-run, and for this reason increase is usually better than in pots, and they require much less attention. The disadvantages of planting bulbs in beds are that recovery of the bulbs as they increase is more difficult, and the more vigorous and freely increasing may swamp the more delicate; furthermore bulb frames are perhaps not the most beautiful feature of a garden.

Growing bulbs in pots, in a greenhouse or a frame, has the advantage that the bulbs can be given individual attention, especially in regard to watering; they can be enjoyed in comfort in all weathers; they can if desired be brought in the house for brief periods to be admired; or they can be exhibited at shows. Although not things of great beauty, greenhouses are more acceptable visually to most gardeners than artificial raised beds with their overhead covers. The disadvantages of pots as compared with frames is that they require more attention and the bulbs may grow and increase less well because of the root restriction.

THE BULB FRAME

Broadly defined this is a prepared bed with some sort of glass (or plastic) covering over it for at least part of the year, to provide dry conditions in summer and if necessary to keep off excessive rain in winter. The bed should be raised to ensure that the drainage is good and that its moisture content is unaffected by the surrounding soil conditions. The height of the walls is not important, but for the comfortable viewing of the plants the higher the better up to waist height. The only disadvantage of a waist-high bed is the cost of walling material, and of the drainage material and compost to fill the space. Excellent results can be obtained from a bed which is only raised by 30 cm

(1 ft), but the details of smaller bulbs can then only be admired 'on all fours'.

The choice of building material for the walls is largely a matter of taste and availability. If appearance is not considered important railway sleepers or any of the cheaper types of concrete or breeze blocks are adequate. For a more elegant frame there is a wide choice of brick, walling stone, or aggregate material. The covering frame itself can be a commercially available frame or run of frames which will rest on the upper surface of the walls. An alternative to frames, which I have used several times, is to cover the bed with standard Dutch lights, possibly the cheapest method for the largest area covered, if a suitable way of supporting them can be found. Here they are supported on galvanized angle-iron screwed into wooden blocks in uprights of galvanized scaffolding poles. The sides are normally left open so that air circulation is perfect, and the small amount of rain which blows under in high wind does not appear to do much damage.

In snow or exceptionally wet conditions I have wooden frames supporting plastic sheet which fit into the front and back spaces temporarily. Dutch lights can easily 'take off' in high winds unless they are held down in some way. If they are supported on angle material they can be held down by metal clips under each corner of the light which can be turned sideways under the angle support.

The greatest advantage of the Dutch lights is that they are more easily removed completely than a run of frames during spring and autumn when the bulbs will benefit from the rain, or artificial watering, in dry seasons. If frames are used it may be simpler to remove the overhead glass from them and keep the sides on.

Ideally in a bulb-frame there should be a depth of good compost of at least 30 cm (1 ft). If the bed is raised to 60 cm (2 ft) or more, the bottom should be filled with rubble or other coarse drainage material with reversed turves over this to prevent the prepared compost washing down into it. A good compost for the general run of bulbs should be based on a good quality top-spit loam, mixed with a third of its bulk of peat, and half of its bulk of coarse grit. The grit is very important and should always amount to at least a third of the total bulk, and more if the loam is heavy. This 'home-made' compost is similar in composition to the John Innes compost used in Britain, which is also suitable but usually requires a considerable addition of extra grit. It is composed of 7 parts loam, 3 parts peat, and 2 parts coarse sand, with a base fertilizer, which consists of hoof and horn, and superphosphate, 1.19 gm per litre of each, and potassium sulphate 0.6 gm per litre. These are the quantities in the No. 1 compost, and approximate to ½ oz of base fertilizer to 1 gallon, and are doubled in No. 2, and trebled in No. 3. In addition to this ground limestone should be added, except for lime-haters, at a rate of 0.6 gm per litre (⅔ oz per 8 gallons). For bulb frames the No. 2 compost is suitable, or the 'home-made' compost with the same quantity of the base fertilizer described or of bone meal. After the first year the fertilizer should be replenished by applying a top dressing of either J.I. Base Fertilizer or bone meal at a rate of 2–3 oz to the square yard (65–100 gm per square metre).

Woodland bulbs do better in the open, but some growers may want to grow them in a shaded raised bed. In that case the compost should contain a higher proportion of peat, or leaf-mould if available, and the lime should be omitted.

The most difficult problem arising from the use of a bulb-frame is that the individual groups of bulbs can easily spread into each other and become muddled, which makes their retrieval difficult when they need replanting or distributing, and one group of quickly increasing bulbs can swamp a more delicate planting. There are various ways of solving this problem. In the first place it is helpful to plant the more difficult, slowly increasing, groups of bulbs together, so that they are less likely to be overwhelmed by their neighbours, and also to plant different genera next to each other because, much as one might like to keep the species of one genus collected together, it will then be difficult to tell where one group meets another when they are dormant.

In addition to choosing the neighbouring groups with care, they can be physically separated in some way. One possibility is to use tiles or similar narrow material between them, but the most popular method now seems to be to plant the bulbs in mesh pots, as used for water plants, and plunge these to their full depth in the bed. This keeps them completely separate and makes them easy to lift, at the same time allowing the roots access to the full depth of soil.

A MIXED FRAME

A raised bed similar to that described as a 'bulb frame' can be planted with alpine plants which require protection from excessive rain, especially in winter, but a mixture of bulbs and alpines is not often planted because of the difference in their watering requirements. However, there is scope for experimenting with this mixture, and a long raised bed with Dutch light cover in my garden, which was first devoted to bulbs and later to alpines, now contains a mixed planting of bulbs requiring fairly dry conditions in summer with some of the alpine plants from regions with a similar rainfall pattern, which I hoped would not resent a shortage of water between early summer and early autumn. This clearly is a compromise and the bulbs are undoubtedly a little wetter than if they were allowed to dry completely in a bulb frame. The soil around the other plants is watered occasionally if they show signs of distress during the summer, and during the autumn and spring the bed is left uncovered. In winter it is covered again as long as the soil remains sufficiently moist, and the lights are removed if it needs water.

Mixing the bulbs with other plants certainly adds to the interest of a bed which would otherwise be bare for about four months, although it may not appeal to the bulb purist. Alpines which tolerate or even benefit from a dry summer, for example *Lewisia tweedyi*, the eriogonums, and some penstemons, many plants from a Mediterranean or similar climate, such as *Catananche caespitosa*, the acantholimons, *Verbascum spinosum*, and *Salvia caespitosa*, all seem to do well in it. Only small bulbs have been chosen as company for them, for example the smaller crocuses like *C. cambessedesii*, the blue and white forms of *C. pestallozae*, *C. danfordiae*, *C. cvijicii*, *Iris hyrcana*, *Narcissus rupicola*, and *N. atlanticus*, *Cyclamen graecum* and several small *Fritillaria* species.

GREENHOUSE BEDS

Rather than devoting a cold or slightly heated greenhouse entirely to pot plants, part of its area can be devoted to a bed, preferably raised, in which bulbs can be planted exactly in the same way as in a bulb frame, with its attendant advantages and disadvantages. The one advantage over a frame is that the temperature can be kept a little higher. An unheated house will give excellent results, but a small amount of heat whenever frost threatens will keep the house frost-free, so the exciting bulbs on the borderline of hardiness can be grown, notably those from

South Africa and South America, such as moraeas, romuleas and dwarf gladioli from the former, rhodophialas, habranthus and zephyranthes from the latter, and many others.

If a large collection of South African bulbs is grown some research is necessary into their water requirements, as some grow in winter and some in summer, and it may be advisable to give the opposite ends of the bed a different watering regime. A truly frost-free bed may not come within the scope of this book, as it involves the use of heat, but an increasing number of these slightly tender bulbs, especially from the Andes, are being grown and exhibited in 'Alpine' shows. Many are worthy of trial outside in the warmest parts of the British Isles, North America and Australasia, and I have described a selection of them later in the book.

BULBS IN POTS

Growing bulbs in pots gives the gardener maximum control over compost, watering, and drying during dormancy, and therefore is the ideal method for the more difficult plants. In addition, if a greenhouse is used to keep them, it gives the opportunity of admiring them in comfort during what is frequently a wet time of year, and also makes it possible to exhibit them at shows, particularly of the Alpine Garden Society and the Scottish Rock Garden Club in Britain, and of the American Rock Garden Society in North America.

The pots of bulbs can be grown in a sunny greenhouse or alpine house, and this need not be heated in winter unless it is intended to include some of the slightly tender bulbs in the collection, in which case a little heat, sufficient to keep out more than a degree or two of frost, will make it possible to grow a more extensive

range. An alternative is to keep the pots in frames. This is a perfectly satisfactory method which I used for many years; its only disadvantages are that the plants are more difficult to study if the frame is at ground level, and that it does not give an opportunity of maintaining a frost-free environment.

Bulbs can be grown in either plastic or clay pots, or indeed in a mixture of the two. Most amateur growers favour clay pots for general use. They dry out much more quickly than plastic pots, which means that they need more frequent watering in dry conditions, even when they are plunged, but in wet conditions they are much less likely to remain excessively wet after watering, a state to be avoided in bulb-growing. Plastic pots need water less frequently and do not necessarily need plunging, but it is essential to use more drainage material in the compost to prevent the ill-effects of over-watering. Perhaps the ideal arrangement is to grow the bulbs needing a drying off period in clay pots, and those needing a permanently moist soil, woodlanders for example (usually better in the garden!), in plastic pots.

Clay pots should be plunged up to their rims in coarse sand or similar material, to reduce the rate at which they dry out, and to protect them from frost in an unheated house. Although it is not essential to plunge plastic pots as they cannot lose moisture through their walls as clay pots do, there is considerable merit in plunging them during winter in an unheated house. In the severe winter of 1982 we lost a considerable number of precious bulbs in unplunged plastic pots, because their pots were frozen solid for two or three weeks. Most of these would probably have survived in the open garden, and this experience suggests that even plastic pots should be plunged, or alternatively some heat should be introduced in severe weather, to prevent the compost freezing for long periods.

Composts for bulb frames have been discussed on page 17 and very similar composts are suitable for plants in pots. For general use I favour a compost of sterile loam 2 parts, peat 1 part, and coarse grit 1½ parts, with John Innes Base Fertilizer (or bone meal) and lime to the strength of John Innes No. 2 (see page 17). Alternatively a ready prepared J.I. compost can be used with added grit to give adequate drainage. If plastic pots are used it is advisable to increase the proportion of grit to 2 parts in 5. For plants needing woodland conditions the proportion of peat can be increased or, ideally, a generous amount of sterile leaf-mould added. The leaf-mould should be sterilized separately from the loam. On a small scale this is easily accomplished by pouring boiling water through it in a fine sieve. If leaf-mould is readily available it can be used in place of the peat, often with better results as it contains some nutrients.

Mention must be made of the increasing use of peat-based and other composts which do not rely on loam, with their nutrients supplied by slow-release fertilizers and trace elements. Although these have largely replaced loam-based composts commercially, they have found little favour with amateur bulb-growers. I suspect that this is due more to a natural conservatism, combined with excellent results from the old composts, than to any failure with the new materials. My own experience is insufficient to recommend them, but some (uncontrolled) experiments a few years ago suggested that most bulbs did at least as well in a peat-based compost, as long as it was very well-drained and its pH suitably adjusted. There is certainly plenty of scope for experiment with some of the less common bulbs. At present the subject is

further complicated by doubts about the use of peat in horticulture, and the need to experiment with other materials like bark and coconut-fibre.

The details of bulb planting in pots depend on the size and number of the bulbs, but as a general rule they should be covered with at least three times their own depth of soil, and planted with a bulb's width between each, unless they are deliberately crowded for exhibiting! Large bulbs may have to be planted nearer the surface to give sufficient space for a reasonable amount of compost under the bulbs. If a generous amount of grit has been added to the compost there is nothing to be gained by putting extra drainage material at the bottom of the pot (a popular myth!), but there is a lot to be said in favour of a generous layer on top of the compost. It makes watering easier as there is plenty of space for the water above the compost, it helps to retain moisture after watering in dry conditions, and it protects the foliage and flowers from splashes of soil during heavy-handed watering with a can or hose attachment.

The watering regime depends very much on the genus and will be discussed further under the individual genus headings. Most bulbs under glass will need a drying-out period during the summer, but it is important not to hurry them into dormancy by withholding water early. Wait until the leaves are turning brown, or until seed is set if they are to be propagated in this way. Usually they can be watered again in early autumn (September in the U.K) but, ideally, early-developing bulbs like narcissi should be started earlier, and some late-flowering bulbs, like calochortus, will need their whole dormancy much later. Recently it has been realized that pots can be dried too much during summer, although a few genera may enjoy being 'baked' thoroughly.

In my experience bulbs are in noticeably better condition at the end of their dormancy when their compost has remained very slightly moist, by accident or by design, than when they have been 'baked'. In practice this is not an easy state to maintain, but it seems better to keep the pots shaded while they are dry, and perhaps to keep the plunge or the material on which the pots are standing slightly moist, rather than keeping them in the hottest sun, as was the past 'teaching'. Some bulbs, especially those from high mountainous areas which may be subjected to rain at any time, should be kept watered at all times, and any woodland species will need to be kept moist and shaded.

Most bulbs need repotting at intervals as they become crowded or exhaust the nutrients in their compost. The frequency with which this is done depends mainly on whether any feeding regime is adopted. The method which I have usually adopted is to repot the bulbs completely every two years, but at the end of the next year to scrape away the old compost down to the level of the bulbs so that they can be examined, and the compost above the bulbs renewed. This gives an opportunity to make sure that the bulbs are healthy, and to remove small bulbs for propagation if they are needed, and it renews most of the compost, so that further feeding is probably unnecessary. The alternative is to leave the pots untouched for the two years and to give some supplementary liquid feeds during the second year after repotting. Indeed some growers only repot when the bulbs are obviously overcrowded and rely on feeding for several years. This has the advantage of being a more labour-saving method, and incidentally gives a good potful for exhibition. The most suitable fertilizer for flowering-size bulbs is one with a high potash content, as used for tomatoes, which should be used at half-strength once a fortnight during active growth.

CHAPTER 3

Propagation

GENERAL

Many of the more popular bulbs increase in the garden if they are left alone apart from occasional lifting and splitting when they become overcrowded. This over-crowding can occur quite quickly in some plants, for example the more vigorous narcissi and crocuses; and it usually results in their flowering less freely, a sign that they will benefit from lifting and splitting up. They can be replanted in fresh soil elsewhere, or in the same position after the soil has been improved with more fer-tilizer, compost etc.

Most of the less common bulbs increase slowly but take several years to become overcrowded if they are left undisturbed in the ground. If propagation is a priority the increase will be quicker if the bulbs are lifted, perhaps after two or three years, their bulbs separated and any tiny bulbs planted separately, in the same way as young seedlings. If the bulbs are grown in pots this can be done routinely at the time of repotting.

The most difficult groups of bulbs are those which do not increase vegetatively or do so very slowly. For these the only methods of increase are from seed, the most important method for amateurs; from micropropagation, which I do not feel comes within the scope of this book although it is becoming of ever-increasing importance commercially; and from simpler methods of 'cutting' the bulbs, from breaking them in half to twin-scaling.

BULB DIVISION

Bulbous plants can increase vegetatively in different ways. During the course of a growing season each bulb may split into two or sometimes more, a little smaller than the original, and will probably be capable of flowering during the following year. Narcissi, and some tulips, crocus, and corydalis are among those which behave in this way. Other plants form small bulbs around the base of the orig-inal bulb, for example many fritillaries, reticulata irises, and gladioli, and in some species these can be extremely small and abundant, as in those fritillaries which produce 'rice-grain' bulbils.

If you want rapid increase of your bulbs it is advisable to remove any tiny bulbs at repotting time and treat them in the same way as seed (see below). Even with larger bulbs frequent splitting and repotting will give the maximum increase. For bulbs in the open ground, they can be exposed while dormant and small bulbs removed as necessary, or they can be lifted and divided.

A few plants are capable of forming stem bulbils in the leaf axils, which provide a simple method of propagation. Lilies are the main genus in which this is found but it also occurs in several *Calo-chortus* species. The bulbils can be detached when they are fully developed at the end of the growing season, and then treated in the same way as other small bulbs.

BULBS FROM SEED

There is a reluctance among many gardeners to attempt to grow bulbs from seed because 'it takes too long'. Most bulbs flower from seed in three to five years, the majority sooner rather than later with good treatment, and many other alpine plants, perennials, and shrubs take as long. In practice if you sow seed of bulbs and other 'slow' plants regularly every year you will have the excitement of seeing new plants flowering annually without remembering just how long they took! Growing from seed enables the gardener to build up stocks of plants which are uncommon and expensive as bulbs, or which are not available in the trade, either because commercial growers cannot increase them rapidly vegetatively, or because they are in demand only by a comparatively few enthusiasts.

Apart from the labour of sowing the seed this method of propagation involves very little work over the years, and even this can often be reduced by some shortcuts. The ideal time to sow most bulb seed is in early autumn, but unless it is home-saved seed it will probably not be available until much later. Seed sown before Christmas will usually germinate after two or three months of cold, during the following spring or early summer. Seed sown later than this will be more erratic and will often fail to germinate until spring a year later.

Most seed germinates after it has had several weeks of cold weather, but if you sow a lot of different species you will find a few of them germinating at unusual times. Early-sown seed may germinate in the autumn, in which case it is best to keep it growing in a frost-free house – indeed this may save a year of growth. Seed sown late in the spring may also germinate unexpectedly quickly without a cold period. This has been very noticeable with *Calochortus* species, which usually germinate within a few weeks and can then be kept growing under glass until they go dormant late in summer.

One suitable material in which to sow bulb seed is what is sold in Britain as John Innes Seed Compost, composed of 2 parts loam, 1 part peat, and 1 part coarse sand, with ground limestone 0.6 gm per litre (approximately 1 oz per 8 gallons), and superphosphate 1.2 gm per litre (2 oz per 8 gallons). It needs to be well-drained, and is usually improved by the addition of extra coarse sand or of a fine grade of Perlite, to a third of its bulk. The pots will probably be kept for at least two years before repotting, so that there is a good argument for using a compost with more fertilizer, and I prefer J.I. Potting Compost No. 1, described on page 17, again with extra drainage, or alternatively a mixture of sterile loam 2 parts, peat 1 part, and Perlite 1½ parts (or coarse sand), with J.I. Base Fertilizer 4 oz or bone meal, and lime 1 oz, to 8 gallons. For woodland or lime-hating bulbs the lime must be omitted and sterile leaf-mould or extra peat added. One part each of loam, peat, and leaf-mould, with adequate drainage, seems to give good results for them.

Although clay pots can be used for seeds, I favour plastic because they require watering less often, and ungerminated seed and young seedlings seem to suffer little from over-watering. I use square pots, which take up much less space than round pots, three-quarters of the usual pot depth, although this is not essential. They are filled with compost to a little below the rim and then flattened down gently so that there is plenty of space above the seed for a surfacing of grit or grit and compost, depending on the size of the seed. Methods of sowing are very much a matter of choice. If the seed is small I find it easiest to sow it direct from the packet with its top torn off, by judiciously tapping it to get one or two seeds out at a time, but the alternative of emptying the packet into the palm and sowing a pinch of seed between thumb and forefinger works equally well. I usually sow large seed separately in the same way. It is most important after sowing to give the seed a generous covering of clean grit to a depth of at least 5 mm (¼ in), as this will stop it being disturbed by overhead watering subsequently. I use either a fine flint grit (chick grit) or fine aquarium gravel for the smaller seed, but for most bulb seed, which is large, the same surfacing grit as for normal potting is satisfactory. For large seed I first scatter sufficient compost from a sieve just to cover the seed before topping it up with a layer of grit which can be up to 12 mm (½ in) deep. The pot must then be labelled with the name of the plant and date of sowing and the provenance.

With the exception of tender species, of which the seed must be kept under glass, the simplest routine for the pots after sowing is to keep them in a shady place open to the weather, watering whenever they become dry, until germination takes place. They should then be brought into more light, preferably in a cold house or frame, and watered regularly until they show signs of becoming dormant, when water can be withheld unless they need permanent moisture. Seedling bulbs will often continue growing for much longer than adult bulbs and they should be encouraged to have as long a growing season as possible. During the dormant period the pots should be kept almost dry but results are better if they retain a minimum amount of moisture.

Some bulbs germinate better with bottom heat, which can be provided in a propagator or by standing the pots over an arrangement of soil-warming cables under the plunge. If their hardiness is doubtful and you have enough seed, it should be split: some should be given the cold treatment described and some sown in heat. I frequently sow seed in this way, using the soil warmth of a mist propagator but covering the pots unless they become dry. I have been pleasantly surprised how many bulbs will germinate within two or three weeks in winter using this method, particularly some of those from the Andes and from South Africa. These are becoming more readily available and can be grown in the cold house, and possibly in the garden in warmer areas. Any bulbs which germinate in winter will need to be kept under glass, preferably in frost-free conditions.

I have decribed the usual method of sowing seed in pots, but an alternative used by some growers for large seed is to sow it in polythene bags. It is sown at the usual time in autumn, mixed with just-moist peat or vermiculite and put in sealed bags, which are then stored in a domestic refrigerator (not a deep-freezer). The bags need inspection periodically because the seed may germinate while still in the cold, in which case it must be removed and planted. In early spring the bags can be brought into a warmer room, and will usually germinate quickly. One advantage of this method is that only germinated seed is planted, theoretically saving some space. The most important use of the method is for seed with hypogeal germination, for example many of the lilies, which normally will not produce leaves until the second spring, after two cold periods, having formed a tiny bulb only in the first season. This seed can be sown in moist peat in a bag and kept at 20°C (68°F), perhaps in an airing cupboard, until it is seen to have germinated and formed a bulb. It is then transferred to a refrigerator for at least two months before being sown normally, when it will produce leaves, thus saving one year.

Having germinated the seed and nursed the seedlings through their first growing season, the next problem is how to treat them subsequently. This depends in part on the particular plant and how well it has grown. Generally at the end of one year's growth the seedling bulbs are small. They may indeed be so small that they are very difficult to find in compost, and any attempt at retrieving them then will result in unnecessary losses. This is particularly true of slow growers like tulips, but it can also be a problem with small white fritillaria bulbs in a compost containing Perlite. The best advice is to leave the pots undisturbed until they have completed two years of growth, by which time the bulbs will at least be large enough to find, and can be repotted in fresh compost as recommended for large bulbs. The seedling bulbs are often at a surprising depth in the compost and the only part that can usually be ignored is the top third where they were sown. If the seed pots are plunged or standing on a material like sand it is worth looking under the drainage hole, as some small bulbs, especially tulips, will often have found their way there. Some bulbs are particularly easy and quick from seed, and if at the end of their first season the young bulbs have made good robust top growth, they can then be repotted, and this will shorten the time to flowering, the only possible danger being the loss of a few of the smaller bulbs. Even when repotting after two seasons one often finds a number of very small bulbs, which probably result from delayed germination until the second spring. During the second season's growth in the original pots some liquid feeding with a general fertilizer every two or three weeks will help the development of the bulb although they seem to do surprisingly well without it, judging from my own experience.

The best time to repot the bulbs is at the end of their dormant period, so that they can start into growth immediately in the fresh compost, which will be moist. Separate the bulbs and repot them in the same way as adult bulbs into the compost suggested for them, using a pot or pots of whatever size is necessary to accommodate them. An alternative is to replant the whole potful into a larger pot without disturbance. This saves work but it means that much of the compost available to the bulbs is the old compost, and that they will therefore need extra feeding.

An excellent way of saving labour, particularly applicable to the easier bulbs and also to woodland bulbs which do better generally in the garden than in pots, is to sow extra thinly in the first place and to plant the whole potful in the garden after two seasons. Many of the most exciting woodland species, like trilliums and erythroniums, are very slow to reach flowering size and need many years of repotting. Instead they can be planted out into a well prepared woodland bed or peat bed and left alone, apart from watering when necessary, until they flower. Then if they appear crowded they can be lifted and divided and replanted.

OTHER METHODS

Most other methods are based on the principal of breaking or 'cutting' bulbs into pieces. At its simplest, it can consist of breaking a bulb into two halves, and planting them separately. This method works well for some simple fritillary bulbs. A similar operation can be used in large bulbs with multiple growing tips, like old cyclamen tubers, which can be cut into large pieces, each with a growing point, the pieces treated with fungicide, and potted separately.

Simple cutting

In bulbs with a basal plate, most methods rely on the plate's inherent ability to form bulbils. In the simplest method, the bulb can be lifted and the basal plate cut through to a depth of 50mm (½in) in several directions. The bulb is then kept in damp peat or vermiculite in a polythene bag in a warm place, preferably around 21°C (70°F), until bulbils are forming along the cuts. The bulb should then be planted upside-down in a very well-drained humus rich compost for a further year, after which the bulbils can be separated.

Scaling

This method is used mainly for lily bulbs, but can be used with other bulbs composed of detachable scales, for example fritillarias. The scales, as many as required, are broken off the parent bulb with a portion of tissue from the basal plate in late summer, soaked in a fungicide such as Benlate, and mixed with damp Vermiculite or peat, and kept in a sealed polythene bag in the dark at approximately 21°C (70°F) for three months. They should then be transferred to a refrigerator (not a deep-freeze), until bulblets form on the scales, usually after 6–8 weeks, when the scales with their bulblets still attached should be planted in a suitable well-drained compost with the scales just below the surface, in a greenhouse or frame. After the growing season the small bulbs can be separated from the scales and replanted.

Twin-scaling and chipping

Twin-scaling is a development of the previous method, in which the whole of a bulb with scales is used. The roots and the tip of the bulb are removed, keeping the basal plate undamaged. The bulb is turned upside-down and cut vertically into small sections, each with a piece of the basal plate. Each section can then be pulled apart into pairs of scales, which must be soaked or dusted with fungicide, and then treated as described for scales.

Chipping is an operation similar to twin scaling, and can be used for most bulbs. The bulb is cut vertically through the basal plate in the same way, usually into 4, 8, or 16 'chips', depending on the size of the bulb, each with a proportion of basal plate. Great care should be taken to keep the knife absolutely clean and to treat the chips with fungicide, before treating them as for scales. At the extreme development of this method, used commercially, bulbs can be cut into a great number of 'chips', or into the much smaller pieces used in micropropagation, a method which is beyond the scope of this book, but is becoming increasingly important in building up stocks of 'difficult' bulbs.

PROPAGATION OF THE MAIN GENERA

Cultivation and propagation of bulbs have been described in general terms in the previous chapters, without specific suggestions in regard to individual genera or species. I will discuss any special requirements of the larger genera in this section, and deal with the smaller genera as they are mentioned in the seasonal chapters.

Anemone

The tuberous anemones fall mainly into three groups in their requirements. The shade-loving species, *A. nemorosa*, *A. ranunculoides*, and *A. apennina*, together with *A. blanda* which enjoys sun or partial shade, spread quickly by increase of their elongated tubers, and often by seeding also, and if necessary they can be increased by division. If the various colour forms of *A. blanda* are planted in groups well apart from each other they are less likely to hybridize and produce wishy-washy intermediate seedlings, which can eventually overwhelm the originals with their good clear colours.

In contrast to these, the sun-loving round-tubered species *A. coronaria*, *A. hortensis*, *A. pavonina* and *A. fulgens* do best in warm well-drained soils, preferably but not necessarily alkaline. These species increase much less freely in the ground than the popular groups derived from their hybridization, 'De Caen' and 'St Brigid', but they can be raised easily from seed. The third group are the more difficult species with similar tubers, from Turkey and Iran, *Anemone tschernjaewii*, *A. biflora*, and *A. bucharica*, which need cold-house cultivation with a dry period in summer, and are difficult to increase except by seed, which is not always set freely.

Calochortus

These spectacular North American bulbs are not often available commercially in the USA or in Britain, but they appear in American seedlists and in those of the specialist societies in both countries. Fortunately they are easily raised from seed, as described in the last section. The seed is often not available until early spring but it usually germinates within a few weeks of sowing. The young bulbs are small and should not be repotted for two years. Flowering occasionally starts after three years but more often after four or five. Increase by division of the bulbs is usually slow but stem bulbils are sometimes found, occasionally just below the surface of the soil, and these can be treated as normal young bulbs. The different groups of *Calochortus* flower over a very long season and must be treated individually, allowing them a long growing season, which could end in early summer but may continue well into autumn. They therefore need starting into growth later than most other bulbs, after a dry period of

three or four months. Some are woodland species and should not be dried off completely (see page 147).

Colchicum

Most of the colchicums are vigorous autumn-flowering plants with large leaves, which increase freely in the open ground, and indeed may become overcrowded after a few years with diminished flowering. If this happens or if they are to be increased quickly they should be lifted while dormant and replanted immediately into fresh soil. A few species, especially those flowering in spring with small leaves, are more suitable for the cold house or rock garden and do not increase much vegetatively. These should be raised from seed, which may be the only method of obtaining stocks of many of them, but it is a slow process as they usually take at least five years to attain flowering-size.

Corydalis

This genus is becoming increasingly popular among alpine enthusiasts, and contains a large number of widely differing species, from woodlanders to plants requiring a summer baking. Only a few of the bulbous species increase freely in the garden by splitting of their bulbs, for example *Corydalis solida* and its allies, and these can easily be divided when required. Many species seem to require a dry period and are best under glass, and propagation of these may only be possible from seed or by cutting of the bulb (see page 127).

Seed raising, as previously described, is certainly the most important method for corydalis. One feature of corydalis seed to bear in mind is that it is shed very quickly and that germination is much better if it is sown immediately after collection. If the seed is kept dry for long, germination is likely to be erratic at best and non-existent at worst. The long green seed capsules must be watched carefully, as the seed often ripens before they turn brown to any degree, and is then shot out and lost. If there are several seed pods which look full, open one and see whether the seed is black, in which case you can safely open any at the same stage and sow the seed immediately. Otherwise remove the capsules as soon as they show any sign of browning, or as soon as any of them have begun to open. Although the seed must be sown immediately it may not germinate until the following spring, but germination should then be excellent.

Crocus

Many crocuses are easy and freely-increasing in the open garden, but some of the less common species require careful cultivation in a rock garden or under glass, and every opportunity should be taken of propagating these from seed. Here the only problem may be finding the seed, as the capsules of some species are at, or even just below, the surface of the soil, and may spill their seed before the gardener is aware that they have produced it. Whenever crocus 'grass' is turning brown it is advisable to look at the base of the dying leaves for any seed capsules. The seed can be sown immediately or kept for sowing in the autumn. The results are probably the same, but I have a personal preference for immediate sowing of most seed – it saves having too much seed to deal with in the autumn, and it occasionally results in early germination and a shorter wait for flowering.

Cyclamen

Cyclamen only increase naturally by seed, and although it is theoretically possible to cut them up into portions, as long as each has a growing point, this is not a very practical proposition. They are unusual in ripening their seed at roughly the same time of year irrespective of whether they have flowered in autumn or spring. This is generally around mid-summer, when the round seed capsules open and expose the brown seed embedded in a sticky material, much loved by ants who often transport the seed to their nests; hence the frequency with which small cyclamen appear in unexpected places. The ripe seed should be collected and sown immediately, or after washing off their sticky coating. Such coatings frequently contain germination inhibitors, but in the case of cyclamen this does not seem to be the case, and the seed eventually germinates well whether it is cleaned or not.

The ideal compost for cyclamen, whether seedlings or adult bulbs, should contain a large proportion of leaf-mould, preferably sterilized. The seed usually germinates the following spring, but sometimes in the autumn. The seedlings form several leaves quite quickly and can be potted up separately at the end of their first season, but they seem to thrive better if they are in close proximity to other seedlings. It is probably better therefore to keep them in their seed pots and give them liquid feeding in their second season, and only repot them when they become crowded. At that stage the corms intended for the open garden can be planted out, or they can be potted individually. The more tender species should be kept in a cold greenhouse throughout, but the young bulbs of hardy species will do equally well in a shaded frame or even in an open shaded plunge bed.

Fritillaria

This increasingly popular genus is a large one with an immense range of plants from different habitats throughout the northern hemisphere, with different methods of increase and different cultural requirements.

Many of the easiest species for the garden, *Fritillaria meleagris*, *F. pyrenaica*, *F. pontica* and others, only increase slowly by division of their bulbs when left in situ, and establishment of a large colony over the years is probably more dependent on self-seeding than on vegetative increase. They are very easy to raise from seed, of which they set an abundance if they are not dead-headed, and if a large stock is wanted they lend themselves to sowing the seed in the open or in a frame with prepared soil. The majority of the species which are less robust and which do not form bulbils are best grown from seed in the normal way. Many of these bulbs can also be increased, by brave gardeners, by cutting or breaking each bulb in half, as described in the previous chapter.

Vegetative increase is also very variable. At the one extreme are plants which occasionally split into two or form an occasional bulbil; at the other extreme are species which form a multitude of tiny bulbils, for example *Fritillaria acmopetala*, *F. affinis*, *F. recurva*, and *F. pudica*. These small bulbils can be 'sown' like seed and grown on in the same way, possibly but not necessarily flowering a little quicker than from seed. If you are not looking for maximum increase they can be left on or around the parent bulbs, when some at least should eventually reach maturity, although others will probably disappear. A compromise which I have found successful is to separate some or all of the bulbils when repotting and sprinkle them at a higher level in the pot over the mature bulbs.

The most obliging species, not as many as one would like unfortunately, are those which produce several larger bulbils each year, which can be potted up separately from their parents and will probably mature in a couple of years. Several of the Middle Eastern species behave in this way, *Fritillaria crassifolia*, *F. hermonis*

amana, *F. aurea*, and others, as well as a few American and European species. More details will be given under individual species.

Galanthus

Snowdrops are generally easy to grow in partial shade in humus-rich soil with adequate drainage; and most of them increase freely by splitting of their bulbs, eventually becoming overcrowded, so that propagation is simple by division. Galanthus enthusiasts seem satisfied that this division should be carried out 'in the green' while the plants are in full growth. If this is done soon after flowering one can enjoy the flowers before they are disturbed. This method certainly works well and the plants become established and flower for the next season. I am not entirely convinced that it is any better than dividing the clumps of bulbs while they are dormant, as long as they are in moist soil and are immediately replanted into moist soil. There is little doubt that if dry stored bulbs are planted they will establish more slowly with considerable losses. In the case of the commonest species which are sold cheaply in large quantities, sufficient of them will usually survive for the losses to be scarcely noticeable, but the many more precious species and varieties should be kept moist at all time, storing the bulbs in damp peat if they cannot be replanted immediately.

The less common species can be grown from seed, usually taking three to four years to flowering, but unless the different species are kept well apart, hybridization will often be a problem.

Iris

The bulbous irises of interest to the rock gardener fall mainly into the two sections Juno (subgenus *Scorpiris*) and Reticulata (subgenus *Hermodactyloides*), which differ greatly in their requirements.

The Juno irises are characterized by having permanent storage roots below the bulb. These can be as big or bigger than the bulb, and are vital to the survival of the bulb. They are easily broken off the bulb in handling, and when purchasing Juno bulbs it is essential to ensure that they are still attached. In practice it is easier to persuade the detached roots to form new bulbs than the bulbs to form new roots, but neither is very successful. Make sure you have both from the start, but do not discard the pieces, unless you are sending them back to the supplier!

Juno irises will increase by splitting of their bulbs and roots, but in most species this is a slow process and it is easier to build up stocks by growing them from seed. The seed should have a cold period, but even then germination is notoriously erratic, odd plants sometimes appearing intermittently over several years. For this reason it is advisable, unless there has obviously been good germination, to move the whole potful into a larger pot of fresh compost. Progress of the young plants is usually sufficiently good for the repotting to be done after one season's growth. In some species, for example *Iris cycloglossa*, full germination is seen during the first spring, and the plants can then be potted individually at the end of their dormancy, or they can be planted several to a pot, ensuring there is plenty of space for the spreading storage roots.

The Reticulata irises are among the most satisfactory dwarf bulbs, most of them increasing freely both by the bulbs splitting into two or three and by the formation of small bulbils around the base of the bulb. In this way large clumps will build up rapidly in good well-drained soil, and these can be divided when necessary. The rarer species can be grown from seed. Their capsules may not be obvious at the end of the season , because like those of some crocuses, they are at or partially below soil level. The bulbs are slow to develop in the early stages and often take five years to attain flowering size.

Lilium

There are a few lilies small enough to be considered here, and their propagation is generally different from other bulbs. They can be increased from scales as described above, but as far as the smaller species are concerned they are more often grown from seed. Treatment of the seed can be the same as for other bulbs until after germination, preferably using a compost containing sterile leaf-mould as recommended for woodland bulbs. Germination usually takes place in early spring, but may be delayed until the second spring after sowing unless it is given a hot and cold treatment in polythene bags as described earlier (page 24).

After germination the pots should be brought under glass and the seedlings will often produce further leaves quite quickly. For maximum growth the best results seem to be obtained from repotting the young plants at this stage, while they are in full growth, three seedlings to a 3¼ in (8 cm) pot, or more in a larger pot. A more labour-saving method is to repot the whole potful into a considerably larger pot and then repot individually or at a wider spacing in the autumn. The young plants should develop quickly and they can be planted into suitable soil in the garden after two or three years, or repotted frequently if they are to be kept in pots. If repotted frequently *Lilium formosanum* var. *pricei* will often flower in its second season.

Narcissus

This is another widely varying genus: with some species enjoy woodland conditions, others thrive in normal garden soil, and yet others need a well-drained soil in the warmest possible place, or need to be grown under glass. In many species and hybrids the bulbs increase well by splitting into two or even three each year, eventually building up into over-crowded clumps, which should be divided and replanted.

There are several species which remain uncommon because their vegetative increase is slow or because they have special cultural needs, and these should be grown from seed, or possibly by cutting up the bulbs (see page 26). The seed can be dealt with in the usual way, but the seedlings of those species which benefit from a dry summer resting period, mainly native to North Africa or southern Spain, should be kept almost dry during their dormant period, whereas the majority can be kept watered at all times. Seedling bulbs are very small and hard to find in compost, so they should not be repotted for two years. The majority take four or five years to flower.

Trillium

These excellent woodland plants increase gradually by forming new growth buds along the sides of their rhizomes, so that it may be possible to divide their clumps after several years. They can be left for a long time before they will suffer from overcrowding. Vegetative increase can be improved by means of special treatment of the rhizomes. These are exposed after the leaves have died down by scraping away the soil, and then the growing point at the end of the rhizome is cut out with a sharp knife, leaving a concave depression. This will prevent flowering from that growing point but it will encourage formation of small bulbs around the cut surface, which can be removed later or left to grow large. Another method is to make a longitudinal cut to the depth of 2 mm along the rhizome, which will encourage bulbil formation along the length of the

cut. Whichever method is used the cut surface should be dusted with a fungicide before the rhizome is replanted.

They are not difficult to grow from seed but it is a slow process. In the first place no leaves are produced until the second spring after sowing, after which the seedlings should be kept well-watered and shaded until they appear large enough to repot. At that stage it is usually simpler to repot the whole into a larger pot rather than disturb them. An excellent alternative, mentioned previously (page 25), is to plant the whole potful into a specially prepared shady bed of rich soil with plenty of leaf-mould, where they can be left until they flower; be careful to keep them moist at all times and free from weeds.

Tulipa

The tulips nearly all need a sunny position in well-drained soil. A few of them increase rapidly and can be propagated by division after a few years, but more often this is a slow process and, given the required patience, seed raising is an excellent method. In my experience they are less slow to raise than their reputation might suggest. Some years ago I was given seed of a collection of species from Russia which I anticipated might take six or seven years to flower, but the first, the beautiful *Tulipa tschimganica*, flowered after four years and most of the remainder flowered the following year.

Tulipa sprengeri, a spectacular, very late-flowering species, is a most satisfactory candidate for growing from seed, as it is easily grown but expensive to buy, and it will flower in three or four years from seed. In many gardens it seeds itself around if established colonies are left undisturbed. As it sets an abundance of seed it also lends itself to sowing outside in drills in a frame or prepared bed.

CHAPTER 4

Bulbs for Autumn

After the burgeoning of summer, in which bulbs play a minor role, autumn brings a reawakening of interest in them. It is impossible to say with any certainty when 'autumn-flowering' bulbs will bloom. In North America the Fall varies enormously from season to season and from State to State, and in areas with dry summers it is dependent on the onset of rain. Even in Britain it can vary by several weeks, but the beginning of September in the south of England usually sees the earliest flowering of the *Cyclamen*, *Crocus* and *Colchicum* species, which can be major contributors to the autumn scene in the rock garden and borders.

CYCLAMEN

Cyclamen purpurascens (*C. europaeum*) is usually the first to flower in Kent, often opening the odd flower before the end of August. The leaves are generally almost circular, plain green in the centre but mottled to a variable extent with silvery green towards the periphery, occasionally even being unmottled. There is a rare form with pure-white flowers, but generally the flowers are pale to deep reddish-pink and are deliciously scented, a quality found in only a few cyclamen.

This is a beautiful species, and its very early flowering and scent make it particularly desirable, but unfortunately most growers find it more difficult to grow than *Cyclamen hederifolium*. Deep planting seems to help. My experience is that it is easy to raise from seed and I have a group of seedlings established in a shady part of a raised bed where they seem happy, but they do not increase by self-sown seedlings in the same way as *C. coum* or *C. hederifolium*, and past experience suggests that they may eventually dwindle rather than form a good colony.

1. *Cyclamen hederifolium*

Cyclamen hederifolium is the commonest and most widely grown species, and possibly the most valuable of all bulbs for autumn. It is easy to raise from seed, and it even grows reasonably well from the dried corms, which are frequently available cheaply but are not usually to be recommended, because a proportion of them will never form roots. Always buy cyclamen as growing plants if possible, and then raise more from seed. They are tolerant of a variety of conditions in sun or shade, with a preference for the latter in drier areas. In fact they are remarkably tolerant of dry shade under trees or shrubs, especially if the ground has been well prepared initially with plenty of compost or leaf-mould, which all cyclamen seem to relish.

Many years ago in this garden we were fortunate in being given a large quantity of freshly lifted corms, some of them very large indeed. They all established without difficulty and over the years have produced scores of self-sown seedlings, some of them a long way away from the original planting, thanks to the ants which enjoy the sugary coating and presumably take the seeds to their nests. The rain tends to wash the seed to the front of the bed, from which one can remove tiny growing plants to put elsewhere or give to friends. We now have a bed 1.5 metres wide and several metres long in which the leaves, mainly of *C. hederifolium* and of *C. coum*, form a continuous carpet from autumn until early summer; the display of flower in all shades is remarkable, first from late summer to mid-autumn, and then again from late winter to late spring. The bed was originally shaded by a large apple tree, which succumbed to a hurricane, but it is now in almost full sun with no ill effects to the cyclamen.

The leaves of *Cyclamen hederifolium* are beautifuly marbled with grey in a variety of patterns, and some good leaf forms have been selected, which come almost true from seed. These include one with particularly spectacular markings, offered in catalogues as 'Bowles Apollo'. The plant was first raised by E. A. Bowles, and one must assume that only its seedlings are now in cultivation; but the group under this name seem to have well fixed markings, even if the pundits feel that they are different from the original. Plants with almost uniformly grey-green leaves, and others with strikingly long and narrow leaves are sometimes seen, and the possible variation in a large group is remarkable.

The flower colour is also very variable, from pure white to deep magenta with all shades of pink between. Most of the white forms usually have some pink colouring on the 'nose', and pure whites are much sought after.

Cyclamen cilicium is a smaller, more delicate-looking plant than *C. hederifolium*, but in spite of appearances it is easy to grow and hardy in most of the British Isles, requiring the same conditions as *C. hederifolium*. The leaves are small and rounded, dark green, sometimes unmarked but usually with some marbling. Forms with pure white flowers are not uncommon and can sometimes be purchased as such, but most commonly the flowers are pale to deep pink with darker shading at the base of the petals.

Cyclamen intaminatum was originally included as a subspecies of *C. cilicium*, but it has now acquired specific status. It is a delightful little plant with small rounded leaves, considerably smaller than those of *C. cilicium*, usually plain green, but in some forms marbled. Specialist nurseries list the two forms separately. The flowers are tiny, among the smallest of all the species and are most commonly plain white or pale pink with no basal blotching. Its small size makes it ideal for cultivation in a pan in an alpine house or cold greenhouse but, given a site where it will not be swamped by more robust neighbours, it grows perfectly well in the garden in sun or partial shade.

Cyclamen mirabile is a comparatively recent introduction from Turkey, and closely resembles *C. cilicium*. The rounded leaves have toothed margins and are strongly marbled, with deep-purple shading on the reverse. The flowers are similar to those of *C. cilicium*, usually on shorter stems, and sometimes with a frilled edge. It is an excellent plant under glass, but has not proved as easy to grow outside.

The remaining autumn-flowering cyclamen are usually grown under glass, but in areas warmer than southern England they would probably be good garden plants. Even here there is scope for experiment, and *Cyclamen cyprium* has survived several winters in a sheltered area of this garden, although admittedly it has not flowered as well as those previously described. On the other hand *C. graecum* has grown and flowered well in a raised bed with the protection of overhead Dutch lights only. It is evidently hardy down to at least -5°C (23°F) if it is planted deeply; the corms in this bed being at least 15 cm (6 in) beneath the surface, partially protected by a lump of tufa. *Cyclamen africanum* and *C. rohlfsianum* are too tender for the open garden except in areas where there is no danger of frost.

Cyclamen cyprium is similar in size to *C. cilicium* but the rounded leaves have a strikingly toothed border and well-developed marbling at the edge, which is only rarely absent. The flowers are white or pale pink with a well-marked dark-purple blotch at the base and generally do not appear until most of the other autumn species have finished.

C. africanum resembles *C. hederifolium* very closely, especially in flower, but the leaves are usually much bigger and their petioles rise straight upwards from the tuber, rather than lying horizontal before turning upwards as in *C. hederifolium*. Unfortunately it is much more tender.

Cyclamen rohlfsianum can be a spectacular species, but it is more difficult to grow than the others and is almost completely frost-tender. Grown under glass it is very liable to rot if care is not taken with watering. The plants should be kept dry during the summer, and watered sparingly at first when signs of growth appear, or in early autumn. During the growing season it should be watered more freely, but it should be kept out of direct sun light. The large leaves are generally broader than long and are partially lobed with toothed margins and have purple backs. The flowers are deep rose with darker colouring towards the base, and are usually scented.

Only *C. hederifolium* and *C. purpurascens*, among the autumn-flowering species, are hardy in Zone 5, but they all make excellent pot plants. The best time to pot them or to transfer young seedlings into larger pots is towards the end of the natural dormant season in late summer. They can be grown in plastic pots but care must be taken to ensure particularly good drainage, as the tubers can rot if kept in sodden poorly drained soil, especially if they are kept wet during the summer. If clay pots are used there is less danger of overwatering. Various composts can be used, including proprietary peat-based, or John Innes No. 2 or similar loam- based composts, but they will almost certainly require extra drainage to be added, to make up at least a third of their bulk. A good home-made compost is one part of sieved leaf-mould, one part of peat or peat-substitute, one part of loam, and two parts of coarse grit with some additional lime, or of limestone chippings, with bone meal or John Innes base fertilizer (see page 17) to the strength of John Innes No. 2 compost, that is to say 1 oz to one gallon of compost.

When potting the tubers they should, in most cases, be planted with the surface of the tuber level with the surface of the compost but covered by a top dressing of grit. *Cyclamen graecum* and *C. purpurascens* are better planted deeper in the pot with at least 3 cm (1 in) of compost over them. During the growing season they should be kept moist at all times, but after the leaves die down watering should be reduced until growth recommences. Ideally during this time *C. graecum* and *C. africanum* should be kept dry, and the other species should be kept 'just moist', a desirable state not easy to achieve as they will obviously have a wet period each time they are watered, unless they can be watered by immersing the bottom of the pot in shallow water for a short time. Cyclamen seem to flower better if they are slightly pot-bound, so it is advisable to pot them into the smallest size which will accommodate the roots comfortably, and only to repot when they become pot-bound.

CROCUS

There are a large number of autumn-flowering crocus species, most of which appear to be hardy in Zone 5, and possibly lower. Many of these are uncommon in cultivation except in the collections of crocus enthusiasts, but there remains a good range available from nurserymen which are easy to grow in the open garden. It seems strange that the name 'autumn crocus' conjures up a picture of a colchicum for many gardeners, and that the true genus is not as popular as it should be: it has none of the disadvantages of the colchicum – enormous leaves which make their placement difficult, and a certain uniformity of colour. Everyone loves crocuses in spring and, apart from the absence of accompanying leaves in most of them, the autumn-flowering species are of equal merit, usually long-lived in the garden and increasing freely.

The ideal situation for them is a raised bed or rock garden, but they are equally at home in any sunny border as long as the drainage of the soil is reasonably good. In heavy soils it is certainly advantageous to incorporate extra grit, as for most bulbs. The more robust species can be naturalized in grass. They are very satisfactory pan plants for the cold greenhouse where they can be enjoyed in comfort, unbattered by the autumn rains; although very few actually need a drying-off period in summer, as do some of the winter- and spring-flowering species.

The earliest crocus to flower, usually in August, is *Crocus scharojanii* (*C. lazicus*), an exciting high-mountain plant which is rare and difficult; it is the only yellow-flowered crocus flowering in autumn, most of the commoner yellow crocus-like plants being sternbergias. It can be grown outside in soil more humus-rich than is appropriate for most species; and it resents excessive drying in summer if it is grown under glass. The flowers are slender and deep golden-yellow, appearing before the leaves.

Most of the species flower in September and October, and into November (in the northern hemisphere) and I will consider the most easily grown first. *Crocus speciosus* is tall with a very long tube and large flowers, sometimes looking almost coarse. The colour of the flowers is variable from white through some wishy-washy shades of cream or palest lavender to a good deep purple, usually veined with darker purple lines on the exterior. The anthers are yellow. Some of the best forms should be obtainable as named varieties: for example 'Aitchisonii' pale lavender, 'Albus' a good white, 'Artabir' pale lavender with prominent veining,

'Cassiope' pale violet with a yellow throat, 'Conqueror' mid-blue, and 'Oxonian' deep blue. Their names may not always be accurate in catalogues, but at least they are all excellent garden plants.

Crocus pulchellus 'Zephyr' is very similar to these, pale lilac-blue in colour and another very easy plant. The true *C. pulchellus* is less often seen. It has smaller, more globular flowers of a good deep purplish-blue, with a yellow throat and white anthers, and there is also a white form. *Crocus medius* was at one time one of the most common species in catalogues. Although not quite so freely available now, it is another very easy species, which increases moderately. The flowers should be a good deep purple, with yellow stamens and deep-orange, branched style, but paler colour forms are sometimes seen, and there is a rare pure white.

Crocus serotinus is one of the species which flowers with the leaves and thus strikes one as more like a spring-flowering species. It is usually available as its subspecies *salzmannii*, or under the name *C. asturicus atropurpureus*, which is also a form of ssp. *salzmannii* and is one of the darkest-flowered species of all with deep-purple segments. The colour of ssp. *salzmannii* is very variable from palest blue to purple. All the varieties seem easy to grow and can even be established in grass.

Crocus sativus is the Saffron Crocus, characterized by the style's having three long, bright-red branches which are used to make saffron. It is not a very good garden plant as it rarely flowers freely, except in warmer climates. I have a long-established clump in a sunny border which produces an abundance of leaves every year but only a few flowers, which are lilac, streaked with darker purple. *Crocus cartwrightianus* is closely allied to *C. sativus*, but it has smaller flowers, varying in colour between white and purple, usually with some darker streaking, and it

flowers more reliably if it is given a warm, sunny position.

Crocus longiflorus is another free-flowering species for the open garden, The colour varies but is generally pale purple, with some darker feathering and a yellow throat; the anthers are orange and the stamens yellow, and like *C. sativus* and *C. serotinus* it usually has leaves by the time it flowers.

Crocus nudiflorus is a favourite species in my own garden. It is said to flourish particularly well in grass, but here it is in a rock garden, where the slender, deep-violet-purple flowers appear before the leaves in early autumn. They never make a dense cluster of flowers but are well spaced, because the corms are 'stoloniferous', tending to spread sideways freely. *Crocus kotschyanus* is another splendid plant, especially in the form of its subspecies *leucopharynx*. The type species has large pale lilac-coloured flowers, with yellow blotches or a general yellow staining at the throat, and white stamens; whereas the subspecies has flowers of a similar colour but with a conspicuous white throat, a very cool combination which makes it among the most beautiful of all the easily grown autumnal species. Although all the crocuses do best in full sun, this species has certainly been very succesful in a partially shaded position, in a rich but very well-drained soil, where it increases and flowers well.

If I was limited to three autumn-flowering crocuses I would have little hesitation in choosing *Crocus kotschyanus* ssp. *leucopharynx*, *C. banaticus*, and *C. goulimyi*. The flowers of *C. banaticus* are unique in shape bacause the spreading outer segments of the flower are much larger than the inner segments, which are upright. The result is a flower which resembles an iris in shape, hence its old name of *Crocus iridiflorus*. The colour is usually a uniform pale lavender, even in the throat, but the various clones seem to vary and some are a much deeper shade. The anthers are yellow, and the styles are large and much branched, either white or of a colour similar to the segments. There is a very beautiful white form, which remains rare. *Crocus banaticus* is not difficult to grow but it seems to do best in partial shade in a moist bed with plenty of leaf-mould or other humus, rather than in full sun.

Crocus goulimyi is a comparatively recent introduction from southern Greece, which has proved a very successful garden plant, increasing well and flowering reliably rather late in the autumn, in well-drained soil in sun. The flowers have an exceptionally long tube for their size and somewhat rounded segments, the colour being pale lilac. There may be a slight difference in shade between the inner and outer segments, and some forms are bicoloured with the outer segments deep lilac and the inner almost white. There is an exceptionally beautiful white variety of nursery origin which is as easy to grow and increase as the type, and has recently been named 'Mani White', and also a less robust white form of wild origin, var. *leucantha*.

Crocus goulimyi is sometimes said to be a little tender, but in Kent it has proved much hardier than some other southern Greek species, surviving the severe winter of 1982, when the temperature reached as low as -20°C. This killed various forms of *Crocus laevigatus* and several *C. niveus* and *C. boryi,* that I was then growing in pots in an unheated house with the result that they were frozen solid for two weeks. The *C. laevigatus* varied greatly in colour: some were white, others lilac, most of them with most attractive darker feathering on the outside of the segments and yellow in the throat, and yellow branched stigma and white stamens. They were among the most beautiful of the smallest species. *C. boryi* resembles a white *C. laevigatus* but it

Fig. 2. *Crocus banaticus*

2. *Crocus goulimyi* var. *leucantha*

is a more robust plant with considerably larger and more globular flowers. *C. niveus* is also white or very pale lavender, and the flowers are very large, without feathering and with yellow stamens and stigma. *C. hartmannianus*, from the same area, is smaller, with a yellow throat and often with a purplish tube and slight purplish streaking on the exterior. The form from Mt Parnassus differs in having a white throat. Corms of *C. cancellatus*, from the same area of Greece, have survived and increased slowly for several years in a raised bed with winter protection. This is a variety with white flowers heavily marked with deep violet on the outside. It is said to be more difficult to please and is generally grown in a pan or in a bulb-frame. These species are only tender in

exceptional circumstances – they should survive in well-drained soil in most British gardens; and in Zone 7, and possibly lower, in North America.

Several other less commonly available species are sometimes available, and I have described these briefly in the table below.

COLCHICUM

Colchicums can provide one of the most colourful features of the autumn garden, and at that season one can readily forgive them for their large leaves later in the year. The problem is that the flowers *per se* are small enough for them to look ideally placed among rock plants and small perennials, but such a situation has to be

OTHER AUTUMN-FLOWERING CROCUS SPECIES AVAILABLE

NAME	SIZE	COLOUR	PROTECTION ADVISABLE	COMMENTS
C. asumaniae	small	white or pale blue	frame or a.h.	recently available
C. cambessedesii	tiny	pale purple dark feathering	a.h. or frame	too small to appreciate in the open
C. karduchorum	medium	lilac dark veining	none	white branching stigma
C. ochroleucus	small	white with yellow throat	none	easy
C. oreocreticus	medium	purple with buff exterior	none	close to *C. cartwrightianus*
C. pallasii	medium	lilac variable	frame or sheltered	Close to *C. cartwrightianus*
C. robertianus	large	very pale lilac with paler throat	a.h. or frame	recently available
C. tournefortii	large	lavender blue	none	orange branching stigma; flowers open without sun
C. vallicola	medium	white with yellow throat	none	best in peaty soil kept moist

avoided because the large coarse leaves will flop over and kill any small plants within reach. It is difficult to find the ideal site for them, but in groups among shrubs, near the front of borders so that the flowers can be enjoyed, is the one favoured in my own garden. Care is still needed when planting other smaller plants to remember just where the colchicum leaves are likely to be. They can be established in grass, but this also presents difficulties because, although some of the species are sufficiently robust to compete with grass, mowing has to be postponed until the leaves have died down.

The autumn-flowering species are hardy both in Britain, and in Zone 5 – and possibly lower – in North America. They seem to be undemanding as to soil, although the smaller species do better if drainage is good. Ideally they should be in a sunny position, but the easy *Colchicum autumnale* and *C. speciosum* seem to grow quite well in partial shade. The remarks I have made regarding siting apply only to the large-leaved plants; there are a number of small species which are more difficult, in some instances better grown in the alpine house or a bulb-frame.

Colchicum autumnale and its varieties are the easiest to grow and most reliable to increase, although the flowers are not as striking as those of *C. speciosum*. They all have excessively large leaves. *Colchicum autumnale* itself has clusters of rather slender, pale purplish-pink flowers, the individual segments 6–8 cm (2½–3 in) long with no chequering on the outside. The anthers are yellow. Each corm produces a succession of several flowers over several weeks. There is an excellent pure-white variety, *C. autumnale album*, of equal vigour, and both the pink and the white have double varieties 'Pleniflorum' (*roseum plenum*) and 'Alboplenum' which may appeal but have a somewhat ragged

appearance. 'Waterlily' is a more satisfactory double with larger and more substantial flowers. It is probably a hybrid with *Colchicum speciosum*. A deeper purple colour is seen in *C. autumnale atropurpureum*.

Colchicum speciosum is one of the most magnificent of all autumn-flowering bulbs with very large flowers of substantial texture and almost globular shape, followed by leaves of equal opulence. The colour is variable, in shades of purplish-pink with no chequering, and usually with an extensive area of white on the throat. The anthers are yellow. There is a very fine white form 'Album' with equally large flowers, and a darker-flowered form is sometimes listed under the name 'Atrorubens'.

Two species very similar to *C. speciosum* are *C. giganteum* and *C. bornmuelleri*, both available in commerce. *C. giganteum* has very large flowers but they are more funnel-shaped rather than globular. *C. bornmuelleri* from northern Turkey also

3. *Colchicum speciosum* 'Album'

has very similar flowers but the leaves are very much narrower, usually less than 5 cm (2 in) wide, whereas the leaves of *C. speciosum* are frequently over 10 cm (4 in). *C. cilicicum* is a very easy plant in the garden. Its flowers are usually unchequered with segments up to 7 cm (2¾ in) long.

The species so far mentioned have no chequering on the outside of the segments, but it is a very striking and attractive feature of others. This tessellation is probably most marked in *Colchicum variegatum*, which I have frequently admired on some of the Greek Islands, producing its widely open, heavily chequered flowers on very short stems among the rocks, even before the earliest rain. Unfortunately it does not seem to be an easy plant for the garden, although it can be managed in a bulb-frame with a good summer drying. *Colchicum agrippinum* is a similar but much easier plant to grow in the open. It is not of wild origin and is thought to be a hybrid beween *C. variegatum* and *C. autumnale*.

Colchicum bivonae (*C. bowlesianum*) is a larger-flowered species with well-marked tessellation, and it is a good garden plant for the open ground. The segments are up to 7 cm (3 in) long, of the typical purplish-pink, varying in depth of colour, with brown anthers. Several excellent large-flowered hybrids with some degree of chequering have been raised with *Colchicum bivonae* as one parent. These include the very large 'The Giant', pale pink with a white throat, and 'Violet Queen', a dark bluish-purple with darker tessellation and a white throat. *Colchicum macrophyllum* has even larger flowers, usually paler with a white throat, but it is considered to be more tender than the other species mentioned and is probably only hardy in the open in the south of England or in warmer countries (Zone 8).

In addition to all the species with outsize leaves there are a number of small-

OTHER COLCHICUMS

NAME	SIZE	COLOUR	PROTECTION ADVISABLE	COMMENTS
C. corsicum	small	lavender	a.h. or frame	good a.h. plant; flowers slightly tessellated
C. hierosoly mitanum	medium	pinkish purple	a.h.	tender
C. kotschyi	small	white or pale pink	none	starry flowers
C. lingulatum	medium	pinkish purple	none or frame	long narrow leaves
C. lusitanum	medium	pinkish purple	none or frame	slight tessellation
C. parnassicum (laetum)	medium	pale pink	none or frame	resembles C. lingulatum
C. troodii	small	white or pale pink	a.h.	tender
C. turcicum	medium	deep reddish purple	a.h. or frame	deep colour
C. umbrosum	small	white or pale pink	none	poor starry flowers

leaved species. Many of them flower in spring but the following species are autumn-flowering. *Colchicum cupanii* is a delightful little plant with leaves appearing with the flowers. These are purplish-pink, only up to 3 cm (1¼ in) high, with characteristically dark anthers, almost black until their yellow pollen is revealed. Another small species is *C. pusillum* which has much narrower leaves and generally very pale-pink flowers. *C. boissieri* is unusual in having stoloniferous corms which spread sideways, and leaves which are longer and narrower than those of *C. cupanii*. The flowers are of similar colour but slightly larger.

These small species of Colchicum are not such good garden plants as the larger. They can be grown on the rock garden in the company of smaller plants, but are better plants for pot cultivation in the cold house, or for a bulb-frame. The exception among those mentioned is *C. boissieri* which will grow well in well-drained soil in a sunny place.

OTHER GENERA

Allium

Onions seem to be becoming increasingly popular over recent years as gardeners discover their variety and beauty. Many of them are suitable for the rock garden but only a few of these flower during the autumn months. One that has been grown widely for several years is *Allium callimischon* – not a great beauty but well worth growing for its late flowering and neat habit. The length of the flowering stem is variable, usually 10–15 cm (4–6 in) but sometimes twice this height. At the top of each stem is a cluster of small flowers which are a slightly wishy-washy shade of pale greyish-pink. The whole head can be up to 3 cm (1¼ in) across, with 10–20 individual flowers. There are two subspecies in cultivation, ssp. *callimischon* and ssp. *haemostictum*, the latter differing in having red spots within the segments, and being at the lower end of the height range.

Allium thunbergii is a more striking plant which has only recently appeared in the trade. It is proving an excellent rock garden plant, easy to grow and very late-flowering, with rounded heads of deep reddish-purple flowers with very long protruding stamens and style. Although said to be up to 30 cm (1 ft) high in flower, my own plants have generally been about 18 cm (7 in) with little variation. As well as the typical plant I grow one with pure white flowers which is otherwise identical.

Allium wallichii is a much taller plant, growing up to 80 cm (2 ft 8 in), and has flowers of an even deeper purple colour than *A. thunbergii*, in loose umbels up to 5 cm (2 in) wide. It flowers very late and seems to be a good garden plant. Native to wet areas of the Himalayas, it does better in humus-rich soil that does not dry out in summer.

Biarum

The biarums are an interesting autumn-flowering genus that is very little grown. The easiest species in the open is *Biarum tenuifolium* which flowers in early autumn before the leaves appear. The spathe (the main part of the typical aroid flower) rises from ground level to a height of about 15 cm (6 in). It is pale to deep purplish-brown in colour and is narrower than that of most arums, often with a distinct twist in it. The elongated spadix is the same colour and protrudes a little from the top of the spathe. The three or four leaves do not appear until after flowering. They are usually 8–12 cm (3–5 in) long and vary considerably in width from 2.5 to 10 mm. This seems to be an easy, freely increasing plant, but it does not always flower as well as one might wish.

Biarum davisii is now offered by several nurseries. It must be admitted that it is more interesting than beautiful and will make little impact in the garden, its small size and probable slight tenderness making it more suitable for a pan in the alpine house. The hooded spathe is 4–6 cm (1½–2½ in) long, cream-coloured, marked inside with abundant pink spots. It has a somewhat grotesque appearance, very squat with a broad base sitting on the ground, and a wide mouth facing upwards and outwards, in which the short, pinkish spadix can be seen. I find that it flowers regularly as a pan plant but does not increase much for me.

Caloscordon neriniflorum

This is a monotypic species which I have only recently had the opportunity of growing, and which I think should be a valuable addition to the range of autumn flowers, if it proves hardy. It certainly makes a good pan plant, and should survive in the open where temperatures do not drop much below -5°C for long periods. It is a most attractive plant, in appearance between an allium and a nerine. The narrow leaves appear in early spring and die down in late summer. The flowers, in early autumn, are in broad loose umbels 6–10 cm (2½–4 in) across, on stiff stems up to 20 cm (8 in) high. The individual flowers, up to twenty in number, are star-shaped, 8–12 mm across, deep reddish-purple. The flowers open over a long period and set plenty of seed, so that it should be easy to build up stocks with which to experiment in the open ground.

Galanthus

Gardeners enjoy seeing the occasional plant flowering totally out of season, and there is one snowdrop which can be relied upon to flower regularly in mid- to late autumn – *Galanthus reginae-olgae* (*G. cor-*

cyrensis). It resembles the common *G. nivalis* very closely, differing only in its autumn flowering and in having leaves with a distinct grey band down the centre. The inner segments have a solitary green blotch at the apex. It grows well in the open garden and increases slowly, but it seems to enjoy a sunnier site than most of the other snowdrops and is tender in the coldest climates, where it should have glass protection. Strictly, the autumn-flowering *Galanthus reginae-olgae* is classified as subspecies *reginae-olgae* and the spring-flowering form is ssp. *vernalis* of *G. reginae-olgae*.

Leucojum

The snowflakes are a beautiful genus of spring and autumn-flowering bulbs, which includes one or two robust hardy species for the open garden in spring and early summer, and several smaller plants: of the latter, some can be grown in a rock garden or raised bed and some are only suitable for the cold house or bulb-frame in cold countries.

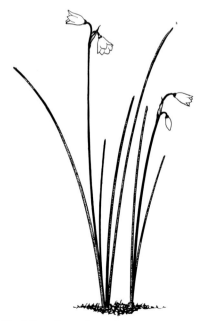

Fig. 3. Leucojum autumnale

The most widely grown autumn-flowering species is *Leucojum autumnale*, which seems to perform much better in some gardens than others, judging by the differences in opinion of growers on its ease of cultivation and its likes and dislikes. Perhaps some clones are easier than others. We have plants growing in two very different situations, but they are reasonably successful in both. The generally recommended site is a warm sunny bed in the rock garden with good drainage, and in such a position here it has increased slowly over the years and flowered well every autumn. We also have several clumps at the edge of a 'peat bed' where it gets some sun around mid-summer but little at other times. Here it has increased much more freely and still flowers well. I suspect that it does best in a soil with plenty of leaf-mould or other humus as well as good drainage,and it will tolerate shade in hotter and drier areas. It is hardy in Zone 6, and possibly Zone 5, in the USA.

It is one of the most dainty bulbous plants with slender upright stems 12–20 cm (5–8 in) high carrying two or three small, nodding or outward-facing white bells usually tinged at the base with the reddish-purple of the upper parts of the stems. The leaves appear soon after the first flowers in early autumn and are very narrow, 10–15 cm (4–6 in) long. Two varieties are in cultivation, var. *operanthum* and var. *pulchellum*, but there is some doubt whether the plants of the first in cultivation are correctly named. Var. *operanthum* differs in being considerably taller and having all the segments toothed at their apices, whereas var. *pulchellum* has its leaves present when the first flowers appear, and has the outer segments toothed and the inner entire.

Leucojum valentinum has only recently come into regular cultivation. It resembles *L. autumnale* in size but the flowers are larger, with pointed segments, the leaves are generally longer, and botanically it is more closely related to the spring-flowering *Leucojum nicaense* in having a six-lobed disc at the base of the ovary. It has not been tried in the open extensively, but as it grows at lower altitudes in Spain and the Ionian Islands it may need some glass protection in countries subject to severe frosts.

Leucojum roseum is a delightful miniature, which is also considered generally to be too tender for the garden, although in Kent it has survived several mild winters in the open. The narrow grey-green leaves are present before flowering; in fact if plants are kept slightly moist at all times they are almost evergreen. In late summer and early autumn the flower stems appear, usually only 5–8 cm (2–3 in) long, each with two or three flowers, smaller than those of *L. autumnale*, pale pink in colour with a deeper pink vein down the centre of each segment. This is a beautiful plant, especially to the lover of miniatures, and it is so easy to grow from the abundantly set seed that a large potful can soon be produced, with spare plants to try outside. The seedlings reach flowering size more quickly than most bulbs, in two or three years.

Narcissus

Although this is not a genus usually associated with autumn, there are two species which flower at this time in their natural habitat, but seem reluctant to grow or flower in cultivation, and are probably only of interest to fanatics! *Narcissus viridiflorus* is a remarkable-looking plant which I would love to grow well. It has uniformly dark-olive-green flowers, solitary, or in umbels of 2–5 if the grower is more successful, on 15–20 cm (6–8 in) stems. The flowers are 2cm (¾ in) in diameter with a very shallow little cup and recurving pointed segments. It needs

4. *Oxalis versicolor*

drying off in summer in a pot or a frame, but only seems to flower after a very hot summer.

The other autumn-flowering species occasionally available is *Narcissus serotinus*, a more orthodox-looking species but one which needs the same conditions to persuade it to flower properly. It is similar in size to *N. viridiflorus* and has similar, narrowly linear leaves appearing after the flowers. These are usually one or two to a stem, white, up to 3 cm (1¼ in) across, with a shallow orange-lobed cup.

Oxalis

The name 'oxalis' may provoke shudders in most gardeners but it is a genus with many fine plants flowering in summer and autumn, some excellent for the open garden and some requiring glass protection in frosty areas. It is always difficult to know how many of the species to include in a book on bulbs, but having recently described many of them in a book on alpine plants, and with an imminent shortage of space, I have elected to exclude the spring- and summer-flowering *O. adenophylla*, *O. enneaphylla*, *O. laciniata*, *O. obtusa*, and *O. inops*, although they have tuberous roots of a

sort, and are highly recommendable. Their descriptions will be found in any book on alpine plants.

The hardiest of the common autumn-flowering species is *Oxalis lobata*, a popular alpine plant for the rock garden where its small size can be appreciated. In spring it produces a cluster of pale-green miniature clover-like leaves to a height of about 4 cm (1½ in), which then die, causing consternation in the uninitiated! In late summer the leaves reappear together with the delightful small, yellow, typical oxalis flowers, which continue in succession for several weeks, after which the leaves die again until spring. Although *O. lobata* has a reputation for slight tenderness it has certainly survived a succession of average winters, down to -10°C or thereabouts.

Two other late-flowering species are probably more tender, but as they both increase very well by division they are worth experimenting with outside, and both have survived our recent mild winters. *Oxalis purpurea* is worth growing for its foliage alone. It develops its leaves in late summer, grey-green, abundantly clothed in silver hairs, each of the three lobes about 1 cm (⅓ in) across. The flowers unfortunately appear rather sparsely, but they are a bright yellow 2 cm (¾ in) in diameter, nestling among or just above the leaves. It grows in South Africa where the usual colour is pale purple, a colour which I have never seen in Britain. The yellow form has been named after that great plantsman, 'Ken Aslet'.

Oxalis versicolor is similar in size, only attaining 2–3 cm (¾–1¼ in) in height, but the flowers are the great attraction, a remarkable chocolate-box effect of red and white candy stripes, produced in great abundance in late autumn and early winter. The small tubers increase very freely, but the plant is too tender to become a menace in gardens subject to frost. I am growing it in a greenhouse border, where the temperature is kept to a minimum of around 0°C and it flowers profusely without getting out of hand. I also grow it in a sheltered bed in the garden where it survived last winter, a mild one (down to -5°C).

Oxalis hirta is a tall species from South Africa with 20–30 cm (8–12 in) hairy stems, bearing three-lobed, almost sessile leaves, and branching towards the tips, each branch bearing a pink flower with a deeper centre, 2.5 cm (1 in) across in autumn or winter. It is not hardy in the garden in Britain but makes an excellent pan plant for the cold greenhouse.

Scilla

Most of the scillas flower in spring, but two species are in cultivation which flower in autumn. *Scilla autumnalis* is 5–12 cm (2–5 in) high with flat heads of small flowers, in shades of pale pinkish to purple, but usually somewhat wishy-washy. Apart from its late flowering it hardly merits a place in the garden. *Scilla scilloides* (*S. chinensis*) on the other hand is a generally underrated plant, with narrow leaves and dense spikes of good pink star-shaped flowers with prominemt stamens.

It seems quite easy in well-drained soil in a sunny position.

Sternbergia

Sternbergia lutea, the most widely grown species, looks to the uninitiated like a yellow-flowered crocus, but the genus is more closely allied botanically to the daffodils, and contains both autumn- and spring-flowering species, all of them beautiful plants for the garden or the cold house or frame.

Sternbergia lutea, flowering in great drifts of yellow beneath the olive trees from September to November, is one of the most spectacular sights around the Mediterranean for the plant enthusiast, who cannot fail to want to emulate it in the garden at home. Sadly this is one of those horticultural spectacles that is difficult to achieve, except in countries with a Mediterranean climate. In the garden the daffodil-like bulbs increase very freely and produce an abundance of leaves in early autumn, but they do not usually flower very freely except after a hot summer, and even then they are much more leafy and have far fewer flowers than in the wild. However a scattering of deep-yellow crocus flowers over a period of several weeks makes them well worth growing.

It is usually suggested that the bulbs should be planted in the hottest and driest bed in the garden and this is probably excellent advice, but the finest display of sternbergias I have ever seen in England was in a very long-established garden in which the owners were not particularly interested. I was astonished to see in the distance a broad drift of yellow a metre wide and 30 metres long, which proved to be a sheet of sternbergias in which the leaves could hardly be seen beneath the flowers. They were growing as a broad edging to a bed which was heavily shaded by Scotch Pines and were said to perform like this every year!

The typical *Sternbergia lutea* has narrow dark-green leaves, up to 6 cm (2½ in) long and up to 12 mm (½ in) wide, and large deep-yellow goblet-shaped flowers, 4 to 6 cm (1½–2½ in) high, which only just overtop the leaves in the garden. In Greece the leaves are absent or only just appearing at flowering time, and this improves the floral display. *Sternbergia lutea* var. *angustifolia* is sometimes offered. This is closer to *S. sicula* and may indeed be a form of it. It differs in having considerably narrower leaves, usually only 6 mm (½ in) wide. Some growers find it more free-flowering than the type.

Sternbergia sicula is a beautiful species which resembles *S. lutea* in shape and colour but differs in being considerably more compact and having much narrower leaves. It is equally easy to grow in a warm garden.

Sternbergia clusiana is a magnificent mid-to-late autumn-flowering plant with much larger, more globular flowers, which always appear before the leaves. It does not seem to be very satisfactory in the garden even in a sheltered position, but makes an excellent pot plant for the cold house or for a bulb-frame. Bulb increase is much slower than that of *S. lutea*. In contrast to *Sternbergia clusiana*, with its large flowers, *S. colchiciflora* is a fascinating and rather uncommon miniature, which again is best grown under glass. The flowers are usually only 2.5 cm (1 in) high and appear to be almost stemless as the tube is beneath the ground. The very narrow leaves are twisted and

appear several weeks after the flowers. It seems to be easy to grow and increases more freely than *S. clusiana*.

Most of the sternbergias are too tender for the open garden in colder areas, but *S. lutea* is hardy in Zone 7 in North America.

Zephyranthes

This is another genus with crocus-like flowers which flowers in autumn. The genus *Habranthus* is closely allied to *Zephyranthes*, and may produce some late flowers in autumn, but as their main season is in summer they will be dealt with in that section of the book.

Zephyranthes candida is unquestionably the best species for the garden, and it is surprising than it is not more widely grown. It has glossy green linear leaves up to 15 cm (6 in) long, mainly upright and often evergreen. The stiff erect flower stems are up to 20 cm (8 in) tall with solitary crocus-shaped flowers 3–4 cm (1¼–1 ½ in) long, which are white, tinged with green towards the base, with yellow anthers. In a sunny border of well-drained soil it flowers reliably every autumn and increases well by splitting of its bulbs. Although it grows in wet conditions in the wild in Argentina it seems to be perfectly tolerate of drought here. It is not sufficiently hardy to be grown in the coldest parts of Great Britain, and is probably Zone 7 in North America.

The only other common zephyranthes to flower regularly in autumn rather than summer is *Z. rosea*. This is a beautiful species with small linear leaves and rose-coloured flowers 2.5–3 cm (1 in) long on short tubes. It is not difficult and is worth trying in warm areas in the garden. It makes an excellent pot plant for the cold house or can be grown in a protected bulb-frame.

For the sake of completeness I will include the late-spring-flowering *Z. atamasco*, a very beautiful species with large pure white flowers, which unfortunately only seems to be hardy in the alpine house.

5. *Sternbergia lutea* (opposite)
6. *Zephyranthes atamasco* (right)

CHAPTER 5

Bulbs for Winter and early Spring

GENERAL

This season is the most difficult for the gardener who likes to enjoy colour all the year round, but it can also be among the most rewarding – any glimpses of colour are extra-welcome during the dreary months of winter. There are some excellent winter-flowering shrubs among the viburnums, prunus, mahonias, and sarcococcas, to name a few, but to have colour under and around these shrubs adds tremendously to the effect. There are a few perennials like early hellebores and *Iris unguicularis* which can be relied upon to flower then, but bulbous plants must be the main contributors.

The period covered here can be taken as from early November to the middle of March, in Northern Hemisphere countries with a climate similar to that of Brit-

ain in a 'normal' season. Winter flowers after Christmas are very much dependent on the weather, and the display which one might hope for in January may be postponed by a long cold spell until the middle of February, or later in cold areas, and conversely a warm period, such as we are experiencing as I write, can bring flowering forward so that the earliest irises and snowdrops have begun to flower in December. Many of the bulbs described in the last chapter will continue to flower into this period and some of those to be described in the next chapter may, in an early season, have started flowering in early March.

I will describe first the major genera, on which one expects to rely for a good display, and then some of the smaller genera, and genera which only contribute one or two species with flowers at this time, but which come into their own later.

ERANTHIS

The Winter Aconites can always be relied on for the first yellow 'colour carpet' at some time during January, and to continue to flower on and off for several weeks, withstanding difficult weather conditions reasonably well. A fall of snow spoils them for the time being but they soon recover with fresh blooms when the snow melts. They do well in the shade of deciduous trees or shrubs and will tolerate

7. *Eranthis hyemalis*

more sunny conditions in cooler climates. In my own garden they are well established in one bed, and their flowers carpet the ground, to be followed by large numbers of scillas and chionodoxas as they fade, all among the spreading roots of *Prunus tenella* 'Fire Hill', which runs about underground and produces striking upright 60 cm (2 ft) stems of pink flowers from reddish buds in late spring. The aconites seed themselves around freely if they are left undisturbed, especially into the edge of a gravel drive, which is always a fruitful source of seedlings from nearby plants.

The two common species of *Eranthis* are *E. hyemalis* and the very similar *E. cilicica*, now often lumped with it by botanists but usually offered in catalogues as a separate species. *Eranthis hiemalis* is almost too well known to need describing, with its large goblet-shaped flowers nestling in a ruff of narrow leaflets (bracts). *E. cilicica* flowers a little later and has more dissected leaves and bracts often with a faint bronze tinge. It does not seem to increase so freely and possibly does better in a sunnier situation.

The two species are the parents of a very fine hybrid, *Eranthis* x *tubergenii* 'Guinea Gold', which flowers three or four weeks later than *E. hyemalis*. The leaves are usually tinged with bronze and it is a more robust plant, taller and with larger flowers of a deeper, more golden yellow. Unfortunately the true plant has become uncommon, because it does not come true from seed, and vegetative increase is much slower than that of the other species.

Two other uncommon species are occasionally available. *Eranthis longistipitata* has smaller yellow flowers which are on short stalks above the dissected leaf-like bracts, whereas in the other species they are sessile. It appears to be more difficult to grow. The other species is *E. pinnatifida*

8. *Eranthis* x *tubergenii* 'Guinea Gold'

from Japan, which has small greyish-white flowers and, because of its small size and rarity, is usually grown in the cold house. I have found it slow to increase and temperamental under glass, and I have not tried it outside.

GALANTHUS

Perhaps snowdrops should have taken pride of place in this chapter as their earliest flowers often appear just before Christmas, and the later flowers of *Galanthus reginae-olgae* may still be appearing a month earlier. Although the later species may flower into late spring this seems such a typically winter-flowering genus that I will consider them all here. They all have similar, typically shaped pendent flowers with three large outer segments, and three small inner segments which are fused to form a cup. These inner segments have green markings at their apices and often at their bases. These markings are important in identification, as are the shape and colour of the leaves, which may be glossy green or glaucous grey-green, with or without a central stripe.

From the writer's point of view perhaps the most difficult problem with the genus is to know which to include out of the vast array of species, forms and varieties, which are available to the specialist. Every gardener loves snowdrops and many are

9. *Galanthus nivalis* 'Flore Pleno' (top)
10. *Galanthus nivalis* 'Lutescens' (left)
11. *Galanthus caucasicus* (above)

probably unaware of their great variety, and are content with growing carpets of *Galanthus nivalis*, the commonest and easiest of them all. I content myself with an increasing collection of those which can be recognised as distinct without requiring picking and studying in detail, and I will describe these first.

As I write this in January, the snowdrops are at their best, with three varieties very much predominant. When we moved here 20 years ago there were a few snowdrops in one small part of the garden, and these were all the double *Galanthus nivalis* 'Flore Pleno', which has increased tremendously and which I have been able to establish as good-sized colonies in other shady places. Double flowers are often spurned, especially among alpine enthusiasts, but these have great appeal because of their vigour and free increase and because, when looking at them from above, it is in fact difficult to know that they are double. They are small and have a broad shallow flower in comparison with others, but to appreciate their 'doubleness' one must pick them or at least upturn their flowers to admire the beautifully arranged frilly cluster of white inner segments, notched and marked with a green V on the outside at the apex, and heavily striped with green within. 'Lady Elphinstone' is sometimes available. It also has double flowers but in these the markings on the segments are yellow instead of green.

The double snowdrop is very small, especially as it flowers when the leaves are only beginning to develop, and contrasts dramatically with our other most successful species, *Galanthus caucasicus*, which stands at least twice as tall at 20–25 cm (8–10 in) and has very broad, 2 cm (¾ in) grey-green glaucous leaves. The flowers are correspondingly large, with very long outer segments and notched inner segments with their outer third

green. If you like your snowdrops large this is an excellent plant which seems to increase very freely here in a rather heavy loam in deep shade, in spite of becoming very dry in summer.

G. caucasicus is a variable plant and some forms may be smaller than I have described. They usually start flowering early in January, but varieties flowering earlier in winter have been described as var. *hiemalis*. Originally we acquired *Galanthus caucasicus* as *G. elwesii*. This is another large and vigorous species, but it differs in having green markings at the base of the inner segments as well as at the tips. 'Straffan' is probably another good vigorous form of *G. caucasicus*.

Several other snowdrops are doing well here but have not increased as rapidly as those mentioned previously. Among them are three very distinct forms of *G. nivalis*. 'Lutescens' stands out as one in which the markings on the segments are yellow instead of green, and the conspicuous ovary is also yellow. This has a reputation for being difficult, but it is increasing modestly in a shady place, in soil well enriched with leaf-mould, a site which suits all the more demanding species. 'Viridapicis' is very unusual in having green markings on the large outer segments as well as on the inner. 'Scharlockii' is distinct in having very long leaf-like bracteoles which stand up above the flower.

There are several other good garden forms of *Galanthus nivalis*, and a wealth of lesser known species and variants, to please the specialist. Of the former, 'Atkinsii' is the tallest , up to 25 cm (10 in), with elegant long flowers. 'S. Arnott is probably in this group and is another tall and vigorous plant but the flowers are fuller and more rounded. 'Magnet' is more slender and is distinct in carrying its flowers well out from the stem on long pedicels.

Galanthus allenii is another tall species with leaves almost as broad as those of *G. caucasicus* and large flowers with their inner segments marked at the apices with green. *G. plicatus* is similar in size but the leaves have a central pale stripe and are plicate, that is to say that the leaf margins are folded downwards, especially when they first unfurl. The green markings are apical only, but there is a subspecies, *G. plicatus* ssp. *byzantinus*, which differs in having green at the base as well as at the tips. *G. gracilis* is a small-growing plant with narrow twisted leaves, and flowers with green markings at the tips and the bases of the segments. *G. rizehensis* is also small, with very narrow leaves and flowers up to 2 cm (¾ in) long, and apical markings.

The snowdrops so far described have grey-green glaucous leaves, but there are a few species in which the leaves are a bright glossy green, giving a very different appearance to the plant. The commonest

and easiest of these is *Galanthus ikariae*, which I first acquired many years ago from a Paul Furse collection as *G. ikariae latifolius*. This grows splendidly in a more sunny place than the others, and has become a favourite snowdrop with its distinctive very broad glossy leaves and late flowering, well into spring. The flowers are otherwise typical, with apical green markings. At the same time as acquiring this species I was also given *Galanthus fosteri*, with similar bright-green leaves. It differs from *G. ikariae* in having more upright leaves and flowers with a broad basal band of green and a narrow apical patch on the inner segments. It has a reputation for being difficult, and it seems to prefer a well-drained sunny position rather than woodland treatment. I found it easy under glass and also grew it successfully outside in a warm sunny bed for several years.

IRIS

This genus gives us some of the most exciting of all bulbous plants, and these fall mainly into the two subgenera *Hermodactyloides* and *Scorpiris*, for which I will use the older names 'Reticulata' and 'Juno', which are more familiar to gardeners. The Reticulata irises generally flower early and will all be described in this chapter, although in many seasons a few of them may flower later in spring. The Junos present more of a problem as many of the fascinating small and difficult species usually grown under glass flower early, and the majority of the larger, more garden-worthy ones flower later, but I will consider all of them here.

Reticulata irises

Even when one has already been enjoying a few early snowdrop or narcissus flowers the earliest irises always provide one of the great thrills of gardening, raising

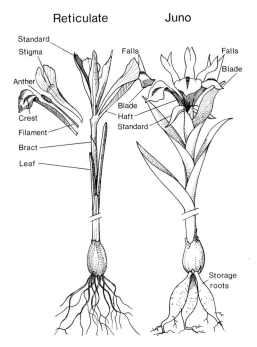

Reticulate   **Juno**

Standard
Stigma
Falls
Falls
Blade
Anther
Blade
Crest
Haft
Filament
Standard
Bract
Leaf
Storage roots

Fig. 4. Comparison of Reticulata and Juno iris

12. *Iris histrioides* 'Major' (above)
13. *Iris* 'Lady Beatrix Stanley' (right)
14. *Iris* 'Katharine Hodgkin' (below right)
15. *Iris* histrio (below)

hopes that spring is in the air. Most of the section are hardy, even in Zone 5. It is always *Iris histrioides* 'Major' that leads the way, never starting before Christmas but never waiting for long afterwards unless the weather is exceptionally hard. The fat greyish buds are always peering through the ground at the beginning of January waiting for a glimmer of warm sun. Once the flowers have opened they are surprisingly weather-resistant, recovering even from being buried for a few days under the snow. The bulbs increase freely by forming a lot of small bulbils around the base of the mature bulb, so that in a well-drained sunny site it is possible to build up a good size group.

There seems at the present time to be some muddle over the naming of this plant. Those I grow were purchased at least 20 years ago when everyone seemed to have the same plant under that name. Now this form seems very uncommon, and on the rare occasions on which plants are available from trade sources, they are variable, some of them resembling more closely the excellent *I. histrioides* 'Lady Beatrix Stanley'. The old clone has very large flowers 8 cm (3 in) wide of a uniform, very deep-blue colour on short stems. Down the centre of the broad blade is a narrow dark-yellow crest with white flecking outwards from it, these markings affecting only the inner third of the blade. 'Lady Beatrix Stanley' flowers a week or two later. It is very similar in size and colour but the blade is much more heavily marked with white; in fact the inner half of the blade appears white flecked with dark blue, the outer half blue with white streaks becoming fainter but almost reaching its periphery. This is evidently a selected clone of *Iris histrioides* itself, as it closely resembles the plate of that species in the Atlas for Dykes on Iris, published in 1935. It seems to be less free in bulbil production but increases slowly

but steadily in the open garden. At the present time all these species have become uncommon.

Iris histrioides var. *sophonensis* is sometimes seen and is quite an easy plant in the garden with very free bulbil production, which makes one wonder why it is so uncommon. The flowers are a very dark blue, smaller and much narrower in all their parts than those of Iris histrioides. As the blade is narrow the white streaking is inconspicuous, but the central yellow stripe stands out well.

Iris 'Katharine Hodgkin' opens its flowers two or three weeks after *Iris histrioides* 'Major'. It is a hybrid between *Iris histrioides* and the yellow *Iris winogradowii* and it is so vigorous that it has quickly become a very popular plant for its early flowering and its ease of cultivation. It increases rapidly both by division of its bulbs and by bulbils, rapidly forming spectacular groups. The flowers are even larger than those of its parents on similarly short stems. The background colour throughout is greyish-white heavily striped with pale blue. On the very broad blades the colour is suffused with yellow especially around the deep-yellow crest. Around the crest also are a few darkest blue, almost black, spots. The overall effect of mixed blue and yellow may not be to everyone's taste but a mass of these flowers in the garden at a dark time of year is spectacular, and remarkably easy to produce. 'Frank Elder' has the same parentage as 'Katharine Hodgkin' but has much less yellow in the flower so that it gives the impression of being pale blue, a pleasanter colour to most eyes. I have only grown it for a short time but it seems to increase more slowly.

What a pity *Iris histrio* is such a rare and temperamental plant! I grew it in pots for several years from collected bulbs, but eventually after some early increase they dwindled and died. To my amazement two years ago a small but healthy-looking colony appeared in a bed mainly devoted to cyclamen, and it has about eight flowers as I write. The explanation for its appearance is that I usually throw old bulb compost on to beds in the garden if there is any possibility of them containing small overlooked bulbils. This has resulted in several pleasant surprises which, incidentally, support the view that many rare bulbs might do better outside. I am sure that a sunny well-drained bed is the best place for all the Reticulata irises. The flowers of *Iris histrio* are smaller than those of *Iris histrioides* and of a much paler blue in most forms. The white markings on the blade of the falls are similar to those of 'Lady Beatrix Stanley' but they affect the whole area up to the margin. Unlike *Iris histrio*, its subspecies *aintabensis* is frequently available from nurseries, though less so than a few years ago. Sadly it is not such a good plant, with smaller pale-blue flowers with narrow blades and less conspicuous markings, but it grows well in the garden and is well worth cultivating.

There are two yellow-flowered species, *Iris winogradowii* and *I. danfordiae*, which usually flower several weeks later than *I. histrioides*. *Iris winogradowii* is a magnificent species with flowers as large as the the biggest forms of *I. histrioides*, and resembling them closely in all respects except that of colour, which is a good bright yellow throughout. The blade of the fall is very broad with a central golden yellow ridge and the same deeper colour in its inner third, flecked with a scattering of very dark greenish-blue dots. *Iris winogradowii* is easy to grow in the garden if its needs are recognised. In warm areas it does best in a partially shaded bed, with abundant humus to ensure that it never dries out. It increases mainly by its bulbs splitting, but it is also easily raised from seed.

It is difficult to take *Iris danfordiae* seriously as a garden plant; it is necessary to purchase it every year to keep it going satisfactorily in most gardens, as the bulbs break up after flowering into tiny bulbils which will only flower after several years, if ever. Fortunately it is inexpensive if you want to treat it as an 'annual'. Much has been written on the subject of getting it to flower year after year, and the consensus of opinion seems to be that the only hope is to plant the bulbs at least 20 cm (8 in) deep and perhaps to feed them regularly with a liquid feed. It is a delightful species with small flowers on 15 cm (6 in) stems, bright yellow in colour with a deep-yellow ridge and a few greenish spots on the falls. The flowers have an unusual squat appearance because the standards are reduced to mere bristles.

Iris reticulata and the range of forms and hybrids, mainly with *I. histrioides*, derived from it, are among the most valuable plants to give colour to the early spring garden, with a long flowering season from late February to early April here. Paul Furse and others collected some very fine varieties of *Iris reticulata* during the 1960's and '70's which gave

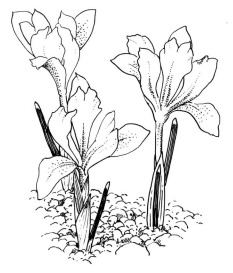

Fig. 5. Iris danfordiae

IRIS RETICULATA VARIETIES

'Alba'	white
'Cantab'	Cambridge blue, yellow crest with white markings to each side
'Clairette'	pale blue, darker blue blade , white crest and markings
'Edward'	dark blue, orange crest and white markings
'Gordon'	light blue, orange crest and white markings
'Harmony'	deep blue, orange crest with conspicuous white streaks each side
'Hercules'	pale blue, crest. yellow
'Ida'	pale blue, crest pale yellow with white around, with blue spots
'Jeannine'	deep violet, falls with orange blotch and white streaks
'Joyce'	deep blue, standards paler, yellow crest with surrounding grey stripes
'J. S. Dijt'	reddish-purple with blue falls
'Natasha'	white with a grey tinge, falls with deep-yellow blotch and greenish veining
'Pauline'	standards deep violet, falls purple with large white blotch streaked with purple
'Purple Gem'	violet with purple falls, blotched white and purple
'Royal Blue'	deep blue with a yellow crest, long narrow falls
'Springtime'	mid-blue with broad bluish-purple falls with white tips and purple spots
'Violet Beauty'	dark purple with orange crest

some idea of its variation in the wild. One with deep reddish-purple flowers resembling the old 'Krelagei' is apparently the commonest in the wild, but there were others of a more violet colour and some striking bicoloured varieties with a background colour of Cambridge blue and a deep-purple blade with golden ridge. Sadly most of these were eventually lost, probably from ink-spot or virus diseases, to which they were particularly prone when nurtured for safety's sake in pots, rather than planted in the garden. Now we have access to a great variety of robust plants, lacking some of the delicacy of the wild plants but making up for it by their excellent constitution and ability to form large colonies quickly.

Iris reticulata of gardens has deepest violet-blue flowers with rather narrow falls and a conspicuous deep-yellow ridge. It flowers and increases well in well-drained soils, especially if they are alkaline, preferably in full sun. Most of the other 'varieties' have considerably larger and fuller flowers. There are a considerable number of these and I have tabulated most of those which are readily obtainable.

Iris reticulata 'Alba' is now very uncommon. Two clones have been available, the true plant which was very difficult and slow to increase, and has possibly died out, and a plant which appeared as 'Cantab alba', which was reasonably easy to grow and which resembles 'Natasha'.

My own experience of these hybrids is limited but one or two are worthy of special comment. 'Cantab' is an old favourite and one of the best of the pale blues. 'Clairette' has a very srikingly marked flower which stands out among the darker varieties. Among the darker blues 'Harmony' and 'Joyce' have excellent large flowers and rapidly increase to form good groups. Several of the newer varieties in the table have very beautiful markings, and are excellent garden plants. Iris 'George' is a fairly recent introduction with very large flowers, evidently emanating from *Iris histrioides* as it resembles that species in size and shape but has the reddish-purple colour of 'Pauline' or 'Purple Gem'. The crest is yellow, with a narrow band of white streaks on each side of it.

Several other Reticulata species are sometimes obtainable. *Iris bakeriana* is a beautiful small-flowered species, which differs from others in the section in having leaves which are eight-sided in cross-section instead of four-sided. The flowers are pale blue, with whitish falls which are dark violet towards their tips and are spotted and streaked with a similar colour.

Iris hyrcana has small light-blue flowers, evenly coloured throughout, apart from a yellow ridge. It has recently become more readily available, and is growing well here in a mixed frame protected from excessive wet. It would probably succeed in the rock garden, like the rest of this section.

Iris kolpakowskiana is one of the most striking species of all. It is unusual in

having narrow grooved leaves, but the flowers are typical in shape, with quite large broad standards and falls. The standards are mid-violet, the falls a much darker velvety colour, contrasting dramatically with the violet-streaked white upper part surrounding the yellow ridge. It seems to grow better in a frame than in a pot and may possibly be successful in a well-drained sunny bed.

Juno irises (subgenus *Scorpiris*)

The Reticulata section includes many of the finest plants for the early spring rock garden or for the edges of sunny borders. The other important group of bulbous irises suitable for the rock garden is the Juno section, which will appeal more to the gardener who enjoys a challenge and can provide the special conditions of a cold house or a bulb-frame, as only a few of them, mainly the larger-growing, will

Fig. 6. Iris bakeriana

16. *Iris* kolpakowkiana

flourish in the open garden except in dry summer areas. Individually they are among the most fascinating of all bulbous plants and anyone who has fallen under their spell will want to grow as many as possible. The Alpine department at the Royal Botanic Gardens, Kew, has a fine collection grown with great skill, and a number of amateur growers are being very successful with them, so it is to be hoped that they may gradually become more readily available, even though they will never be easy.

Cultivation of these irises is discussed in Chapter 3, but in general they all need excellent drainage and a dry summer resting period; the trickier species, which include most of the smaller-growing plants, need care with watering at all times, especially during flowering, as they are very prone to botrytis which can start in the dying flowers and spread to the rest of the plant. Like other irises they are also prone to virus diseases, which resulted in disastrous losses among my own plants some years ago, following importation of some stocks which must have been virused. The moral of this is to be very careful of stocks brought in from outside and to propagate whenever possible from seed. Most of the species are hardy as far as cold is concerned, and most of the difficulty in their cultivation in Britain arises from the dampness of the climate in winter and especially in summer – they are much easier to grow in countries where the summers are dry and the winters are mainly cold but dry. When bulbs are purchased it is important to ensure that they have most of their permanent storage roots intact, as these are easily knocked off and are almost essential for the establishment of the bulb.

Because it is difficult to build up stocks of these species, the number readily available in the trade is limited and, although my policy in this book has been to describe plants available in the trade, I have included a few species which seem to be fairly widely grown in amateur circles, and may be available to enthusiasts.

From the gardener's point of view the species fall broadly into two groups, the larger species which are less demanding and can often be grown outside, and the smaller species which need careful cultivation under glass.

The larger Junos: Many of these plants can be grown in the open garden, given the right conditions, in the drier counties of Britain and in dry areas elsewhere. Excellent drainage is the vital prerequisite, in a sunny position. They have proved successful in my garden in front of a south wall, in a bed which is dryer than most because it has a slight overhang from a building behind it. Many of them set seed in the garden,from which stocks can be raised, usually taking about five years to mature.

The main features of all these plants are similar. They have upright stems enfolded by lush glossy leaves usually overlapping at their bases, from the axils of which the flowers appear successively from the top downwards. The typical Juno flowers are compared with those of a Reticulata on page 52. They have broad falls, usually with a central raised crest of a different colour, and tiny standards which hang down between them.

Iris aucheri (*I. sindjarensis*) is a robust species up to 45 cm (18 in) high, with 3–5 pairs of very large glossy leaves from which up to six flowers appear from the leaf axils. The colour can vary considerably, but in plants I have grown they are pale blue fading to white, tinged with yellow around the yellow ridge and at the tip of the fall, or in var. 'Alba', a creamy white with a similar deep-yellow crest. This is perhaps a rather leafy plant but it is well worth growing in a suitable position in the garden. Some of its vigour has been imparted to three dwarfer hybrids, which are among the very few hybrids raised in this section. There seems to be some confusion about the first two, 'Sindpers' and 'Sindpur'. The first sometimes appears in lists, and is a hybrid between *Iris sinjarensis* (*I. aucheri*) and *I. persica*. The name covers a dwarf plant about 15 cm (6 in) high, a delicate pale blue in colour with purplish shading around the golden-yellow crest. It is a very easy plant to grow under glass and is probably sufficiently vigorous to be worth trying outside. 'Sindpur' is a hybrid between *I. aucheri* and *I. galatica* (*I. purpurea*), and is probably no longer in cultivation, but it must be said that its name occasionally appears mistakenly for 'Sindpers'. The other hybrid 'Warlsind' is a hybrid between *I. warleyensis* and *I. aucheri*, and is described below as it closely resembles the former.

Iris bucharica is one of the best of all Juno irises for the garden, easily grown in a sunny well-drained border. Its lush glossy leaves and habit of growth are similar to those of *I. aucheri*, but the flowers are white with a deep golden-yellow blade and prominent golden crest, in the form most commonly available commercially. During the 1960's Paul Furse collected a number of slightly varying plants under the incorrect name *I. orchioides*, which are now recognized as forms of *I. bucharica*, although they were generally less tall Some of these were a deep yellow throughout, but the most vigorous and easy was pale lemon-yellow, with darker yellow streaked with greenish-blue around the crest. This variety is still in cultivation and can be grown successfully in the open. It is unfortunate that there is confusion in the naming of this species, but plants named *Iris bucharica* from commercial sources are likely to be the white flowered plant with a yellow blade, and those of *I. orchioides* or *I. bucharica* var. *orchioides* will probably be yellow throughout.

Iris graeberiana is one of the tallest and most vigorous species but it seems to have been less readily available during recent years than in the past. Its leaves are again similar to those of *I. aucheri*, but it is often taller with up to twelve leaves and the stem visible between them. The flowers are a delicate shade of pale lavender, except around the blade, which is white at its base and yellow towards its tip, with a white area veined with lavender around it.

Iris magnifica is well named as the tallest and strongest-growing Juno. A colony has grown and increased for many years in a warm sunny bed in my garden, producing a few self-sown seedlings. The height is variable, up to 60 cm (2 ft), with up to 16 large leaves, with the stem visible between. The colour varies a little in

17. *Iris* **magnifica**

depth, but is generally pale lavender with a hint of violet, deepest on the upper surface of the haft and paler on the blade of the fall. The crest is white with deep yellow along its base. A white form is frequently seen – pure white apart from the similar yellow along the crest.

Iris vicaria is an uncommon species in cultivation. It resembles *I. magnifica* closely, but it is not quite so vigorous, and it is probably untried in the garden. The colour is similar and the chief difference botanically is that the haft is winged in *I. magnifica* and unwinged in *I. vicaria*. *I. warleyensis* is another rare species, possibly not obtainably in commerce, although it is not apparently difficult to grow in a sunny border. The colour

varies, but at its best is deep violet except for the blade of the fall, which is margined with white and has a central yellow blotch surrounding the pale-yellow crest. It has been hybridized with *I. aucheri* to produce Iris 'Warlsind', which is more frequently available, similar in appearance and just as easy to grow.

Iris willmottiana var. 'Alba' of catalogues is a 'mystery plant', in that its provenance is unknown and it is not a form of the true *I. willmottiana*, a smaller species probably not in cultivation. In the opinion of Brian Mathew it is possibly a form of *I. bucharica*. Whatever the correct name it has been in catalogues for 40 or 50 years. and is an excellent, easy garden plant. It is similar to *I. bucharica* in habit, but the flowers are pure white except on the falls. The crest is pale at its base but it is deep yellow along most of its length, with a few narrow streaks of violet along each side of it.

One other species must be included in any description of 'easy' Junos – a most exciting plant which is only recently becoming popular, *Iris cycloglossa*. This is an unusual plant in several respects. It grows in Afghanistan in wet meadows rather than on dry hillsides like most of the Junos. Possibly for this reason it is much more amenable to cultivation, flourishing and increasing in the garden in a raised bed or a well-drained sunny border. It is also unusually easy to propagate as germination of freshly sown seed is much less erratic than one expects among Junos. Its habit is very different as it is a slender plant up to 45 cm (18 in) high, with narrow leaves and long internodes. The flowers are unusual among Junos in having larger standards, which stand out horizontally between the falls. The wings of the haft, and the blade, are very broad. The colour is pale violet with a striking white area at the base of the falls, around the golden-yellow crest.

18. *Iris* cycloglossa

The smaller Junos: These are much smaller than the lush-looking irises previously described, and they are such exquisite plants that they are worth the extra care needed to maintain them in areas with damp summers and damp winters. They are ideal plants for the alpine house, where their individual needs of exceptionally free drainage, careful watering at all times, and a dry summer rest can be fulfilled.

Many exciting Juno irises were introduced or reintroduced by Paul Furse and the other collectors who followed him in the 1960s and '70s to Turkey, Iran, and Afghanistan. Sadly some of these have been lost and the political situation makes it unlikely that they will be reintroduced in the near future. Other species are 'hanging on', thanks to the skill of a few growers, and it is to be hoped that these can gradually be increased with greater experience, and will become more generally available.

Iris planifolia is the sole European species and is one of the most vigorous in cultivation, as might be expected. It is said to be becoming much less common in the wild, and on a recent visit to Portugal we only saw it once, in enormous abundance on the slopes beneath the walls of a hill town. It is easy to grow under glass without any special care apart from a dry summer period, but after a few years it often succumbs to a virus infection. It usually grows to about 15 cm (6 in) and has 4–8 broad glossy leaves overlapping at the base so that the stem is completely sheathed. The colour is most often a mid- to deep violet blue, with darker violet veining spreading outwards from the deep-yellow crest. There is also a very beautiful white form, but it is uncommon.

Perhaps the most beautiful of these small irises is the rare *Iris nicolai*. In the form collected by Paul Furse the flowers opened when the leaves were only just beginning to develop, the total height being about 12–15 cm (5–6 in). The flowers were white with a flush of palest violet, especially on the tube and beneath the haft, and the blade was deepest violet-purple around and below the very prominent gold crest, dotted with a few violet spots. A similar plant is still in cultivation under this name but is usually a more creamy white so that the colour contrast is less striking. It is considered by botanists that this plant is probably a colour form of *I. rosenbachiana*, but they are so different that gardeners at least would like them to retain different names. *I. rosenbachiana* in cultivation has more fully developed leaves at flowering time and the colour of the whole plant is an unusual shade of deep brownish-purple, with a very narrow white streak on each side of the dark yellow crest. *Iris baldschuanica* is another Furse introduction, now extremely uncommon, which is closely allied to *I. rosenbachiana*, although very different in appearance. The very broad glaucous blue-green leaves are well developed before flowering. The flowers are cream-coloured with a hint of a pink flush especially on the haft. The crest is prominent, dark golden, with a narrow

Fig.7. Iris nicolai

brown band on each side of its base and grey veining spreading out from it to the borders of the blade and the down-turned wings of the haft.

Iris persica and *I. caucasica* and their allies became known to the present generation of gardeners with their reintroduction by Paul Furse and others during the 1960s and '70s. They have similar requirements to *I. nicolai* and can probably only be grown outside in areas with a much lower rainfall than in Britain. In the collected *I. persica* there was a remarkable variation, and some of these varieties are now usually recognized as separate species such as *I. galatica* and *I. stenophylla*. They are all small plants, only 8–10 cm (3–4 in) high, which start to flower while their leaves are only partially developed The flowers are large, at least 5 cm (2 in) in diameter, with a winged haft and a very broad blade to the fall. Looking back at photographs taken after their introduction one can appreciate the range of different colour forms. The ground colour is most often a greyish-cream, but in some flowers it is tinged to a greater or lesser degree with pale purple or a reddish-brown. The blade of the fall is the most striking feature, always with a large dark blotch below and around a prominent, deep-yellow crest. The colour of the blotch varies between blackish-purple, the most usual colour, and a lighter reddish-purple or a coppery brown.

Iris galatica (*I. purpurea*) is very variable and has a similar colour range to *I. persica*. However, it differs from that species in having two green bracts sheathing the lower part of the tube, whereas the latter has one green and one papery bract and they are more erect and not folded round the tube. Its habitat is also different as it grows at higher altitudes in Turkey, and is apparently easier to grow than *Iris persica*. The same can be said of *Iris stenophylla* (*I. tauri*) which differs from *I. persica* in

having bracts similar to those of *I. galatica*, and having blue flowers, darker on the blade; there is a similar yellow crest with a white band on each side of it, usually spotted with purple or dark blue.

Iris caucasica is one of the easier small Junos to grow, and its more robust forms, including those commonly available commercially, are worth trying in the garden in similar conditions to those suggested for the larger species. Typically it grows to a height of 15–20 cm (6–8 in), with 6–8 leaves sheathing the stem and with 2–4 flowers. These are pale greenish-yellow with a broad golden-yellow crest. The haft has only a minimal wing, and this feature differentiates it from *Iris pseudocaucasica*, which was also introduced at the same time as *Iris persica*. It is a very beautiful species, closely resembling *Iris persica* in size and habit, but the deeply channelled leaves have white margins, the haft has very large broad wings, and the flower colour is either a clear pale lemon-yellow or a delicate shade of pale blue. The colour of the crest varies from a slightly darker yellow to a deep orange, seen in some of the blue varieties.

Fig. 8. Iris caucasica

During the last few years *Iris nusairiensis*, from Syria, has become more widely grown and is proving to be one of the easiest smaller species to grow. Like *I. cycloglossa*, described above, its seed also seems to germinate better than other Junos, so that propagation is comparatively easy. As a pan plant it grows to about 12–15 cm (5–6 in), with six very glossy leaves set closely together, and large pale grey-blue flowers, the central area of the blade around the cream-coloured crest white with darker blue veining. It is a most beautiful species which could probably become a good garden plant in dry areas.

Iris kopetdaghensis is another introduction from Iran and Afghanistan, which is being maintained in a few collections and is occasionally offered by a nursery. It is a slender plant with narrow, widely-spaced leaves, up to 25 cm (10 in) tall. The pale-yellow flower is also slender with a narrow unwinged haft and narrow blade and a very prominent tall crest, deep yellow with a greenish band along its base. *I. kuschakewiczii* is another rarity occasionally on offer. It is very similar to the true *I. willmottiana* and is more likely to be obtainable. It is a fairly strong-growing plant with broad glossy leaves and several lavender-coloured flowers, with a cream crest surrounded by a white area, which is streaked or dotted with dark purple. *I. maracandica* is a plant which I have not seen but which is in cultivation and on a nursery list. It is another dwarf species with large leaves and pure yellow flowers with broadly winged hafts.

Several other beautiful species are worthy of mention as they are being grown in a few collections, although they have not recently been offered in catalogues. One of the most striking of all is *Iris fosteriana*, which puts in a regular appearance at the shows of the Alpine Garden Society, and could probably be

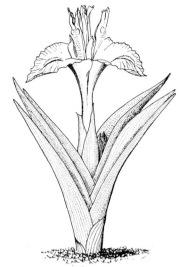

Fig. 9. *Iris nusairiensis*

established in drier climates. It is unusual in having large standards, reflexed downwards and brilliant violet-purple in colour, contrasting with the yellow falls which deepen in colour around the golden crest. *I. narbutii* is a closely allied plant with large dark standards, but the blade is violet with a yellow blotch around the cream crest. *I. microglossa* was another introduction from Afghanistan which is still in a very few collections. It seemed reasonably easy under glass but eventually succumbed to a virus. It grows to about 20 cm (8 in) and has blue-green leaves moderately widely spaced on the stem, and very pale greyish-white flowers heavily veined around the white crest with dark violet-blue streaks, giving an overall effect of pale blue. The haft is broadly winged, the wings faintly veined with grey. The colour probably varies a little and other descriptions suggest that it can be more blue than the description of my original bulbs suggests.

A few other Junos are described in Brian Mathew's monograph on the genus (*The Iris*, Batsford, 1989), but it is doubtful whether they are now in cultivation.

NARCISSUS

This is perhaps the most important of all the genera for spring flowers, with a wonderful selection of species in easily distinguishable groups. Dividing these according to season presents problems as there is so much overlap, but with one or two exceptions the Bulbocodium Section, the appropriately named hoop-petticoat daffodils, contains the earliest-flowering species, to be followed by some of the Pseudonarcissus Section, the trumpet daffodils. I will consider all the bulbocodiums, and the earliest of the pseudonarcissi, in this chapter, and leave the remainder until the next. Most of the plants in these groups are hardy in Zone 5, but *N. romieuxii* and *N. cantabricus* are slightly more tender.

Section Bulbocodium

Of all the dwarf narcissi the bulbocodiums are among the best for the rock garden, and among them the first to flower are usually *Narcissus romieuxii* and *N. cantabricus* and their varieties. There is one exception to this, a plant which has recently become popular for its ability to flower in November, *N. minor* 'Cedric Morris'. There has been some uncertainty as to whether it is in fact a variety of *N. minor* or of *N. asturiensis* but the former

is generally considered to be correct. Certainly in the garden it grows much taller than *N. asturiensis*, usually between 20 and 30 cm (8–12 in). The time of flowering can vary but I have frequently found it flowering in mid-November and it may continue until late January. It is a typical trumpet daffodil with flowers up to 5 cm (2 in) long and segments (petals) almost as long as the corona. Apart from its greater size it is indistinguishable from *N. asturiensis*, but in the garden it seems to increase more slowly, and building up a good group takes several years – a pity as its unusual season is a great asset. It sets seed but I have not yet seen any seedlings in flower

The white-flowered bulbocodiums which grow in Southern Spain and in North Africa are now mainly included in *Narcissus cantabricus*, and are superb early-flowering plants for a cold house or frame, where they can be given dry conditions while they are dormant and enjoyed without their flowers being damaged by the weather. They could probably be grown in a well-drained sunny place on the rock garden in dry areas, a position in which the equally early *N. romieuxii* certainly flourishes.

Narcissus cantabricus is divided into three subspecies, ssp. *cantabricus*, ssp. *tananicus*, and ssp. *monophyllus*, all of which are uncommon but are sometimes obtainable. Ssp. *cantabricus* is further divided into varieties, of which *cantabricus*, *foliosus*, and *petunioides* may be found in catalogues. These are all narcissi of exceptional beauty with their pure-white or sometimes creamy-white flowers, and are well worth searching for or growing from seed if a source can be found.

Narcissus cantabricus ssp. *cantabricus* var. *cantabricus* – a mouthful which I will

19. *Narcissus cantabricus* (left)
21. *Narcissus romieuxii* (opposite bottom)

shorten henceforth to *N. cantabricus* –
grows in Southern Spain. It has flowers of
pure sparkling white with a corona which
is well expanded (but less so than in var.
petunioides), with margins which sometimes flare outwards or may be straight or
even incurved. The style and filaments are
also white but the pollen is yellow. The
leaves are about 1 mm wide and can be
either prostrate or upright in different
clones. It usually flowers in early January,
but may be even earlier.

Narcissus cantabricus var. *petunioides* is
the most spectacular of the whole group,
differing from the others in having a white
corona which is fully expanded, that is
to say that it has opened flat and the
margins may even be a little recurved. It
was originally introduced from North
Africa by Van Tubergens but it remains a
rare plant. Unfortunately, although easily
raised from seed in about four to five
years, it does not come true from seed
reliably, and the best seedlings have to be
selected carefully.

N. cantabricus var. *foliosus* is different
again in having very large creamy-white
flowers, rather than the sparkling pure
white of the previously described varieties. It is also unusual in the group in
having a pedicel. Although the colour is

20.   *Narcissus cantabricus* var. petunioides

less striking it is a very desirable plant and
I find that it is the earliest of the group to
flower. This year a group grown from
seed collected nine years ago were at their
best in a greenhouse bed two weeks
before Christmas and were going over by
late January.

The other two subspecies of *N. cantabricus* to be considered are tananicus and
monophyllus. A plant under the former
name is sometimes offered in the trade,
but there is some doubt whether it is the
true plant or whether it is *Narcissus
romieuxii* ssp. *albidus*, which it resembles in
any case in being off-white. The corona is
less expanded than in the other subspecies
and the style and filaments are yellowish,
but paler than in *N. r. albidus*, and there is
a very short pedicel.

N. monophyllus is characterized by its single, long, very slender and often curling leaf. Otherwise it resembles *N. cantabricus* in the purity of colour, uniformly white apart from the dark, orange-yellow pollen, and with no pedicel. Flower-size varies but they are usually somewhat smaller. Generally it seems rather more difficult to grow and slower to increase even under glass.

Narcissus romieuxii is the best of the winter-flowering species for the open garden. It is sometimes suggested that it is a waste of time trying to grow it in the open because it always flowers in January or earlier, and is therefore spoiled by the weather. In fact it is a splendid garden plant which withstands bad weather particularly well and increases very rapidly in a warm well-drained bed, to give a worthwhile early display of abundant flowers. These, like so many dwarf narcissi, last individually for a long time in the cold weather and are produced in a long succession for a couple of months. The flowers are usually pale yellow with a widely flaring corona and small narrow petals. The style is very prominently exserted and the filaments only a little shorter, and they are yellow rather than white, an important distinguishing feature from N. cantabricus. There is little or no colour variation in my own plants which probably arose from a single bulb twenty or thirty years ago, but it is variable in the wild both in colour and in shape of the corona; darker varieties are sometimes seen in cultivation and may be available as named selections. 'Julia Jane' is an exciting plant which was selected in the wild by Jim Archibald; it has a corona exactly like that of *N. cantabricus* ssp. *petunioides* in shape, but pale yellow in colour.

Other subspecies of *N. romieuxii* offered in the trade are *mesatlanticus*, and *albidus* and its variety *zaianicus*. These may be distinct in gardens but a study of John Blanchard's excellent monograph (see Further Reading) suggests that, apart perhaps from ssp. *albidus* itself, they fall well within the natural variation of *N. romieuxii* as seen in the wild. Subspecies *albidus* is very close also to *N. c. cantabricus*. It has small, pure white, upturned flowers with the anthers scattered, rather than in a cluster as in other varieties.

There may be considerable doubts about the naming of *N. cantabricus* and *N. romieuxii* and their varieties and subspecies, especially among those who have studied them on the ground, but from the gardener's point of view they are all beautiful early-flowering plants and any variations in them are welcome! The cultivar 'Nylon' should be mentioned here, as it sometimes appears in lists. Plants under this name vary greatly between yellow amd white, but closely resemble *N. romieuxii*. The explanation given in John Blanchard's monograph is that it was a name for a batch of seedlings raised from the cross *Narcissus cantabricus* x *N. romieuxii*, which were very variable and should not have had such a 'grex' name applied to them.

The remaining yellow-flowered hoop-petticoat daffodils are included in *Narcissus bulbocodium*, with two subspecies, *bulbocodium* and *praecox*. Subspecies *bulbocodium* is further divided into several varieties, of which the most distinct and most readily obtainable are var. *bulbocodium* var. *citrinus*, var. *nivalis*, var. *conspicuus*, and the dubious but regularly offered var. *tenuifolius*. As with the white species there is confusion concerning the correct names, and even on a short holiday in Portugal in February travelling from far south to far north the immense variety in the bulbocodiums made one doubt how separable they are. For the gardener they are all good plants, flowering in most cases in early spring, easy to grow in sun or partial shade, and very long-lasting in flower. I can think of no other plants which hold their flowers in good condition for as long as these dwarf narcissi. In gardens in the warmer counties of England they seem to flourish most in some shade, preferably in a 'woodland' soil with plenty of leaf-mould.

Any of the varieties of N. bulbocodium are worth growing, and there is so much variation that one can never be quite sure what they are going to look like. In the wild they can vary from a plant fitting the decription of the little N. bulbocodium var. nivalis to one resembling the fat N. bulbocodium var. conspicuus, and it is not surprising therefore that N. bulbocodium itself from trade sources can vary in height from 5 cm (2 in) to 18 cm (7 in); the corona can be quite narrow or widely flaring with petals about two-thirds of its length. Typically the flowers should be small with a narrow corona. Var. tenuifolius is not considered a valid name botanically but it can be obtained from catalogues as a plant similar to N. bulbocodium but with narrower linear leaves. Var. conspicuus should be at the upper limit of the size range, and is the one to look for if you want the most vigorous and largest variety. Var. nivalis is a very low-growing, deep-yellow-flowered plant;

Fig. 10. Narcissus bulbocodium

it has broader leaves and small flowers with a very long, exserted style. Although it is a plant of high altitudes in the wild it seems to be reasonably easy to grow and increase.

Narcissus bulbocodium var. citrinus of gardens is a robust, large-flowered plant resembling var. conspicuus except in colour, which is a pale lemon-yellow. For some reason this is less often grown or offered in catalogues than it was twenty years ago, but it is one of the best in the garden. It is likely that this robust plant is in fact a form of var. conspicuus, and that the name var. citrinus should be applied to an uncommon small-flowered plant from the Picos de Europa.

N. bulbocodium ssp. praecox is a rare plant in gardens which will prolong the season of the yellow bulbocodiums, as it flowers in December and January in company with N. romieuxii. It has large, pale-primrose flowers with anthers which are shorter than the corona, at least in flowers which have not been open long. It is a native of Morocco and is probably safer grown under glass, but given sufficient stock it might prove as easy outside as N. romieuxii.

Section Pseudonarcissus

Apart from Narcissus minor 'Cedric Morris' described earlier, the first of the small trumpet daffodils to flower is N. asturiensis, a perfect miniature with bright yellow trumpets, the corona the same length as, or fractionally longer than, the broad petals, with a distinct constriction in the middle. The height varies a little, but as I look at a group in my garden, they seem to vary from 8 to 15 cm (3–6 in) but are nearer the lower figure on average. I have found that it grows very well and has increased to form a good group in a sunny part of the rock garden in very gritty soil, associating well with Ophiopogon planiscapa nigrescens, which has black leaves, a colour which I have otherwise found hard to use! It is also succesful in light shade with plenty of humus.

CROCUS

There can be few large genera that provide us with such a wealth of plants to appeal to all gardeners, that are uniformly

CROCUS CHRYSANTHUS CULTIVARS AND HYBRIDS	
'Advance'	yellow, exterior violet
'Blue Bird'	white, exterior greyish-blue
'Blue Pearl'	pale blue base bronze
'Blue Peter'	mid-blue, exterior deep bluish-purple, throat yellow
'E.A. Bowles'	yellow, dark brown base
'E.P. Bowles'	yellow, bronze base, purple suffusion from base
'Eyecatcher'	yellow suffused bronze
'Gipsy Girl'	golden yellow, exterior feathered purple
'Goldilocks'	deep yellow, purple base
'Ladykiller'	deep blue edged white, interior white
'Moonlight'	pale yellow, base feathered purple
'Prins Claus'	white, blotched blue
'Princess Beatrix'	mid-blue, yellow base
'Romance'	lemon-yellow, exterior greyish-blue
'Saturnus'	deep yellow, striped purple
'Skyline'	pale blue, exterior violet
'Snow Bunting'	white, base yellow, greyish feathering
'White Triumphator'	white
'Zwanenberg Bronze'	yellow, exterior bronze, margined yellow

worth growing, and that are of a size ideal for the rock garden, for the front of borders, or for pans in a frame or cold greenhouse. Perhaps this is a personal opinion not shared by the majority, but the only crocuses of limited appeal are the 'Dutch Large-flowerd Hybrids' – these seem coarse in comparison with the species and the smaller hybrids, and with the named varieties of *Crocus chrysanthus*. Even they can create a magnificent floral carpet, best viewed from afar, at a time when such sights are difficult to achieve. There are two public gardens near my home in Kent where these large crocuses are planted in their thousands in grass every year and they make a remarkable spectacle during early spring, before the daffodils take over.

In an average season the majority of spring-flowering crocus species flower early, and I will therefore consider them all in this chapter, pointing out the few which usually flower later.

There are several yellow-flowered species to brighten the garden from early to mid-spring, among them *Crocus flavus* (*C. aureus*), best known as the parent of the large-flowered 'Dutch Yellow'. The true species has smaller flowers and is less vigorous. Unlike many of the yellow species the flowers of these have no darker markings on the outside of the segments. In contrast *Crocus angustifolius* (*C. susianus*), the Cloth of Gold Crocus, is almost as vigorous but has dark-brown stripes, or at least some dark staining, on the exterior of the flower. These two crocuses are the most successful in building up colonies in borders or in grass but, like all the yellow-flowered species, they suffer in many gardens from attacks by birds, who nip off the buds or flowers for no obvious reason. Curiously the other colours do not usually suffer, so that crocuses can still be enjoyed. The most effective deterrent, only suitable for owners of small gardens with plenty of time, is to 'cotton' them, weaving black thread supported on short sticks among the flowers, a treatment equally suitable for primroses and polyanthus, which suffer in the same way. Faced with the alternatives of unsightly sticks or nipped off flowers some gardeners give up and grow other plants.

Crocus chrysanthus is almost unknown in the garden except as the parent of the 'Chrysanthus Varieties', a superb range of small crocuses derived from *C. chrysanthus* and *C. biflorus*, which are described briefly in the accompanying table.

C. ancyrensis has similar flowers to those of *C. angustifolius*, but usually without dark markings. *C. korolkowii* is another easily grown, yellow-flowered species, with some dark staining outside. *C. olivieri* has small flowers and is very variable in colour from pale yellow to deep orange. The typical species has little or no dark coloration on the outside of the segments, but this is a well-marked feature in its ssp. *balansae*. *C. olivieri* differs from many of the yellow-flowered species in having a divided style with several slender branches, especially in *C. o.* ssp. *balansae*.

The yellow crocuses so far mentioned have been easily grown species for the open garden. There are several other beautiful species which are uncommon and present more of a challenge to the enthusiast, among them the exquisite *Crocus scardicus*, which has now been in cultivation for many years but has never become common. It does not bloom until late spring. The flowers are large, appearing when the leaves are only an inch or so high, deep golden-yellow paling towards the base of the segments. They open very wide in sunlight so that gaps appear between the segments, a feature seen also in *Crocus cvijicii*. The colouring is remarkable in that the upper part of the tube and the lower part of each segment is suffused with pale violet, a most unusual combination. This seems temperamental in cultivation and is usually grown under glass but, coming from mountainous areas, it resents excessive drying at any time. I was successful with it for several years in a trough, but sadly it succumbed eventually to a mouse – the fate of many a good crocus!

Crocus cvijicii is a very similar plant, but lacks the violet coloration, and is probably a little easier to grow, needing similar conditions. It has grown and increased a little

Fig. 11. Crocus cvijicii

22. *Crocus cvijicii*

over several years, in a raised bed which has not been allowed to dry out too much in summer. *C. gargaricus* is another fascinating little species of recent introduction, which has been little tried in the open, but which I find more successful than the two previously mentioned. It is an unusual species in having remarkably tiny corms, which flower when they are much smaller than expected. The flowers, which are of a uniform golden colour, have short broad segments, giving them a very squat, almost globular appearance. The corms seem to increase reasonably well, at least when it is grown in a bulb-frame or raised bed. It probably benefits from being kept a little moist at all times.

Crocus danfordiae is a small and delicate-looking species, probably safer with some protection. It normally flowers in early spring, but recently in my garden, it flowered in the middle of winter in a raised bed protected from excessive rain with Dutch Lights. The small slender flowers are pale yellow flecked on the outside with grey. It is an unusual-looking species, of which I would like to build up stocks. So far in the frame the bulbs have multiplied slowly.

Many spring-flowering crocus species have flowers in shades of blue, or perhaps more truthfully of lilac, from deepest purple to palest lavender-blue, often with feathering or different coloration on the outside of the segments and at the base. One of the first to flower and one of the most striking in colour is *Crocus imperati*. The interior of the flower is pale reddish-purple but the outside of the segments is cream-coloured with dark purple feathering, so that the flowers are beautiful in bud but give no hint of the colour within until they open in the sunshine. Two similar species with beautiful buds, purple-feathered on a pale background, are *Crocus minimus* which flowers in late

winter and *C. corsicus* which is one of the latest species to flower, both having deep-lavender flowers when they open. *Crocus minimus* is only about half the size of *C. corsicus* but both species are excellent garden plants, doing well with me in the rock garden and in the front of a mixed border.

Crocus sieberi ssp. *atticus* is one of the first crocus to make its mark in my garden. It was raised from one or two seedling corms from the Peloponnese, and has made a cluster of bulbs with 50 or more flowers very early in the year. In this subspecies the flowers are deep lavender with a a very well demarcated orange area at the base of each segment, and a conspicuous deep-orange style with frilly branches clustered together. *C. sieberi* has several other subspecies and varieties in cultivation. *C. s.* ssp. *sieberi* itself is uncommon and more difficult to cultivate than ssp. *atticus*. The colour is variable; however, the base colour is white with a deep-yellow throat but with a purple stripe or purple suffusion on the outside of the outer segments. Ssp. *sublimis* is similar to ssp. *atticus* in being a good garden plant, differing mainly in the corm tunic, but also in having paler flowers with a pale-yellow throat. In the form *tricolor* the yellow of the throat is separated from the lavender of the segments by a white stripe giving a striking tricoloured effect. Of all crocuses, 'Hubert Edelsten' has one of the most unusual colours, and it is also a good grower in the garden. The flowers are white but the outside of each segment is heavily blotched with reddish-purple. Other varieties of *C. sieberi* offered in bulb catalogues are 'Bowles White', pure white with an orange throat, 'Violet Queen', with violet-blue flowers, and

23. *Crocus corsicus* (opposite, main photograph)
24. *Crocus sieberi* (opposite, inset)

'Firefly' with contrasting white outer segments and violet inner segments.

Two other easily grown species with affinities to *Crocus sieberi* are *Crocus dalmaticus* and *C. etruscus*. They are very similar in appearance; the pale-lavender flowers have a pale-yellow throat, and the outside of the segments are cream-coloured with purple streaking, usually most marked in *C. dalmaticus*. The main difference between the species is that *C. etruscus* has one bract around the tube and *C. dalmaticus* has two.

Crocus biflorus is another species with many subspecies, varieties and hybrids which are good garden plants. *C. biflorus* ssp. *biflorus* has white or very pale lilac flowers, of which the exterior is striped with brownish-purple, and the throat yellow. Ssp. *parkinsonii* is considered to be synonymous, although it is sometimes offered separately. Ssp. *alexandri* is one of my favourite crocuses; its flowers white with deep violet on the outside. Ssp. *melantherus* is similar but the outside markings are less prominent and it has almost black anthers. It generally flowers in late autumn or winter, but ssp. *crewii* is almost identical and flowers in early spring. In ssp. *pulchricolor* the flowers are blue with no external markings but with a similar yellow throat.

Crocus pestalozzae in its blue and white varieties is uncommon in the garden but, in my own experience, has proved an excellent plant in a raised bed which never dries out completely. From a very small initial stock it has increased rapidly and can now be tried out in the rock garden. The floral segments are small, up to 2cm (¾in) long, on a comparatively long tube, so that the flowers look unusually small for their height, a feature which in no way detracts from their appeal. The flowers are either a soft lavender or pure white, in each case with a deep-yellow throat with some dark greenish-grey on the outside of

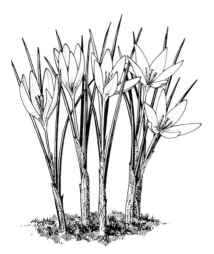

Fig. 12. Crocus pestalozzae

it, and deep-yellow anthers and an inconspicuous reddish-orange style.

Crocus vernus ssp. *vernus* has flowers in shades of lavender with a white or uncoloured throat, but it is best known as the parent of the large Dutch Hybrids, so popular for planting in grass. *C. vernus* ssp. *albiflorus* is a very different plant in cultivation. It is the high alpine species of the European Alps with small flowers which may be blue or white. For many years I grew some bulbs of each colour, originally collected many years ago from an enormous population on Monte Baldo. After a few years the blue-flowered corms had disappeared, but the white-flowered have increased slowly but surely, thriving better in a bulb-frame than in the rock garden. This very small-flowered subspecies seems sadly to be a temperamental plant, in spite of its enormous abundance in the Alps.

In contrast to this, *Crocus tommasinianus* is notable for its enormous abundance in many gardens, an abundance which is frequently rued by the garden's owners. It is capable of increasing by seed and division at a prodigious rate and should not be planted in any place where it can compete with more desirable bulbs – this is definitely a plant for grass or for the wild

25. *Crocus malyi* (opposite)

garden, where it can make a spectacular feature in early spring. There are several named varieties which are better-behaved, including the white 'Albus', 'Pictus' with white tips and darker exterior markings; the darker-coloured 'Barr's Purple', 'Ruby Giant', and 'Whitewell Purple'; and the pink 'Roseus'.

Some white-flowered crocus have already been mentioned, generally albino forms of blue-flowered species and a few hybrids, but there are further species which are typically white, including two outstanding plants which flower very early in spring in the open garden. *Crocus fleischeri* is one of the earliest, with small, pure-white flowers with a yellow throat, contrasting brilliantly with a prominent cluster of orange-red feathery style branches. I find that it does not increase as freely as I would like, but we have enjoyed a small group for many years in a well-drained border.

Crocus malyi has only recently become freely available but it has now proved itself one of the best of all crocuses. In my own garden it has increased very rapidly indeed to give us several good patches to brighten the border in earliest spring – or rather in late winter; it would be rash to assume that winter is over as I write on February 1st, with the *Crocus malyi* at their best! The flowers are large, perhaps twice the size of *C. fleischeri*, with the same glistening white segments and contrasting orange style and yellow anthers. The style is less finely divided and there is no yellow in the throat.

I have briefly described some other uncommon species of *Crocus* in the accompanying table. For full descriptions and an eminently usable key the reader should consult Brian Mathew's excellent monograph *The Crocus* (Batsford and Timber Press, 1982).

OTHER SPRING-FLOWERING CROCUS

NAME	SIZE	COLOUR	PROTECTION ADVISABLE	COMMENTS
C. abantensis	medium	rich blue, yellow throat	cold glass	excellent colour
C. alatavicus	medium	white, exterior flecked dark grey	cold glass	slow to increase
C. antalyensis	medium	pale to deep lilac, exterior lilac or buff, flecked violet	none	very variable
C. baytopiorum	medium	sky blue	cold glass or none	unique colour
C. biflorus ssp. *adamii*	medium	lavender, exterior feathered purple	none	feathering may be absent
C. biflorus ssp. *tauri*	medium	pale to mid lilac, no striping	none	
C. reticulatus	small	white, exterior feathered violet	cold glass	dry in summer
C. versicolor	medium	white, lilac or purple, striped purple	none	good garden plant
C. veluchensis	medium to large	pale to deep violet, throat white or lavender	none	very variable

For many of these species the protection of a cold house has been recommended, but this is mainly because of their rarity, and there is scope for experiment outside. The majority have been found to be hardy in Zone 5 in North America.

CYCLAMEN

A few cyclamen flowers can often be found throughout the winter, especially if a collection of them is grown under glass, with the autumn-flowering species continuing to Christmas, to be followed, or even overlapped, by the first flowers of *Cyclamen coum*. Most of the other species will be in flower by mid-March in a normal season in Britain, and so I will consider them all here, although they may well continue to flower until early summer. They vary in hardiness and this will be discussed under the individual species, but it seems likely that the only species reliably hardy in areas as cold as Zone 5 are *C. coum*, and probably *C. hederifolium* and *C. purpurascens*.

Cyclamen coum is one of the great joys of late winter and early spring, a few flowers usually appearing in my garden as early as Christmas, with the main season in an average winter in Britain from early February to late March. As a result of a generous gift many years ago, we have a considerable range of different forms which display variation in flowering period as well as in colour, leaf markings, and leaf shapes. *Cyclamen coum* is generally considered less easy to grow than *C. hederifolium*, but we have found that the two species, mainly planted in the same bed, have formed colonies of almost equal vigour, with an abundance of self-sown seedlings appearing among the original ancient corms. A bed in partial shade with plenty of leaf-mould incorporated in the soil is the ideal site for *C. coum*.

The great variability of *Cyclamen coum* has always created problems for taxonomists, and 20–30 years ago there were many subspecies and varieties, depending particularly on leaf markings of plants in cultivation. Much more study of the species in the wild has now been undertaken and most of the old names have now been 'lumped', and we are left with an immensely variable plant with only two subspecies and a large number of forms or cultivars, some of which come true from seed and have been named. *Cyclamen coum* ssp. *coum* is the plant most widely grown. Its leaves are rounded and can be unmarked deep green, or can be patterned with white to any degree, culminating in the 'Pewter Leaf Group' with leaves evenly shaded silver-grey. This named group seems to be reasonably well fixed and comes true from seed, but is probably not as robust as the others in the garden. The flowers of *Cyclamen coum* also vary greatly in colour from white, through shades of pink, to deep magenta. They all have a deep-purple blotch at the base of each lobe surrounding a double white or very pale-pink eye.

Cyclamen coum ssp. *caucasicum* differs from ssp. *coum* in having longer, more heart-shaped leaves with distinctly toothed edges, and flowers which lack the typical white eye within the basal blotch. It appears also to be more tender and therefore less suitable for the open garden in cold areas.

Cyclamen trochopteranthum is very similar in many respects to *C. coum*, but the flowers are scented, and the corolla lobes are spread out horizontally and twisted, resulting in a propeller-like appearance. Like the flowers of *C. c.* ssp. *caucasicum* they have no white eye and the colour is variable, but no white forms have been found. The leaves are always marked with silver to some degree and resemble those of *C. c.* ssp. *coum* in shape.

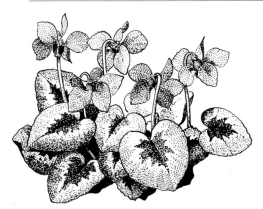

Fig. 13. *Cyclamen trochopteranthum*

C. trochopteranthum is as hardy as *C. coum* and should succeed in the garden in similar conditions.

Cyclamen parviflorum is also allied to *C. coum* but it is one of the smallest of all cyclamen. Its leaves, carried only just above the ground, are orbicular and are unmarked. The flowers are very small with short lobes giving a squat appearance. They are generally deep purplish-pink, with a deep-purple blotch without a pale eye. *Cyclamen parviflorum* is a plant of higher altitudes than *C. coum* and is absolutely hardy, but its small size make it most suitable for a pan or a trough or a carefully chosen place on the rock garden or peat bed, where it cannot be swamped by other plants. It dislikes hot situations and should be kept moist and shaded at all times.

Cyclamen libanoticum is one of the finest of all cyclamen, and usually flowers early in spring, especially when grown in pots as is generally recommended. It is a native of Lebanon where it grows at moderately high altitudes, and it seems surprising that it has acquired a reputation for tenderness which it does not deserve. In my garden in Kent I have been growing it in a shady bed of well-drained soil for the last ten years and it has survived temperatures down to -12°C (10°F) on many occasions and to -18°C (0°F) on one. Like several other species from hot countries which might be expected to relish a sunny position, it does better in shade, especially when grown under glass, where it resents strong sunlight, which causes premature leaf-fall. It is an excellent pot plant in a very well-drained compost, kept moist and shaded during the growing season and allowed to get almost dry during the summer months. Propagation from seed is easy, the seedlings taking 3–4 years to flower.

Cyclamen libanoticum has large cordate leaves with conspicuous grey marbling, and with a red flush on the under-surface. The corolla lobes are broad and overlapping at the base, the flowers among the largest of the genus. There is very little colour variation in this species, the lobes being very pale pink, deepening slightly towards their tips, with an irregular dark band of deep purple across the base.

Cyclamen repandum is the most widely grown of a group of three closely allied species, the others being *Cyclamen balearicum* and *C. creticum*. It has three distinct subspecies, ssp. *repandum*, ssp. *peloponnesiacum*, and ssp. *rhodense*. They flower later than the species previously mentioned. The first of these is an easily grown species for shady parts of the garden, which usually proves hardy except in the most extreme winters. Britain's very cold

Fig. 14. *Cyclamen repandum*

26. *Cyclamen repandum*

(for here) winter of 1982 with persistent temperatures below -12°C (10°F) resulted in the loss of many plants in a colony of *C. r. repandum*, but the remainder have seeded around and they are now better than ever. The other subspecies are much less hardy, although they have survived the mild winters that we are now enjoying, with temperature not dropping much below -7°C (21°F) They make most attractive pot plants, with similar treatment to that suggested for *C. libanoticum*.

Cyclamen repandum ssp. *repandum* has dark green somewhat pointed cordate leaves, usually heavily marbled with broad bands of grey. The lobes are long, narrow, and twisted, deep magenta in colour, darkening towards the base with very little variation apart from the occurrence of white forms which have a little pink around the mouth. Ssp. *peloponnesiacum* differs both in leaf and flower. The leaves are unmistakeable as they are speckled to a greater or lesser extent with small white spots, rather than marbled. They are usually considerably broader and less pointed. Two forms have been recognised, differing in flower colour. The common form has deep to mid-pink flowers, a little darker around the mouth, but a further

form has now been recognised (forma *vividum*) with the typical speckled leaves of the subspecies but with the magenta flowers of the type.

Ssp. *rhodense* has leaves of variable shape, but they are usually similar to those of ssp. *peleponnesiacum* in form, but with similar marbling to those of *C. repandum*. The flowers are white or very pale pink with deeper pink round the mouth.

Cyclamen creticum is a small-flowered species from Crete. One's first impression on visiting the island is that it is uncommon, until one realizes that it only grows in the shade and seems in fact to grow at the base of every suitable bush. Unfortunately it is more tender and more difficult (for me!) than *C. repandum* but it can make a good pot plant in skilled hands, with similar requirements to *C. libanoticum*. It has small slender scented flowers which are usually described as being pure white or rarely very pale pink, and certainly most of the plants one sees exhibited at shows are white. Surprisingly we found that plants with pink-flushed flowers were almost as common as white in Eastern Crete, and were even more attractive. Flower size is variable and some of the forms in cultivation are very small when compared with those in the wild. The leaves are grey-green, heart-shaped, usually with a pointed tip, marked with an irregular grey band or with grey blotches.

Cyclamen balearicum is very similar to *C. creticum* but the flowers in most forms are smaller, with shorter lobes, white or greyish-white often faintly veined with grey. In some forms the flowers are very small indeed. The leaves are large and similar in their greyish colour and markings, but they usually have a more rounded point and their margins tend to curve inwards. *C. balearicum* seems to hybridize freely with *Cyclamen repandum*, and an abundance of such hybrids have appeared in my alpine house over the years in the gravel in which the parents were once plunged together. They have all had the typical grey leaves of *C. balearicum* and very small short white flowers with pink noses – unusual but not very garden-worthy!

In an earlier chapter I pointed out that a frost-free house, although frowned upon by many alpine enthusiasts, adds to the range of bulbs which can be grown, and such a house is certainly necessary for *Cyclamen persicum*. This is the species from which the florists' cyclamen, so popular as house plants, were developed, and it is a most beautiful species for those with a suitable house. The flowers are very variable in size but they are always long and slender and often have twisted petals, held well above the leaves, in a range of colours from white through shades of pink to deep magenta. It seems surprising that selection from such elegant flowers should have produced the somewhat bloated flowers of the house plants. Breeding work has been done, notably by Wye College, to produce more compact plants with smaller flowers which have

retained more of the charm of the wild species, often with a good scent, and these are becoming popular with the public. *C. persicum* itself is easier to keep over several years than the florists' cyclamen and this applies to some extent to the small hybrids. They take a little longer to raise from seed, usually two years, and they must be kept frost-free at all times and allowed to become dry during their summer dormancy.

OTHER GENERA

Anemone

This is an invaluable genus containing many spring-flowering bulbous plants for the rock gardener, with species for every purpose, from the carpets of flowers of the very hardy *Anemone blanda* and *Anemone nemorosa* to the delicate beauty of *A. tschernjaewii* and *A. biflora*, which need careful cultivation under glass. They also cover a long season, from the earliest flowers of *Anemone blanda* which often accompany the later snowdrops, to the late-flowering varieties of *Anemone nemorosa*; and their descriptions will be split between two chapters accordingly.

In an average season in the south of England the first flowers of *Anemone blanda* appear in February with their main season in March, but they are very dependent on the weather. They seem to grow and flower well in my garden in rich soil in a partially shaded position, but in a nearby garden with pure chalk a few inches below the soil surface they are even better, planted in full sun. The flowers are large, wide open, and up to 5cm (2 in) in diameter with 10–16 segments, giving a semi-double appearance. They are produced in a long succession to give one of the best colour displays of spring. *A. blanda* can be obtained in at least eight named varieties in shades of blue, pink, and white. It is advisable if possible to keep these varieties some distance apart, as they hybridize freely, and the resulting seedlings, which will be flowering after two or three years, are usually distinctly wishy-washy, though quite attractive when they mingle in quantity.

The typical plant has mid- to deep-blue flowers, the darkest blue being found in the varieties 'Atrocaerulea' and 'Ingramii', which are probably identical. Various different shades of blue are found in 'Blue Shades' of nurseries. 'Rosea has good clear pale-pink flowers, and 'Charmer' has deeper pink flowers. At least three white varieties are in cultivation. 'White Splendour' has the largest flowers with a reddish flush on the outside. 'Bridesmaid' and 'Fairy' have pure-white flowers, which are a little smaller in the latter. 'Violet Star' has deep-amethyst flowers with a white exterior. 'Radar' has deep-magenta flowers with a conspicuous white centre, and 'Scythinica' is white with a blue exterior.

Anemone caucasica is a rare plant which is only occasionally available. It resembles a very small *Anemone blanda* with pale-blue flowers, and is said to enjoy similar rich but well-drained conditions.

Anemone apennina is very like *Anemone blanda* in appearance, in its blue or white forms. It differs in having long thin rhizomes, and seed heads which remain upright, whereas *A. blanda* has rounded knobbly tubers and seed heads which turn downwards as they develop. From the gardener's point of view the most important difference is that *Anemone apennina* definitely prefers shady conditions. It is a delightful, very easily grown plant, which will spread freely in humus-rich soil in the shade of shrubs – too freely for the rock garden or peat bed. The flowers are of similar size to those of *A. blanda* but the varieties in cultivation are always blue or white, the two being equally easy to grow.

The remaining species of Anemone to be considered in this chapter are allied to *Anemone biflora*, and are very different in their requirements from those described above. They are among the most beautiful bulbs for the alpine house but they seem to need considerable care. My own experience based on plants collected by Paul Furse is of *Anemone biflora*, *A. bucharica*, and *A. tschernjaewii*, and these are the species most likely to be seen in cultivation, with the addition of the exquisite *A. petiolulosa* which appears occasionally at Alpine Garden Society Shows. They all need a very well-drained compost and a dry dormant period, in a frame or preferably a cold house. Unfortunately they do not seem to increase vegetatively, but they sometimes set seed from which young plants can be raised with care.

Anemone biflora has finely divided, pale-green basal leaves with a whorl of similar stem leaves. The flowers, two or three to a stem, open vivid scarlet from cream-coloured buds, with small blackish-purple ovaries and yellow stamens. Later the flowers become greenish cream and then bronze, lasting in good condition for several weeks. *Anemone bucharica* has very similar flowers, but the leaves are much more finely divided, the dark ovary is even more prominent, and the stamens are blackish-purple. The segments have a cream shading on the outside, whereas those of *A. biflora* are scarlet throughout.

Anemone tschernjaewii is one of the most beautiful of all alpine plants. The leaves are three-lobed with toothed margins, but the flowers are identical in size and shape to those of *Anemone biflora* and are pure white with a contrasting reddish-purple ovary and similar-coloured stamens. It needs the same treatment as *A. biflora* but seems to be a little easier to please. *A. petiolulosa* resembles *A. bucharica* in having finely divided carrot-like leaves, but the flowers are of a clear yellow, more

27. *Anemone blanda* 'Rosea' (top left)
28. *Anemone blanda* and *A. blanda* 'White Splendour' (top right)
29. *Anemone apennina* (above)
30. *Anemone blanda* with *Narcissus* 'Queen of Spain' (right)
31. *Anemone biflora* (below)

Fig. 15. Anemone tschernjaewii

open than the goblet-shaped flowers of A. biflora, with a greenish-yellow ovary and spreading yellow stamens.

Chionodoxa

In the genus *Chionodoxa* we have some excellent easy-going plants for the open garden, which are hardy even in Zone 5. Unfortunately they are suffering from problems of nomenclature. Twenty years ago most of the chionodoxas in cultivation were named *Chionodoxa luciliae*. This had several flowers to a stem, and could be obtained in pink and white forms, as well as the common pale blue with a con-

32. *Chionodoxa siehei*

spicuous white eye. A larger-flowered species with one or two flowers to a stem was also available as *C. gigantea*. In 1976 an outstanding *Chionodoxa* with several much larger blue flowers and only a small white eye was given an Award of Merit as *C. siehei*, and has subsequently proved to be an excellent plant for the garden.

The next step in the saga was that '*C. luciliae* of gardens' was found not to be the plant originally described by Boisssier, the latter being in fact identical with *C. gigantea*, which thus becomes a synonym of *C. luciliae*. '*C. luciliae* of gardens' was therefore referred to *C. siehei*, the AM plant being a particularly vigorous form of it. The picture for the poor gardener remains confused, since most trade sources still use the old name of *C. luciliae*. Also I suspect that two different vigorous plants are being described as *C. siehei*, one with a large white eye and one with a small eye.

Whatever the names, the large-flowered species of *Chionodoxa* are excellent garden plants which will readily colonize a position under shrubs or in the wilder part of the garden, increasing by division and by self-sown seedlings. The 'old' *C. luciliae*, now *C. siehei*, is the best for naturalizing as it increases so freely. The flowers are a good deep blue with a big white eye. 'Pink Giant' is a fine large variety with several flowers to a stem, of a good clear pink. There is also a white variety 'Alba'. The plant generally offered as *C. siehei* is more robust: it has very large flowers with a less obvious white eye. It does not increase as quickly and is suitable for a more choice situation. *C. gigantea* (*C. luciliae*) has very similar large flowers, but only one or two to a stem.

The true *Chionodoxa forbesii* is uncommon in cultivation. It has a few flowers to a stem, and these are smaller and deeper blue than those of *C. siehei* or *C. gigantea*.

Chionodoxa sardensis differs from those described in having no white eye and flowers of a richer deeper blue. The flowers are also smaller and increase may not be quite so free, but it is one of the best species for the garden. *C. nana* is a much smaller plant with one or two flowers to a stem, pale blue with a white centre. Although it is usually grown in the cold house or frame it will do quite well in a rock garden with good drainage and full sun.

Scilla

The more widely grown scillas are similar to the chionodoxas in being extremely hardy, and easy to grow and increase, and they will carpet the ground with their flowers even in the wilder parts of the garden in sun or in the shade of deciduous shrubs. When we came to our present garden 22 years ago there were few flowers in the wilderness, but in one shady area overrun with brambles and weeds, there were several scillas and chionodoxas. In reconstructing the area these became scattered and and the whole area is now a sea of blue every spring, which associates well with the yellow of the daffodils subsequently planted with them. Once established and seeding around they are almost indestructible as I found when I decided a few years ago to limit them to only one bed! Now I leave them to be enjoyed, but I interplant them with more robust plants which will not suffer from a surfeit of bulbs and dying leaves around them in late spring.

The few autumn-flowering species have been considered in the last chapter, and some other species, especially the 'Blue-bells' and some larger species, will be described in the next chapter. The commonest species for early spring flowering, and the species most suitable for natural-izing, are *Scilla bifolia*, *S. siberica*, and *S. mischtschenkoana* (*S. tubergeniana*), and

their varieties.

Scilla bifolia is a small plant, usually 5–10 cm (2–4 in) high, with two narrow leaves and a somewhat one-sided cluster of up to a dozen small star-shaped flowers; these are deep blue with a hint of mauve, with a prominent ovary and style, which are a little darker in colour. This is the species which has become naturalized in my own garden with *Chionodoxa siehei*, and has hybridized with it to produce a range of bigeneric hybrids. The hybrids are usually labelled *Chionoscilla allenii*; they resemble the *Scilla* but have slightly larger flowers with their segments joined at the base, as in *Chionodoxa*. *Scilla bifolia* also has an attractive pink variety, 'Rosea'.

Scilla sibirica is an equally good garden plant suitable for sun or partial shade, or for growing in grass. It is of similar height to *S. bifolia* but has larger flowers, fewer to a stem; these are bell-shaped and nodding and are of a purer and often deeper blue, especially in its excellent popular variety 'Spring Beauty'. There is also a good white variety, 'Alba'.

Scilla mischtschenkoana has long been a popular species for the garden under the easier name of *S. tubergeniana*, the name usually found in bulb catalogues. It is a dwarf species which starts to open its flowers as soon as they begin to come through the ground in early spring, the spikes eventually up to 15 cm (6 in) high. The two or three glossy pale green leaves, 1–2 cm wide, develop after the first flowers. The flowers open more widely than those of *Scilla sibirica*, and are palest blue in colour with a dark blue stripe down the centre of each segment.

Several other species of scilla flower in early spring and are suitable for the rock garden or any well-drained sunny bed. Among Paul Furse's collections was a scilla labelled *S. hohenackeri*, which has been established in my garden ever since. Although perhaps not in the first rank of plants for the garden, it has remained entirely trouble-free and has given a good display of flowers in earliest spring; they arise from an untidy mat of weather-beaten leaves up to 45 cm (18 in) long, which appear during the previous autumn. Four to eight flowers, larger than those of most of the scillas mentioned, are borne on a stout upright scape 20–30 cm (8–12 in) high. The flowers, 2–3 cm (¾–1¼ in) in diameter with narrow spreading segments, are mid lavender-blue, the stamens with pale filaments and dark blue anthers. Subsequent work by botanists has shown that this plant is in fact *S. greilhuberi*, and that *S. hohenackeri* is a slightly smaller plant with fewer flowers to a stem, and leaves which only appear in spring, so that they are less untidy-looking.

Scilla amoena is similar to *S. bifolia* but usually a little taller with 3–6 upward-facing flowers to a stem, a little paler in colour but with a dark blue central stripe. *S. bithynica* and the similar *S. messenaica* also flower early. They have more leaves to each bulb than *S. bifolia* and a much denser spike of smaller pale-blue flowers with prominent dark stamens. *S. messenaica* has a looser spike and more leaves than *S. bithynica*, and is more freely available. *S. puschkinioides* bears some resemblance to *S. mischtschenkoana* in its pale flowers with dark stripes; but it is less tall and the flowers are much smaller, and it is not therefore such a good garden plant.

Scilla rosenii is an exciting recent introduction but it seems to be difficult to grow well. It has one or two very large blue flowers with white centres, which tend to open as they come through the ground, before a scape has developed, so that they are ruined by rain splashes off the soil. The secret of success is said to be to grow it in the open in the coolest possible conditions, in order to encourage growth to start as late as possible.

Puschkinia

Puschkinia scilloide is closely allied to scillas and chionodoxas, and is another first-class, fully hardy, dwarf plant. The flower stem is about 12 cm (5 in) high with a rather short dense spike of flowers which are very pale blue or occasionally white, with a central deeper-blue stripe down each segment, and cream-coloured anthers. There is an excellent pure-white form.

Colchicum and Merendera

Colchicum: In the last chapter the majority of the colchicums were described, including all the popular large-flowered 'Autumn Crocus' which can be such a spectacular feature of the autumn garden. In contrast to these the spring-flowering species are small plants which are generally considered to need the protection of a frame or cold house, although some of them can be grown in a sunny well-drained bed. Most of them flower early in spring and will be decribed in this chapter.

The two most unusual species, both of them reliable plants for the cold house, are *Colchicum luteum* and *C. kesselringii*.

Fig. 16. Colchicum luteum

C. luteum is the only yellow species, a cluster of short-stemmed flowers appearing above the unfurling leaves soon after they begin to develop. The flowers are golden-yellow with the segments the same colour on the outside as on the inside. They are up to 4 cm (1½ in) wide when they open into a star-like shape in the sun, and unlike the crocuses the flowers remain at least partially open on dull days. After flowering the glossy green leaves lengthen to 10–15 cm (4–6 in), but never attain the dimensions of the autumn-flowering species.

Colchicum kesselringii has always appealed to me since Paul Furse collected bulbs of it in the 1960s, although it is so diminutive that it can only be appreciated fully as a pan plant. As in C. luteum, the flowers appear when the shiny green leaves are only a centimetre or two high. The segments of the slender flowers are 2–3 cm (¾–1¼ in) long on a tube of similar length. They are very narrow, pure white in colour, with a striking dark violet band along the centre of the exterior of each. Even after flowering the leaves only attain 5–8 cm (2–3 in). It seems to increase modestly when grown in a cold greenhouse.

There are several other species which resemble the smallest-flowered of the autumnal species and are grown by a few specialists, for example *Colchicum falci-*folium, *C. szovitsii* and *C. triphyllum*, but the only one of these currently available commercially is *C. hungaricum*. This an attractive little species which makes a good pan plant. It is pale lavender or white in colour with conspicuous dark brown anthers, the segments only 2–3 cm (1 in) long. The leaves are very short at flowering time but eventually may reach 20 cm (8 in) long.

Merendera: These are very closely allied to *Colchicum*, differing in that the flowers have no tube, so that the segments are entirely separate. The autumn-flowering species were described with the autumn-flowering colchicums. The best of the spring-flowering species are only distinguishable from spring-flowering colchicums by close examination to see whether the segments are indeed separate; in a few species this is obvious because the segments fall apart, making an untidy flower. They are all small plants most suitable for pan cultivation with a dry period in summer, and several of them are in cultivation. The strange *Merendera sobolifera* was introduced by Paul Furse and grows and increases well in a bulb-frame or in a pan. However, it might be considered more interesting than beautiful as it has very narrow leaves and equally narrow white flowers hidden among them. *M. kurdica* is a much more substantial plant with leaves up to 4 cm (1½ in) wide, only just developing at flowering time. The flowers are a good deep pink, up to 4 cm (1½ in) in diameter in the best forms. *M. trigyna* and the very similar *M. raddeana* are lilac-pink in colour with narrower segments and narrower leaves than *M. kurdica*. *M. trigyna* usually has three leaves from each corm and *M. raddeana* two.

The only other spring-flowering species commonly grown are *Merendera robusta* and the very similar *M. hissarica*, which both have pale-pink or white flowers

Fig. 17. Colchicum kesselringii

and tend to suffer from their segments falling apart when the flowers are fully developed.

Leucojum

The autumn-flowering snowflakes were described in the last chapter, leaving the majority of species to be considered here.

Leucojum vernum, the Spring Snowflake, is usually the earliest to flower and is a beautiful plant for the open garden, thriving in partial shade in a bed which contains plenty of humus. It will also grow well in full sun as long as the ground is not too dry, and it can be planted in grass. The first flowers generally appear with the snowdrops in earliest spring, when the broad glossy-green leaves are only an inch or two high. The height of the plant in flower depends on growing conditions but is usually 10–20 cm (4–8 in). The flowers may be solitary or in pairs, white with a faint greenish tinge, broadly cup-shaped with the tips of the segments pointed and slightly recurving and blotched on the outside with green. Two varieties of *L. vernum* have been described. Var. *car-*

Fig. 18. Leucojum vernum

pathicum differs from the type in having yellow tips to the segments instead of green. Var. *vagneri* is a more robust plant than the type, and can be considerably taller, with two flowers on each stem.

The other spring-flowering leucojums are smaller and more tender plants, usually grown in the cold house except in warm, nearly frost-free areas. They need a well-drained compost and should be allowed to become almost dry during the summer months after the leaves have died down. The easiest of these to grow is *Leucojum nicaense*, an exquisite plant which is easily raised from seed and increases also by splitting of the bulbs. It frequently retains its leaves in summer, especially in seedling plants – if this is the case the pots should be kept just moist. It has narrow glaucous grey-green leaves and stems up to 10 cm (4 in) high, each carrying one or two small white pendent flowers having widely spreading segments with pointed tips and conspicuous yellow anthers.

Leucojum trichophyllum is another delightful plant for a pot, but is less reliable in its flowering than *L. nicaense*, only performing well after a good baking during summer. It has a few very long narrow pale-green leaves which often start dying back before the flowers mature. The segments are narrower and less spreading than those of *L. nicaense*; they may be pure white or flushed with pink at the base or may be a beautiful shade of pale pink throughout. This pink clone is sometimes available in the trade. *L. longifolium* is a rare species similar in its cultural requirements to *L. trichophyllum*. It is slow to increase vegetatively but can be grown from seed. It has long narrow dark-green glossy leaves and slender upright stems with several small white nodding bell-shaped flowers.

Leucojum aestivum is usually somewhat large to consider here, and it flowers in late spring and early summer. It is a very easy plant in moist soils, and will even grow satisfactorily in grass, producing long strap-shaped leaves, and umbels of nodding bell-shaped flowers, white with green tips, on stems up to 60 cm (2 ft) high. It varies considerably in flower size, and one of the best clones is available as 'Gravetye Giant'.

Romulea

The genus *Romulea* has never been popular with gardeners, although the best of the species are beautiful plants, especially when grown under glass. Their lack of popularity results mainly from the fact that they only open their flowers when the sun shines brightly, and their buds are almost invisible when compared with those of crocuses. There are several species with very squinny flowers and an infinite capacity for seeding around under glass or in the garden, and these may have given the genus a bad name. They are mainly either Mediterranean plants or South African, and are more tender than their near relations the crocuses. They are not hardy when temperatures are as low as in Zone 5.

The South African species usually flower in late spring and will be considered in the next chapter. Most of the European romuleas flower early in spring and will be described here. They are easily grown under glass in very well-drained compost in full sun, and in warm areas they flourish on the rock garden. Care should be taken not to grow the small-flowered quick-seeding species or untried species outside, as they are not easy to 'deadhead' and quickly produce an excessive number of seedlings in a rock garden.

All the romuleas have unstriped linear leaves and very short wiry stems with funnel-shaped flowers: these open very wide in sunlight and their segments, which are much shorter than those of crocuses, are often recurved at their tips. The

most widely grown is *Romulea bulbocodium*, a common plant around the Mediterranean with flowers varying greatly in size and colour. In a good form this has upright leaves 10–20 cm (4–8 in) long and flower stems about half this length. When the flowers are fully open they are up to 3.5 cm (1½ in) wide, pale to deep lavender-blue in colour with a broad golden-yellow throat. The exterior of the outer segment is greyish-brown with a tinge of yellow and green and a central pale stripe. There is an excellent form with pure white flowers with the same golden throat and a yellow exterior with a greenish stripe. In both forms the white branched style protrudes considerably above the yellow stamens. *Romulea bulbocodium* var. *clusiana* is very similar but generally has large flowers of a good deep lilac with a yellow throat.

Romulea crocea resembles *R. bulbocodium* closely except in its colour, which is deep yellow throughout, apart from some brownish coloration on the exterior of the segments. It is a beautiful species but seems less easy to grow than *R. bulbocodium*.

Romulea nivalis is also similar to *R. bulbocodium* in colour but the flowers are smaller than those of the best forms and

Fig. 19. Romulea bulbocodium

the plant is more stiffly upright, with several stems closely grouped. It grows well under glass and should be sufficiently hardy to try in the rock garden as it comes from mountainous areas in Lebanon. It increases slowly by division and also sets seed, which is easily raised to flower in three to four years.

Romulea tempskyana is another large-flowered species, the flowers deepest purple with no yellow in the throat. *R. linaresii* is sometimes on offer, and this also lacks the yellow throat, but has deep violet flowers. *R. requinii* is a delightful small species, which has been collected in the past from Corsica. The flower stems are only 5 cm (2 in) long, and the leaves twice this length; and the flowers, 1.5–2 cm (½–¾ in) wide, are of a rich violet colour. In view of its small size it is better enjoyed in a cold house or frame. It is not a species which seeds excessively.

This short account covers most of the good European species available from trade sources. Some of the more spectac-ular South African species will be described in the next chapter.

Sternbergia

Although the autumn-flowering *Stern-bergia lutea* is the best known of the genus, there are two species which flower in early spring.

Sternbergia fischeriana closely resembles a small-flowered *S. lutea* but the segments are shorter and the flowers more open. It seems to need drying off in summer and should therefore be grown under cold glass. *Sternbergia candida* is a most beau-tiful recent introduction from Turkey. It has erect or semi-erect leaves, appearing before the flowers. The stems are up to 18 cm (7 in) high, with 1–3 funnel-shaped flowers, which are 5 cm (2 in) in diameter and pure white, with golden-yellow anthers. It seems to be quite easy to grow under glass and is probably sufficiently hardy to try in the rock garden in the warmer counties of England, and in Zone 7 elsewhere.

CHAPTER 6

Bulbs for mid- to late Spring

GENERAL

This is the peak season for bulbs. In most gardens it coincides with the flowering of many early shrubs and trees, so that there are opportunities for combinations of colour with the shrubs underplanted with carpets of bulbs. When the bulbs are first planted some thought should be given to the colour of any nearby shrubs which might coincide in their flowering time, unless you belong to the school of thought which maintains that flowers cannot clash! Every year I regret a planting of a large orange-cupped narcissus beneath a low-branching *Magnolia* 'Leonard Messel', an uncomfortable combination of orange and deep pink in close proximity. With so many pink-flowered *Prunus, Magnolia,* and *Rhododendron* species flowering at the same time as the daffodils, the combination of pink and yellow is inevitable and only jars when the yellow is too harsh or mixed with orange. It can be softened by adding the blues of easily established scillas, chionodoxas, anemones, and muscaris, which combine well with both pink and yellow, greatly improving the appearance of the most 'ordinary' planting of forsythia, for example.

'Mid-spring' is difficult to define as it varies from season to season and from country to country, and the bulbs already described fully in the last chapter, for example *Cyclamen, Crocus, Scilla* and *Chionodoxa*, will often overlap with those in this section. *Narcissus, Iris,* and *Anemone* continue to play an important part, and their later-flowering species will be considered here. Several 'new' genera come into their own at this time of year, the most important being *Fritillaria, Tulipa, Corydalis,* and *Muscari*, together with some important shade-lovers, for example *Trillium* and *Erythronium*. Many other smaller genera also flower at this time and will be described later.

NARCISSUS

There are few genera among bulbous plants with the diversity of structure seen in *Narcissus*, a diversity which has made it

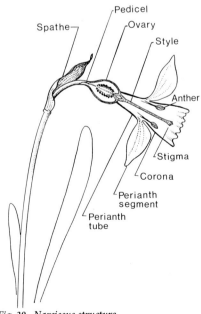

Fig. 20. Narcissus structure

possible for botanists to divide them into several well-defined Sections, outlined in the last chapter. I described there the Section Bulbocodium, which contains some of the most appealing of dwarf daffodils for the rock gardener with their typical 'hoop-petticoats' – broad cups and small narrow segments, and the smallest of the trumpet-flowered Pseudonarcissus Section, *N. asturiensis*, an exact miniature of the common trumpet daffodils. In addition to further species in this Section, including the unique *N. cyclamineus* with its narrow trumpet and narrow reflexing segments, the Sections of most interest to the rock-gardener are the Jonquillae and Apodanthae – they contain *N. jonquilla* and *N. rupicola*, with one to several flowers to a stem, with a long tube, small cup, and widely flaring segments; and the Ganymedes Section, containing *N. triandrus* with pendent flowers with a longer cup and segments which reflex, less markedly than those of *N.cyclamineus*. In addition to these there are a few species from the Tazettae and Narcissus Sections, most of which are too large for the rock garden and its environs, and a galaxy of small hybrids. Many of these species are hardy to Zone 5, but *N. jonquilla*, *N. x odorus*, and *N. canaliculatus* are probably only hardy in Zone 6.

One of the most valuable attributes of all the dwarf daffodils is that they remain in perfect condition for a remarkably long time after the flowers first open, so that those previously described will often still be flowering a month later than I have suggested, especially the various Bulbocodiums which have a long flowering season between them.

Narcissus cyclamineus is to many eyes the most exquisite of all the small narcissi. It is usually around 15–20 cm (6–8 in) tall with deep-green glossy leaves, 8–10 mm wide, and solitary pendent flowers, which are deep yellow with a long narrow

trumpet beneath fully reflexed, equally long narrow segments, the whole flower only 1 cm wide but up to 5 cm (2 in) long. *N. cyclamineus* is easily grown if it is given suitable conditions. It needs a moist, humus-rich soil in partial shade, a 'peat bed' being ideal. Superb colonies can be seen in moist woodland in the Savill Gardens at Windsor and at Wisley, but in spite of its apparent abundance in certain gardens it has become much less common than in the past, possibly because of a failure of stocks in Holland. In the right conditions in the garden it seems to increase well by division of the bulbs, and it can also be raised from seed, the seedlings taking four to five years to flower. *Narcissus cyclamineus* has been used extensively for breeding, and has produced some beautiful hybrids which inherit the attractive recurving segments. Some of those small enough to appeal to the rock gardener are described in a later table.

Section Ganymedes

The Section containing *Narcissus triandrus* is one of the most appealing to rock-gardeners, and the evocative name of 'Angel's

Fig. 21. Narcissus triandrus

Tears' has probably added to this appeal. As with so many of the sections there has been much argument and discussion about the classification of the species within it, and from the gardener's point of view the main requirement is that the names in catalogues or in nurseries should represent recognizably distinct species. I have only once had the pleasure of seeing narcissi growing in Portugal, but that was sufficient to encourage a pro-lumping rather than a pro-splitting viewpoint, and a study of John Blanchard's excellent monograph (see Further Reading), clearly written from a vast experience of the species in the wild, certainly encourages that view. For this Section he has only one species, *Narcissus triandrus*, with four varieties: var. *triandrus*, var. *cernuus*, var. *concolor*, and var. *loiseleurii*. One or two other names are popular. Var. *concolor* may be found in lists as *N. concolor*. *N.triandrus* 'Albus' is a common catalogue name which is applied to pure white forms of var. *triandrus*. Var. *pulchellus* should be included in var. *cernuus,* and is discussed there.

None of these plants are very easy to grow in the garden, but they do best in well-drained, acid, humus-rich soil in partial shade. It was very noticeable in Portugal that they were always growing in the shade of trees, but they may also be found there on open north-facing slopes at higher altitudes. They only increase slowly by splitting of the bulbs, but they can be raised from seed.

All the species have narrow green leaves which may be upright or semi-prostrate. The flowers may be solitary or in umbels of up to six, with cup-shaped coronas 10–14 mm wide, and reflexing petals, a delightful shape which, like *N. cyclamineus*, it imparts to its hybrids. The petals are generally 25–30mm (1 in) long, creamy white or deep yellow but intermediates may be seen occasionally.

Narcissus triandrus var. *triandrus* is the plant generally available in the trade as *N. triandrus* 'Albus'. The leaves are 4–5 mm wide. The flowers may be solitary but are generally three or four to a stem, occasionally six. The flowers are usually white but occasionally have a little yellow on each petal. The corona is cup-shaped with parallel sides and an entire margin. Var. *cernuus* (ssp. *pallidulus*) differs from this description in having narrower leaves, only 2 mm wide, and a corona which is variable but usually has incurving margins, entire or lobed or fringed. The colour is much more variable, from creamy white to pale yellow, with the corona the same colour or a little darker. This includes var. *pulchellus*, which is considered to be of garden origin and has bicoloured flowers with the petals darker yellow than the corona.

N. triandrus var. *concolor* (*N. concolor*) is a plant we were fortunate to see in Portugal in early March, flowering on a shady roadside bank. The flowers were an unvarying shade of deep yellow throughout, and seemed to me to resemble the plant of the same name available for many years from trade sources. Apparently in Spain it appears in much more mixed populations. *N.triandrus* var. *loiseleurii* is a splendid plant occasionally seen in cultivation. Although there is considerable doubt whether it is distinct botanically, the plants in cultivation resemble those of *N. triandrus* var. *cernuus* but they are very much larger in all their parts.

Sections *Jonquillae* and *Apodanthae*

These are not always separated by botanists, but they seem sufficiently distinct, especially to gardeners, to make the separation useful. The Jonquils have narrow, linear, green leaves which are round in section, and their seeds differ in having no strophiole, the white appendage which joins them to the ovary. This is present in the seeds of the Apodanthae, and the leaves are glaucous and channelled down the inside and slightly ridged down the outside. Another feature which will be noticed by gardeners is that the leaves of the jonquils appear in autumn, whereas the leaves of *Narcissus rupicola* and its allies do not appear until early spring.

The species in Section Jonquillae have been a cause of contention among botanists for years, because they are individually variable and their features seem to overlap. This has led to different plants, varieties or even species, being introduced under the same name, thus causing confusion to gardeners also. The differences between most of the species are subtle and perhaps not too important to the gardener.

Narcissus jonquilla itself is the largest and most robust of the group, and is a fine plant for the garden. It can grow up to 40 cm (16 in) high, with the erect leaves overtopping the flowers a little. There are up to five sweetly-scented flowers to a stem, occasionally more, each with a long straight tube, pointing upwards a little, and up to 25 mm (1 in) wide with a shallow cup not more than a quarter of the length of the petals; and with petals which do not reflex, clear yellow throughout. One or two varieties have been described, but the only one in cultivation regularly is var. *henriquesii* (*N. henriquesii*). This differs in having a deeper corona, almost double the depth of the corona in the type plant and in carrying its flowers horizontally, rather than ascending. Generally it is somewhat shorter and has fewer flowers to a stem, but neither of these features is very helpful unless you are comparing a number of plants.

Narcissus fernandesii is not considered very distinct by John Blanchard, as it shares many features with *N. jonquilla*

and its variety *henriquesii*, and with *N. assoanus, N gaditanus,* and *N willkommii.* It differs from *N.jonquilla* in having a shorter tube which is curved, and a longer corona, and in the petals overlapping more at the base, but these are all somewhat variable features. The leaves also may be upright, spreading , or prostrate in plants from different sources. From the gardener's point of view the name describes an excellent garden plant which has been thriving in my garden for many years in a sunny position in very well-drained soil, and has sown itself around. The height varies from 15 to 25 mm (6–10 in) or occasionally a little more, with two to four flowers to a stem. The leaves in these plants are erect, very narrow and round in section. The flowers are ascending, deliciously scented, the tube only slighty curved, the petals reflexing very slightly and just overlapping at the base. The corona is deep, at least half the length of the petals, with parallel sides and a frilled edge. The flowers may appear in early spring, but mid- to late spring is more usual.

Narcissus cordubensis, from Southern Spain, is rarely available from the trade and its status seems to be uncertain – it may well be a good form of *N. fernandesii* – but some bulbs of it were distributed in the past as *N. jonquilla* var. *henriquesii*. It is less tall than these, and the flowers are darker than those of *N. jonquillae*, with overlapping incurving petals which are often lobed. The corona is conical and is also lobed. It is said to be an easy garden plant.

Narcissus assoanus (*N. requienii, N. juncifolius*), under the old name of *N. juncifolius*, has been one of the most popular small narcissi for the rock garden, thriving in well-drained soil in sun, and increasing gradually by splitting of its bulbs. It is usually smaller than those previously mentioned, 10–15 cm (4–6 in) high, but is

Fig. 22. Narcissus assoanus

described as reaching as much as 30 cm (12 in) in some populations. The leaves are usually erect, equalling or slightly overtopping the flower stems. There are usually one to three flowers to a stem, up to 20 mm in diameter. The petals are broad and are not usually reflexed, the corona is darker in colour than the petals (an important distinguishing feature), and it is wide and shallow, with a frilled margin.

Narcissus gaditanus is uncommon in cultivation and is a difficult plant to grow well, only flowering after hot dry summers. The leaves are generally prostrate or spreading, and the flowers, three to six to a stem are much smaller than those of *N. assoanus*, although the plant is of similar height. The corona is comparatively large, almost as long and wide as the individual petals.

Narcissus willkommii (*N. jonquilloides*) is another uncommon plant of doubtful, possibly hybrid, origin. It is more slender than *N. jonquilla*; the leaves are very erect, and may be slightly glaucous. The flowers are frequently solitary, the tube is straight and the corona is proportionately larger

even than that of *N. j.* var. *henriquesii*, cup-shaped with spreading sides and lobed margin.

There are two or three natural hybrids of *Narcissus jonquilla* that are frequently offered in catalogues. *N. odorus* is usually seen in the form of *N. o. rugulosus*, the Campernelle Jonquil, an excellent garden plant for general use. It resembles *N. jonquilla* but is larger with broader leaves and a longer corona. *N. gracilis* and *N. tenuior* are hybrids of *N. jonquilla* and *N. pseudonarcissus*. *N. gracilis* is one of the latest narcissi to flower. It is usually about 30 cm (12 in) high, with two or three flowers to a stem, bright yellow with a darker shallow cup. *N. tenuior* is a smaller plant and is paler than *N. gracilis*, and is said to be less easy to grow.

Although the Jonquillae are attractive garden plants, the species of the Apodanthae have even more appeal to the alpine enthusiast, as they are among the smallest and most beautiful species. They are all excellent plants for pan cultivation but one or two of them present more of a challenge in the open garden. They all have glaucous leaves which appear in late winter or early spring, and they can be simply grouped according to flower colour, which may be yellow or white, creamy in *N. atlanticus*, and according to

33. Narcissus watieri with *Muscari chalusicum*

34. *Narcissus rupicola* with *Cyclamen repandum*

whether the flowers are solitary or in umbels. Thus *N. rupicola* and *N. cuatrecasasii* have solitary yellow flowers, *N. atlanticus* and *N.rupicola* ssp. *watieri* (*N. watieri*) have solitary white flowers, and *N. scaberulus* and *N. calcicola* have yellow flowers in umbels.

Narcissus rupicola is the best garden plant of this section, a delightful miniature 10–15 cm (4–6 in) high with erect or semierect glaucous grey-green leaves first appearing in early spring, and solitary flowers, which are 25–30mm (1–1¼ in) across. The broad overlapping petals are held at right-angles to the corona which curves outwards from the base and usually has a lobed margin. It is one of the later dwarf species to flower in spring, and it increases well vegetatively in a well-drained sunny bed, or makes a beautiful pot plant with long-lasting flowers.

Narcissus rupicola ssp. *marvieri* is very similar except in size. It is not usually much taller but the flowers are appreciably larger, and the corona is proportionately deeper and darker. It is an excellent pot plant and grows quite well in the rock garden, but it does not increase as freely as *N. rupicola*. It is easy to raise from seed, taking four to five years to reach flowering size.

Narcissus rupicola ssp. *watieri* (*N. watieri*) is one of the most beautiful dwarf narcissi, with clear sparkling-white solitary flowers, resembling in all other respects *N. rupicola*. Unfortunately it has a poor reputation as a garden plant in Britain, and it is often said to flower sparsely even under glass but, in warmer areas at least, one frequently sees beautiful pans of it with every bulb flowering, and the bulbs increase reasonably well under glass. The main secret of success seems to be to keep it dry after the leaves turn brown; it is one of the few bulbs which actually appreciate 'baking' during its dormancy. It is not often attempted in the open, but it has grown, increased, and flowered regularly in a warm gritty bed under a south wall in my garden, where it had some protection from excessive rain in summer from an overhang. In climates with drier summers it should thrive outside.

Narcissus cuatrecasasii is another species which usually has solitary yellow flowers. It is uncommon in cultivation, although it is not a diffficult plant to grow. It is similar in height to *N. rupicola*, but it occasionally has two flowers to a stem, and these are slightly darker and larger with a longer pedicel, and more overlapping petals. The corona is more cup-shaped with its margins entire and tending to incurve.

The two other yellow-flowered species are *Narcissus calcicola* and *N. scaberulus*, but these usually have several flowers to a stem. Sadly *N. calcicola* is very rare in cultivation and is not often offered in the trade. We were able to admire it in one of its two very localized sites in Portugal, growing on an exposed rocky hillside. It has erect glaucous leaves and stems 12–18 cm (5–7 in), with one to three flowers to a stem, horizontal or ascending, with petals quite widely spaced and not recurving. The corona is deep with parallel sides and an entire margin. *N. scaberulus* we also saw in Portugal growing on a damp bank partially shaded by trees in humus-rich soil, which would almost certainly dry out in summer. It was very similar to *N. calcicola*, but somewhat smaller. The leaves, although variable, tended to be more spreading or even prostrate, and there were up to six flowers to a stem, which were smaller with a deeper corona with an incurved margin. Although their habitats seemed very different these two species will tolerate similar growing conditions, in rich but very well-drained soil, kept almost dry in summer. They do well as pot plants or in a bulb-frame, and could certainly be tried in the garden in a similar situation to that for *N. rupicola*.

Narcissus atlanticus is a beautiful small species with solitary flowers, which are always creamy-white, in contrast to the pure white of *N. rupicola. ssp. watieri*. Its origin is a mystery, as it was raised from seed collected in 1936 by E.K. Balls in the High Atlas, and has never again been found in the wild. It is similar in height to *N. rupicola* or a little shorter, with upright leaves, the cream-coloured petals reflex a little and the corona is deeply cup-shaped with no incurving of the margins. It is not usually considered an easy plant, but it will grow and increase modestly in a pot with the same treatment as *N. r.* ssp. *watieri*. I have a photograph of it well established in a raised bed in a plantsman's garden about 20 years ago and it would certainly be worth trying in the open if one could build up sufficient stocks. The bulbs split into two occasionally, but seed is the best method of propagation.

Section Pseudonarcissus

This Section contains all the trumpet daffodils. The smallest of these, *N. asturiensis* was described in the previous chapter, together with *N. minor* 'Cedric Morris', which flowers so extraordinarily early. *N. minor* is now considered to include some other species still recognized by some botanists as distinct, for example *N. nanus* and *N. pumilus*. *N. nanus* (*N. lobularis*) is a good garden plant which flowers later than *N. asturiensis* and grows well in the open ground or even in grass. It is taller than *N. asturiensis*, with wider leaves and flowers a little larger, held horizontally, yellow with a slightly darker central zone to the petals. The corona is less constricted in the middle than in *N. asturiensis* and has a frilled margin. *N. minor* var. *pumilus* (*N. pumilus*) is taller, intermediate in height between *N. nanus* and *N. minor*, flowers later and has a more deeply frilled corona.

Although these forms of *Narcissus minor* are larger than *N. asturiensis*, they are small enough to look good on the rock garden as long as they are not associated with the smallest alpines, and they are large enough to make an impact in borders associated with shrubs and larger perennials. In considering the remaining trumpet daffodil species – mainly forms of *N. pseudonarcissus* – I will confine my descriptions to plants likely to be less than 30 cm (12 in) high. Although these may be considered a little large for the average sized rock garden they grow particularly well in 'woodland' conditions, in the partial shade of taller trees and shrubs, associating beautifully with other bulbs and low-growing perennials which revel in similar conditions, such as the varieties of *Anemone nemorosa*, and *A. ranunculoides*, erythroniums and trilliums, and the cardamines and pulmonarias.

One of my favourite narcissi for such a position is *Narcissus pallidiflorus* which just keeps within my height range. Its first flowers open a week or two after *N. cyclamineus*, which enjoys the same conditions, and the open flowers last well and continue to appear over a period of three or four weeks. It is a most attractive colour, sometimes described as creamy or straw-

35. *Narcissus pallidiflorus*

coloured, but very pale with a hint of lemon, and a tinge of green towards the base. The petals have a slight twist and are paler towards their edges. The corona is a little longer than the petals and slightly darker, with a frilled spreading margin. The only fault of *N. pallidiflorus* is that the bulbs seem very reluctant to divide, and it must be raised from seed if you want a good-sized colony. Seed is set abundantly and the seedlings will flower within four to five years.

Narcissus pseudonarcissus has a number of varieties and of subspecies. Several of the latter are still considered to be species by some authorities and some catalogues. Most of them are less than 30 cm (12 in) high, although this varies considerably with different growing conditions. They are generally easy garden plants which can even be grown in grass, but they thrive best in the conditions suggested for *N. pallidiflorus*. The typical species has pale-yellow flowers held horizontally or drooping slightly, with the corona darker than the petals and straight-sided. *N. p.* ssp. *obvallaris* (*N. obvallaris*), the Tenby Daffodil, is a robust garden plant of similar height to the type plant, with broader more overlapping petals and a slightly fringed corona, all of a deep-yellow colour. Ssp. *moschatus* (*N. mosch-*

atus) is an unusual-looking species with creamy white flowers angled acutely downward, with drooping petals and a long straight-sided corona. It increases rather slowly by division and unfortunately never seems to set seed.

Narcissus nevadensis is classed as a subspecies of *N. pseudonarcissus* in *Flora Europea*, but many authorities consider it a distinct species and the differences seem fairly convincing. It frequently has more than one flower on a stem and can have up to four. The flowers are bicoloured, with the petals white or very pale, and the corona lemon-yellow, the same length as the petals with straighter sides. This description could be applied to *N. longispathus*, which is rarely cultivated and is possibly the same species. It is said to differ in being a deeper shade of yellow throughout with a more expanded trumpet, but paler forms also exist.

Section Tazettae

The only species small enough to be of much interest to the rock gardener is *Narcissus canaliculatus* Hort. This is the name under which it has been popular as a garden plant for many years and which will probably remain in catalogues, although it is considered doubtful by botanists. It may be a small form of *N. tazetta* ssp. *italicus*. It is usually about 15–20 cm (6–8in) high with erect glaucous leaves and three to six flowers to a stem. The flowers are 12–16 mm in diameter with pale-cream, semi-recurved petals and a bright yellow cup-shaped corona with slightly incurving sides and entire margins. In a sunny well-drained soil in the garden the bulbs increase very rapidly, often without flowering as much as one would wish. In a very warm bed in front of a south wall I seem to get a fair number of flowers after a hot summer, but it is a pity such a delightful plant is not more free-flowering.

Dwarf hybrid narcissi

There are an enormous number of hybrids in cultivation, and I have selected most of those 20 cm (8 in) or less in height as being of most interest to the rock-gardener, and I have tabulated their most important features. All these hybrids are good garden plants which should thrive in well-drained soil in a sunny position. I have included the Division to which each belongs, as this is a guide to the general appearance.

Divisions

1 Trumpet hybrids
2 Large-cupped hybrids
3 Small-cupped hybrids
4 Double hybrid
5 Triandrus hybrids
6 Cyclamineus hybrids
7 Jonquilla hybrids
8 Tazetta hybrids
9 Poeticus hybrids
10 Species and wild hybrids

DWARF HYBRID NARCISSI

NAME	DIVISION	SEASON	HEIGHT	PETALS	CORONA	COMMENTS
April Tears	5	late	20 cm (8 in)	yellow	pale yellow	3–4 to a stem
Bambi	1	early	15 cm (6 in)	creamy white	deep yellow	easy
Bebop	7	late	18 cm (7 in)	yellow, becoming paler	yellow	single-flowered Jonquil
Beryl	6	late	20 cm (8 in)	pale yellow	orange	
Bobbysoxer	7	late	20 cm (8 in)	pale yellow	orange with yellow edge	one or two to a stem
Goldsithney	2	mid	20 cm (8 in)	yellow	yellow	
Hawera	5	late	20 cm (8 in)	pale yellow	pale yellow	2–5 to a stem excellent grower
Jack Snipe	6	mid	20 cm (8 in)	white	yellow	
Jumblie	6	late	20 cm (8 in)	yellow	yellow	2–3 to a stem
Lintie	7	late	20 cm (8 in)	yellow	orange	1–3 to a stem
Little Beauty	1	mid	12 cm (5 in)	white	yellow	
Little Dancer	1	mid	18 cm (7 in)	white	yellow	
Little Gem	1	early	12 cm (5 in)	yellow	yellow	
Little Witch	6	mid	20 cm (8 in)	deep yellow	deep yellow	
Midget	10	early	20 cm (8 in)	yellow	yellow	*N. nanus* form
Millennium	1	early	18 cm (7 in)	pale yellow	lemon	
Minnow	8	mid	15 cm (6 in)	cream	pale yellow	1–5 to a stem

36. *Narcissus* 'Hawera'

/DWARF HYBRID NARCISSUS.

NAME	DIVISION	SEASON	HEIGHT	PETALS	CORONA	COMMENTS
Pencrebar	5	late	15 cm (6 in)	yellow	yellow	double jonquil
Petrel	5	late	20 cm (8 in)	white	white	2–5 to a stem
Piper's Barn	7	mid	20 cm (8 in)	deep yellow	deep yellow	
Quince	6	early	18 cm (7 in)	pale yellow	yellow	sister to Tete-a-Tete
Rip van Winkle	4	early	15 cm (6 in)	pale yellow and green		fully double
Segovia	3	late	18 cm (7 in)	white	yellow	flat cup
Snipe	6	early	20 cm (8 in)	white	pale yellow fading cream	
Stocken	10	late	10 cm	deep yellow	deep yellow	best under glass
Sundial	7	mid	15 cm (6 in)	deep yellow	greenish yellow	usually twin flowers
Sun Disc	7	late	15 cm (6 in)	yellow fading cream	yellow	shallow cup
Tete-a-Tete	6	mid	12 cm (5 in)	yellow	yellow	very easy even in grass
Topolino	1	early	15 cm (6 in)	white	pale yellow	
Taffeta	10	very early	15 cm (6 in)	deep cream	deep cream	Bulbocodium
Xit	3	mid	15 cm (5 in)	white	white	like large *N. watieri*

ANEMONE

Fig. 23. *Anemone nemorosa*

37. *Anemone nemorosa* 'Robinsoniana'

Many species of *Anemone* were described in the previous chapter, but there remain a few which flower in late spring and early summer to consider here. One of the most important groups of anemones for the gardener is of the woodland species, *A. nemorosa* in many varieties, and its allies *A. ranunculoides,* with hybrids between them, and *A. trifolia.* All these grow from slender rhizomes, and therefore are not strictly within the compass of this book. However they are invaluable fully hardy plants distributed by bulb growers and I propose to describe them briefly in tabular form. They all have similar requirements in the garden, thriving in light or deep shade in a soil with abundant humus, preferably leaf-mould, which never becomes completely dry. In good woodland conditions they spread quickly to form a carpet of colour in late spring.

There is a large number of named varieties of *A. nemorosa*; their names are not 'cut and dried', and the same plants may be obtainable from different sources under different names. The majority of those generally available are listed below, but a few more may be found in specialist collections. No description is given of the leaves as they are all composed of three lobed leaflets, generally deep green in colour.

ANEMONE NEMOROSA AND ITS ALLIES

Species or Variety	Flowers	Other comments
Anemone nemorosa	white, often pink-flushed	the native species; suitable for the wild garden
'Alba Plena'	double white, irregular centre	
'Allenii'	large, deep lavender, paler outside	reliable old variety
'Atrocoerulea'	medium, deep purplish-blue	
'Blue Beauty'	large, pale blue, exterior pale	leaves bronze-tinged
'Blue Bonnet'	large, blue	late-flowering

38. *Anemone ranunculoides*   39. *Anemone coronaria*

ANEMONE NEMOROSA AND ITS ALLIES (*cont*)		
SPECIES OR VARIETY	FLOWERS	OTHER COMMENTS
'Bowles Purple'	purple	
'Bracteata Plena'	large, inner petals white narrow, outer green	
'Flore Pleno'	double variety of the species	
'Hilda'	semi-double white	
'Leeds Variety'	very large, white, flushed pink with age	
'Lytchette'	large white	
'Monstrosa'	large, segments deeply cut, green	
'Pentre Pink'	large, whitish rapidly changing to deep pink	
'Robinsoniana'	large. lavender, exterior grey	excellent old variety
'Rosea'	medium, white fading to pink	
'Royal Blue'	deep blue	
'Vestal'	double white, symmetrical centre button	
'Wilks' White',	large, white	
A. *ranunculoides*	small, bright yellow; double form available	excellent, rapidly increasing
A. × *lipsiensis* (× *seemannii*)	medium, soft primrose	beautiful and easy; earliest leaves bronze-tinged in × *seemanii*, green in 'Pallida'
A. *trifolia*	large, white or faintly pink-tinged, anthers pale blue	reasonably easy in good conditions

A group of four closely allied species of anemone from low altitudes around the Mediterranean is suitable for a sunny and sheltered place in the garden. They may not prove hardy in areas colder than Zone 7. *Anemone coronaria* is one of the joys of spring in Greece, but it is not widely grown in its beautiful wild forms, which have finely cut leaves and semi-double flowers in shades of red, blue and white. It differs from *A. pavonina*, which often grows in the same area, in having a ring of finely divided stem leaves, whereas in *A. pavonina* the stem leaves are undivided, and the flowers have a conspicuous white or cream eye, in a similar range of colours. These two species have given rise to the 'St Brigid', 'De Caen', and 'St Bavo' anemones, which are so popular as cut flowers and could be grown in the garden in dry climates, but seem somewhat coarse in comparison with their wild parents.

Anemone hortensis resembles these but grows in southern France and the Balkans and has more fully double flowers in shades of pink and purple. *Anemone fulgens* is similar but the leaves are less finely cut and the flowers are brilliant scarlet. It is thought to be a hybrid between *A. hortensis* and *A. coronaria*, and requires a similar well-drained soil in a sunny situation.

FRITILLARIA

This is another genus with which one must associate the name of Paul Furse. Although several species were widely grown before his introductions, he found so many new and exciting ones that many gardeners took up the challenge of growing them. Now they are one of the most popular genera of bulbous plants, especially among rock gardeners. With greater experience, more and more

species are being found to be suitable for the garden. In the wet conditions of much of Britain, those needing a summer resting period are easily grown under glass. In areas which have drier summers, most species, other than some of the Asiatics and Americans which suffer from drought, will flourish in a well-drained rock garden.

This is a large genus and in the following pages I propose to split it geographically into European, Middle Eastern, Asiatic, and American species. This may seem an arbitrary division but it it is relevant to the cultural conditions which the species generally require.

European Fritillaria species

The *Fritillaria* species native to Europe contain many of the most valuable easy garden plants, including *F. meleagris*, *F. pyrenaica*, and *F. messanensis*, and most of the remainder are likely to succeed in good conditions on the rock garden or raised beds; all except the few Mediterranean species from low altitudes are hardy in Zone 5 and possibly Zone 4.

Faced with choosing the best *Fritillaria* species for the garden, most gardeners would probably pick the British native Snakeshead Fritillary, *F. meleagris*, but for ease of cultivation and the ability to build

40. *Fritillaria meleagris*

up into good long-lived groups, *F. pyre-naica* is probably even better. Apart from its ease of cultivation in a border or in grass, in sun or in partial shade, *F. melea-gris* is also one of the most beautiful species, with its pinkish-purple hanging bells strongly chequered with darker purple on 20–30 cm (8–12 in) stems. The colour can vary considerably and at one time several named clones, selected in Holland, were available, but these seem to have become uncommon. There is a superb white form which can be pur-chased as a separate cultivar, 'Aphrodite', or as part of a mixture. The white bells usually have a greenish tinge and may have a little darker tessellation. The white forms often seem to be dominant when they are allowed to self-seed, so that even-tually they may become more plentiful than the purple from an original planting of a mixture.

F. *pyrenaica* flourishes in the rock garden or a sunny well-drained border, and will increase freely from self-sown seeedlings. It is similar in height or a little taller than *F. meleagris* and the colour of

the flowers can vary considerably. The most common clone has dark chocolate-brown bells with some chequering, with margins recurving to show the greenish-yellow interior. In a mixed planting from seed derived from several sources the colour ranges from this deep chocolate to pale greenish-yellow with every interme-diate shade, but the interior colour varies little. A very attractive pure-yellow cul-tivar is sometimes available, a brighter colour than any of my mixed seedlings.

South of the Pyrenees, Spain and Por-tugal are the homes of *Fritillaria lusitanica*. At one time it was split into the Spanish *F. hispanica* and the Portuguese *F. lusi-tanica,* but these now have been 'lumped' into the one somewhat variable species. This is a slender plant, very variable in height from 15 to 30 cm (6–12 in), with narrower leaves and narrower flowers than *F. pyrenaica* but with similar variable colouring, reddish-brown with well-marked chequering being the most common. Although usually grown as a pot plant it can be grown in the rock garden, except possibly in areas with a very high summer rainfall.

Two species can be found in the South of France, not far north of the Riviera. *Fritillaria involucrata* is locally abundant on roadside banks, partially shaded by trees. It grows up to a height of about 30 cm (12 in) with very slender blue-green leaves in pairs up the stem, and in an involucre of three above the flower. The flowers are a soft pale-green in colour, sometimes with no tessellation, sometimes with quite heavy reddish chequering.

In the same area, *Fritillaria montana* (*F. nigra*) is much less common (I could not find it!), but it has a wide distribution from there eastwards. It is a tall species, up to 45 cm (18 in), with one to three flowers to a stem. The leaves are narrow

41. *Fritillaria pyrenaica*

and opposite, with two or three above the flowers, which are a very dark chocolate colour. *F. ruthenica* is an almost identical species, differing only in the presence of curling tendrils at the tips of the involucral leaves. Both species are easy plants for the garden if the drainage is good. *F. orientalis*, from the Caucasus, is also very similar but it has larger flowers. I have no experience of it in the garden but it is so similar that it also would probably grow well in the open garden.

In higher locations in the Maritime Alps two beautiful dwarf fritillarias grow, *F. tubiformis* (*F. delphinensis*), and its subspecies *moggridgei*. These are usually only 10–15 cm (4–6 in) high with proportionately very large flowers 5 cm (2 in) long. In *F. delphinensis* the flowers are reddish-brown, heavily tessellated, and with a striking grape-like bloom on the segments. *F. t.* ssp. *moggridgei* is even more attractive, the flowers being of similar size and a clear bright yellow, with faint reddish markings. These can be grown in the rock garden but they do not increase well vegetatively, and should be raised from seed whenever possible. They have

Fig. 24. Fritillaria tubiformis ssp. *moggridgei*

strikingly similar 'counterparts' among the Middle-Eastern species and these will be discussed later.

Greece and the Greek Islands are the homes of a number of species. In the north-east of the country and in adjacent Bulgaria grows *Fritillaria drenovskii*, with two very different forms grown under this name, both of them excellent plants for the alpine house, and worth trying outside by anyone who can build up a sufficient stock. The first form is a dainty little species 10–15 cm (4–6 in) high with very narrow glaucous lanceolate leaves, the uppermost below the flower. The flower is a slender 2 cm-long hanging bell, which is pale reddish-brown with a narrow yellow margin to each segment. This is one of the most attractive of the smaller species and it is a pity that it does not increase by splitting of the bulbs. In order to encourage setting of seed it is worthwhile to cross-pollinate the flowers with a brush, an operation which pays dividends in any of the less common species.

The other form of *F. drenovskii* is more common in cultivation and is more robust. It grows taller and has slightly broader leaves, the uppermost very narrow and protruding above the flowers, which are carried one to three flowers to a stem. They are among the darkest of all the species, deep blackish-purple. This seems to be an easier plant to grow and will probably succeed in the rock garden.

Fritillaria graeca is a very variable plant in the wild, and several different forms are in cultivation. The most attractive is a small plant from Mount Parnassus, which is only 6–7 cm (3 in) high, with quite broad, glaucous leaves and solitary (usually) flowers 2 cm long; these are the typical dark chocolate colour, but with a broad green band down the central half of each segment and slight greenish chequering. Plants that we saw in the Peloponnese were twice this height with shorter and broader bells, one or two to a stem, deep brownish-chocolate with minimal chequering. Most of the plants in cultivation are intermediate between these two forms, with greenish-brown bells with some darker tessellation and at least a narrow band of green.

Fritillaria graeca ssp. thessala (F. thessala) is a much more vigorous plant and is one of the best easily-grown species for the rock garden or sunny border. It is 20–30 cm (8–12 in) high with the uppermost leaves in a group of three above the flowers, as in F. involucrata. It has one to three large bells to a stem, twice the size of those of the type plant. They are chequered with the inner half of each segment pale green and the outer half light, reddish-brown.

F. gussichae (F. graeca var. gussichae) is another robust plant which has been associated with F. graeca, but has major differences. It is similar in size to F. g. ssp. thessala with very glaucous leaves, but there is only a solitary upright leaf above the flowers, which are often solitary but may be up to three to a stem. They are untessellated and typically are pale green, apart from a narrow margin of reddish-brown to each segment.

Fritillaria davisii from the Mani Peninsula resembles some forms of F. graeca in its flowers, but the leaves are deep glossy green, the basal leaves very broad and the stem leaves narrower, with a solitary narrow leaf above the flower. The flowers are lightly chequered dark reddish-brown, with no green band. F. davisii was only introduced within the last 25 years; it has become established as an excellent species which grows and increases well under glass and, like F. graeca, is reasonably successful in the garden. F. epirotica is another very dwarf species from high altitudes in northern Greece. It has recently been available from nurseries, but I have no experience of it in the garden. It has much narrower twisted leaves than those of F. graeca and dark flowers with no green on them.

Fritillaria messanensis has a wide distribution in Europe and North Africa, and this includes Greece. It is one of the best species for the garden, growing and increasing well in sun or in partial shade, in any reasonable soil which is adequately drained. It is usually 20–30 cm (8–12 in) high with very narrow blue green leaves, two or three in a whorl above the flowers. These are borne one to three to a stem and are reddish-brown with a variable amount of green in the centre of the segments, and usually with strong tessellation, the pale green of the interior sometimes visible along the margin of the bell. F. messanensis seems to be a very variable species. F. gracilis is now considered a subspecies, and indeed some of the plants under this name are very similar to the type, especially when they are grown in the garden and become more robust. Typically it should be a little smaller with narrower leaves and untessellated reddish-brown flowers, but one suspects that intermediate forms are being grown. Similar problems arise with the North African varieties which have been named var. atlantica. For many years I grew plants of F. oranensis, which is now included in F. messanensis var. atlantica. They were less easy to grow and never increased. They were considerably shorter plants with much broader leaves, apart from those above the flower. The flowers were very large for the height of the plant but were otherwise similar to those described for F. messanensis. These were almost certainly alpine forms from higher altitudes, and plants from lower levels resemble the type more closely.

Fritillaria obliqua is a very striking species with almost black flowers, which, sadly, is now extremely rare in its habitat in Central Greece. Fortunately it is well established in cultivation and is not difficult to grow under glass, or on the rock garden where summers are not too wet . The height varies but it is usually between 12 and 15 cm (5–6 in). The leaves are broadly lanceolate, very glaucous with a single upright leaf above the pendent flowers. These are usually solitary but there may be up to three to a stem, glossy blackish-purple throughout. F. tuntasia is very similar to F. obliqua but it is taller and more vigorous, with slightly narrower leaves and up to five flowers to each stem. It grows on the Greek islands of Kythnos and Serifos.

Greece is the home of three or four delightful small species with pure yellow flowers, and several more are found in Turkey and in the United States. The Greek mainland species F. conica only grows on the western 'prong' of the Peleponnese, where it is very local among low scrub. It is 10–15 cm (4–5 in) high with broad glossy green basal leaves and much narrower stem leaves. The flowers are solitary and definitely conical, 1.5–2 cm (¾ in) long, bright yellow with a greenish tinge towards the base. F.euboeica is similar in size and colour to F. conica but the leaves are bluish-green and the bell-shaped flowers are not conical but slightly constricted just below the tips of the segments which tend to reflex a little. It was only known from high on a mountain in central Euboea but we found it by chance almost at sea level in the north-east of the island, so it is evidently more widely distributed than was once thought.

Two other species grow on Euboea. Fritillaria rixii has just been described by Martyn Rix. I have not seen it but it is described as resembling a yellow-flowered F. drenovskii. F. erhartii grows abundantly at the southerm tip of the island. It is a very small species, the stems only 5–10 cm (2–4 in) high, above a pair of broad basal leaves which are green with a slight grey

tinge. The 2–4 stem leaves are narrowly lanceolate and the solitary nodding bells, which widen towards the mouth, are deep blackish-purple with a yellow tip to each segment, the flowers thus closely resembling the Turkish species F. zagrica. The above description fits the plants in the wild and those usually in cultivation, but a plant recently exhibited differed in being almost twice the size described. It is a curious fact that extra vigorous forms of Fritillaria species seem to appear from time to time in cultivation.

Other Greek Islands have endemic Fritillaria species, including F. rhodokanakis from Hydra, F. rhodia from Rhodes, and the variety of F. pontica, var. substipitata, which is confined to Lesbos. F. rhodokanakis is a delightful small species only 10–15 cm (4–6 in) high with greyish-green lanceolate leaves, much broader at the base than up the stem. The solitary bell-shaped flowers are pendent, 2–2.5 cm (1 in) long, with segments widely flaring towards their tips. Most commonly the flowers are deep chocolate with the outer third yellow, a combination which it shares with the popular F. michaelovskii and several other species. Occasional plants are seen which are creamy yellow throughout. F. rhodokanakis is an excellent little species under glass and would probably survive on the rock garden. F. rhodia is another yellow-flowered species which is rarely in cultivation. It is a slender plant which may grow up to 25 cm (10 in) high, with narrow glaucous leaves, and solitary narrow greenish-yellow flowers.

Fritillaria pontica is one of the easiest species to grow in the garden, thriving in any sunny place with reasonable drainage. It grows in Northern Greece and adjoining countries, and in Northern Turkey, so that it forms a link with the next group of species. It is a strong-growing plant up 30 cm (12 in) high, with broad blue-green lanceolate leaves scattered widely up the stem, the upper leaves in a typical involucre. The flowers are large unchequered bells, pale green with a variable amount of reddish-brown, which is usually most marked on the base and on the tips of the segments, and sometimes along the margins. It is sometimes absent, the flowers being a uniform pale green. *F. pontica* increases slowly by splitting of the bulbs, but it is easily raised from seed and this is the better method of propagating it. Var. *substipitata* is a particularly vigorous variety from Lesbos. The leaves are usually narrower than those of the type, and the flowers have stronger reddish-brown markings.

Middle-Eastern Fritillaria species

In this section I describe the large number of species from Turkey and adjoining areas. For the most part these are plants from similar habitats, with an extreme climate, very cold and dry in winter, and dry for several months in summer. Consideration of this climate has induced unnecessary pessimism in growers in Britain, who have naturally considered it advisable to imitate the natural conditions by growing them under glass: so they are kept dry during the summer months, and are protected from excessive wet in winter. They are, indeed, all very easily

grown under glass in pots or a bulb-frame, but in practice a surprising number of these species can be grown on the rock garden and will increase there from year to year. Many areas of the USA and Australia have a climate similar to that of Turkey, and all these species can be grown there under ideal conditions in the open ground, especially if irrigation is kept to a minimum.

Fritillaria aurea is one of the earliest of these species to flower and has become one of the most popular, as an outstanding plant for the alpine house. It is easy to grow and increases freely by formation of small bulbils. It is almost a replica, in size and shape of flower, of *F. tubiformis* ssp. *moggridgei*, only 8–12 cm (3–5 in) high, with greyish-green lanceolate leaves and very large yellow bells spotted with brown. The main difference from the gardener's point of view is that the latter is much more difficult to propagate. *F. collina* from the Caucasus is very similar to *F. aurea*, very heavily spotted and with more pointed segments. It is also less easy to propagate. The type *F. tubiformis* also has a 'look-alike' here in *F. latifolia*, particularly in its dwarf variety *nobilis*, which is similar in all respects to *F. aurea*, except in colour which is reddish-purple, lightly chequered, and in the fact that it does not form many bulbils. *F. latifolia* is a variable plant, and in addition to its very desirable dwarf variety there are much larger clones available from nurseries which are easy to grow in the garden but appear a little coarse, with very large greenish bells heavily chequered with reddish-purple on stems up to 30 cm (12 in) high.

Turkey is home to several small species with yellow or green flowers, which are mainly easy plants under glass but have not had much trial in the open. The

42. *Fritillaria carica*

species with bright yellow flowers are among the most attractive, for example *F. carica*, *F. sibthorpiana*, *F. minima*, and *F. forbesii*. The first two of these are very similar, and may in some cases have been confused. *F. carica* is a delightful small species, 10–12 cm (4–5 in) high with four to six narrow, grey-green, alternate stem leaves and small bright yellow bells, with segments recurving at their tips. The subspecies *F. c.* ssp *serpenticola* has recently been introduced. It is a dwarfer plant with broader leaves.

F. sibthorpiana is a rarer plant in cultivation. It is taller, with only two or three alternate stem leaves and slightly larger flowers. *F. minima* is a most beautiful species when seen in the mountains of Eastern Turkey, but it seems to be one of the most difficult to grow. In the wild it is similar in height to *F. carica* but has glossy green leaves. In cultivation it is usually much smaller – my attempts could only be described as squinny – and the flowers tend to turn reddish with age. *F. forbesii* is a taller, very slender species, up to 20 cm (8 in), with upright linear glaucous leaves and slender yellow bells, green towards the base and recurving at the tips. It is a beautiful plant, but it is not easy to grow. and does not always flower freely.

Among the green-flowered species, *Fritillaria bithynica* is the most widely grown, probably because it is easy and increases by bulbil formation. It is variable in height from 10 to 20 cm (4 to 8 in) with intensely glaucous grey-green leaves, very broad towards the base and narrowing up the stem, with a whorl of two or three above the flower. The flowers are yellowish-green, somewhat conical in shape, and are sometimes carried two to a stem in strongly growing plants. The rare *F. viridiflora* resembles a more robust form of *F. bithynica*.

Fritillaria alfredae also has green flowers but is a more slender, and often taller

plant, with much narrower leaves. Its subspecies *glaucoviridis* differs considerably in having very broad leaves at the base and a larger whorl of leaves above the flower. The whole plant is extremely glaucous, and the rather narrow flowers are exactly the same colour as the leaves with an intense bluish bloom. *F. chlorantha* seems to have become very uncommon. It is a tiny species, very reluctant to increase, only about 5 cm (2 in), high with a pair of glossy bright-green leaves and narrow bright-green flowers 1.5–2cm (¾in) long with conspicuous large yellow anthers.

Fritillaria armena is the smallest of a group very similar to the green and yellow species just described but having generally brownish flowers. It closely resembles *F. chlorantha* in all respects except the flower colour which is a deep reddish-brown inside and outside the segments. *F. zagrica* is a very similar plant with more glaucous leaves and yellow tips to the dark brownish-purple flowers, closely resembling the habit and colouring of *F. erhartii*. *Fritillaria caucasica* is similar in colour to *F. armena* but is a taller plant, up to 20 cm (8 in), with a more elongated flower which is typically wider in the centre and constricted towards the margin of the segments; the dark flowers have an even more marked bloom on the surface. This describes the plants originally introduced in the 1960s and '70s, which are still in cultivation, but there is now a much more strongly growing selected plant under this name with one to three flowers to a stem. It is considerably larger and the segments have straight sides sometimes recurving at their tips.

Fritillaria pinardii and *F. assyriaca* (*F. canaliculata*) can also be considered in this group.. They are very variable in size but commonly 10–15 cm (4–6 in) high with three or four blue-green lanceolate leaves, 8–10 mm wide, and narrow flowers with strongly recurving tips to the segments. The colour is basically dark brownish-purple but in these species the interior of the flower is yellowish-green and is visible in the mouth of the bell and frequently around the margins of the segments in *F. pinardii*. *F. assyriaca* differs from *F. pinardii* in being a little taller and having much narrower leaves, usually only half the width of those of *F. pinardii*. It also has a stouter style, and in some forms has a longitudinal green band down the centre of each segment.

None of these brown-flowered species is very vigorous, but they present little difficulty under glass, and would be good rock garden plants in climates with dry summers. Two somewhat similar species have proved easier to grow and are very satisfactory garden plants even in the wetter areas of Britain. *F. minuta* became well-known after its introduction as *F. carduchorum*. It is variable in height in cultivation from 10 to 20 cm (4 to 8 in) and is unusual in having bright green glossy leaves. It carries one to three flowers to a stem, and these are similar in shape to those of *F. pinardii* but a unique brick red colour with an external bloom. It has a tendency to hide its flowers among the

Fig. 25. Fritillaria minuta

leaves, but it it is such an easy plant that it is certainly worth a place on the rock garden. *Fritillaria uva-vulpis* is an equally easy plant which was first introduced as *F. assyriaca*, a name correctly applied to the species described above, which first appeared as *F. canaliculata*. It is similar in height, and in its glossy green leaves, to *F. minuta*, but the colour of the flowers is deepest chocolate-purple with conspicuous yellow tips, and these are borne, one to three to a stem, well above the leaves.

These easily grown plants lead us on to a group of species which were introduced by Paul Furse as various forms or subspecies of *F. crassifolia*, which have now been largely renamed as a result of the work of Martyn Rix and others. Most of them increase well by formation of small bulbils, and it has been a pleasant surprise to find that many of them, especially the taller species like *F. hermonis* ssp. *amana*, grow quite strongly in well-drained sunny beds in the rock garden or elsewhere, despite their hot and dry habitat in the wild. *F. crassifolia* and its subspecies are much smaller and have been tried less often in the open, but they make excellent plants under glass, and will flourish outside in drier climates.

F. crassifolia ssp. *crassifolia* is 7–10 cm (3–4 in) tall, with alternate grey-green leaves, narrowing from the base to the top of the stem. The flowers can vary in colour, but typically they are solitary, widely bell-shaped, 2–3 cm (1 in) long, pale green or deeper greenish-yellow with heavy brownish chequering. *F.c.* ssp. *kurdica* is more widespread in the wild and is extremely variable. At one time I was growing more than a dozen different varieties collected by Paul Furse and no two of them were alike. They are similar in height to the type, or slightly taller, and sometimes have two flowers to a stem. The main difference is in the leaves which are considerably wider. The base colour of the flowers varies from green to yellow to brownish-purple, and the amount of tessellation is also variable, but most commonly they appear more reddish-brown than green. Although easy to maintain under glass, they increase much less freely than *F. c. crassifolia*. There are two other very rare subspecies, which are among the tiniest of fritillaries. Ssp. *hakkarensis* has a cluster of broad green leaves and almost stemless, widely open pale-green bells, moderately tessellated with faint brown. Ssp. *poluninii* is also only about 5 cm (2 in) high with a short stem with narrower grey-green leaves, and widely open greenish-white flowers, green longitudinal veining and nectaries, and prominent yellow anthers – a delightful little species but, sadly, almost impossible to propagate.

Fritillaria hermonis ssp. *amana* is a very variable plant which was introduced in a variety of forms during the 1960s and '70s as *F. crassifolia* 'Lebanon form', and was previously grown in the excellent form from S.E. Turkey, collected by E.K.Balls. It is distinguished from *F. crassifolia* botanically by the shape of its nectaries, which are short and wider than the linear nectaries of *F. crassifolia*, which are half as long as the segments. From the gardener's point of view it is a taller more robust plant, which is easy to grow in the open and multiplies very rapidly by small bulbils. It is generally 15–20 cm (6–8 in) tall with very glaucous alternate leaves, the topmost usually erect above the flower. The large flowers are usually solitary, but can be up to three to a stem, and are variable in colour and in tessellation. In forms I have grown the flowers are green, almost the same shade as the leaves, sometimes with minimal darker chequering but sometimes unchequered, and sometimes with a dark chocolate border to the segments. I have described the subspecies *amana*, because the subspecies hermonis is much less common in

cultivation. It is a shorter plant and the flowers are heavily tessellated with reddish-brown. This feature is also seen in *F. kotschyana*, which is becoming increasingly widely grown, and only differs appreciably from *F. hermonis* ssp. *hermonis* in its style, which is smooth, whereas that of *F. hermonis* is papillose.

The finest form of *F. hermonis* ssp. *amana* differs considerably from those described above. It was introduced by E.K.Balls in 1934, and has remained in cultivation since. The total height is only 10 cm (4 in), with light green glossy leaves, and the flowers are exceptionally long, up to 4 cm (1½ in). The outer segments are pale green with only a hint of chequering. The inner segments are reddish-brown with pale chequering and a broad central pale-green stripe. This clone is sometimes offered as 'E.K.Balls'. and is an excellent plant, which increases by forming a few bulbils, usually larger than those of other forms of *F. h. amana*.

Two other species with affinities to *F. crassifolia* are *F. whittallii* and *F. olivieri*. The former is an attractive species which has recently become more readily available, and is proving easy under glass in Britain and, considering its affinities, may prove a good rock garden plant. It grows to 15-20 cm (6-8 in) high, and has narrower glaucous leaves than *F. hermonis*, none of them above the flowers. These are about 2.5 cm (1 in) long, pale bluish-green with very well-marked purple chequering.

F. olivieri was found by Paul Furse in Iran in extremely wet areas, which would have dried out completely later in summer. In spite of its slightly unusual habitat it is proving an easy plant in the garden, given normal well-drained conditions, growing to 30 cm (12 in) or more, with sparse, very narrow alternate green leaves up the stem and a whorl of two or three above the flowers, which are borne one to three to a stem. These are at least

Fig. 26. Fritillaria michaelovskii

2.5 cm (1 in) long, similar in colour to the E.K. Balls form of *F. hermonis* ssp. *amana*, with a brown edge to the segments, giving the impression of alternate green and brown bands, with little or no tessellation.

Fritillaria michaelovskii is one of the finest smaller species for the rock garden or under glass. It was introduced by Brian Mathew in 1965, rapidly became popular, and is now produced in quantity by Dutch nurserymen. It grows 10–20 cm (4–8 in) high with one to three flowers to a stem. The leaves are grey-green, broadly lanceo-

late at the base, narrowing up the stem. The striking flowers are darkest chocolate-purple towards the base with the outer third bright yellow. In the best forms the two colours are sharply demarcated, but there are some less attractive forms in which the margin is 'muddled', and the purple area less dense or stained with yellow. It is thought that some of these may be hybrids with *F. c.* ssp. *kurdica*.

There are several other tall species which do not fit readily into the previous groups, and are good open garden plants. The best known of these is *Fritillaria acmopetala*, one of the easiest of all to grow and notable for the freedom with which it produces abundant small bulbils, which will eventually flower more quickly than those grown from seed. However it is always valuable to grow any *Fritillaria* species from seed periodically, even if it increases freely vegetatively, as the plants may be more vigorous and will certainly be free from virus. *F. acmopetala* grows from 20 to 35 cm (8–14 in) high with long narrow lanceolate grey-green leaves up the stem, and a cluster of broad leaves

around the base, arising from the bulbils. The flowers are often solitary but may to be up to three. They are large bells with the segments reflexed at their tips and characteristically waisted a little above their tips. The ground colour is pale green with varying markings, but in the best forms the inner segments are deep brownish-purple throughout or in a conspicuous blotch towards the base, so that the flowers appear to be alternately striped pale green and brown.

Fritillaria elwesii is similar to *F. acmopetala* in height and in its rapid increase; but the leaves are even narrower, and the flowers are very slender, only a third of the width of those of *F. acmopetala*, with uniformly deep-purple inner segments and pale-green outer. This has now been established for many years in my garden and even after a wet summer it has shown no signs of deterioration. *F. latakiensis* is almost identical to *F. elwesii* except in its flowers, which differ in having a smooth rather than papillose style, and from the gardener's viewpoint in having much less distinction between the inner and outer segments, as the latter are also heavily stained with purple, thus losing the 'striped' effect. *F. stribrnyi* is a rare plant of recent introduction, which I have not grown. It is another slender plant, 10–40 cm (4–16 in) high, with narrow glaucous leaves and narrow bells which are similar in colouring to *F. latakiensis*.

Two rare plants which are in some amateur collections, and therefore might become more readily obtainable, are *F. straussii* and *F. reuteri*, both among the collections of the 1960s and '70s. *Fritillaria straussi* is an unusual-looking species with broad, bright green glossy leaves in pairs up the stem and a further whorl of slightly narrower leaves above the flowers. These are pale green, one to three to a stem, heavily chequered with reddish-brown. It is sad that this unusual species has become so uncommon. I lost a considerable stock of it during a very severe winter when the pots were frozen for a long time, but prior to that it had seemed reasonably easy in a pot or a raised bed and it increased from moderate-sized bulbils.

F. reuteri is another rare plant, very similar in flower colour to *F. michaelovskii* with its bicoloured brownish-purple and yellow effect, but a taller and more slender plant with green leaves and smaller, very narrow flowers, frequently several to a stem. Its habitat in Iran is similar to that of *F. olivieri*, so one would not expect it to be too difficult to grow.

Asiatic Fritillaria *species*

The more eastern Asiatic species can be considered in two groups. The first contains the Rhinopetalums and several other tall species from eastern Iran and Russia, for example *F. persica*, *F. pallidiflora*, and *F. sewertzovii*, and also *F. imperialis* and its allies, which are mainly too tall to consider here. The second group contains species from the Himalayas, China, and Japan. These species are all very hardy, surviving in Zone 5, except the Rhinopetalum group, which is doubtfully hardy in Zone 6.

The Rhinopetalum group are among the most beautiful of all fritillaries, and are very distinct from other species, characteristically having widely open flowers with very deep nectaries at the base of the segment which protrude as horn-like projections from the back of the flower. They all grow in areas with very hot dry summers, and are therefore usually grown in pots or in a covered bulb-frame. *Fritillaria bucharica* is the easiest species to grow and has succeeded outside in Britain, and all the species are suitable for a rock garden in areas with a very low

43. *Fritillaria acmopetala* (opposite, left)
44. *Fritillaria elwesii* (opposite, right)

Fig. 27. Fritillaria stenanthera

summer rainfall. Vegetative increase tends to be slow, by formation of sparse bulbils, but they are quite easily raised from seed. Most growers seem to have difficulty in keeping them over a long period, and they should be raised from seed whenever possible.

Sadly only two species are generally offered commercially, *Fritillaria bucharica* and *F. stenanthera*. The former, in my experience, grows and increases more freely than any of the others. It usually grows from 12 to 17 cm (5–7 in) high, with shiny grey-green alternate leaves, four times as long as broad, and a cluster of up to six flowers, when it is growing strongly. The flowers are white with a greenish tinge and green nectaries, and are widely conical, the segments overlapping at the base but widely separated at their pointed tips.

Fritillaria stenanthera in its best forms has flowers of a good clear pink, an unusual and desirable colour in the genus. It is similar in habit to *F. bucharica* but does not usually grow as tall or as vigorously in cultivation. The flowers vary in colour from pinkish-white to a strong pink, with

very prominent dark greenish-purple nectaries, and little or no spotting or tessellation. *F. gibbosa* is grown in several collections. It differs from *F. stenanthera* in having more widely open flowers, which are pink, and are veined, spotted, or chequered with pale brown. *F. karelinii* is a very similar rare species which differs from *F. gibbosa* in the shape of its seed capsules, which are not winged. *F. ariana* is also sometimes seen, as a most attractive pot plant. It is generally shorter, with very broad basal leaves and no markings on the flowers, which vary in colour from white to clear deep pink.

In contrast to the Rhinopetalum Group, which are fascinating but rather more difficult to grow than most, *F. persica* is one of the easiest garden plants, at least in areas where the summers are not excessively wet. It is also one of the largest, apart from *F. imperialis*, I have several groups originating from Furse collections, still persisting and even increasing in the garden, their only fault being a reluctance to flower freely except after hot summers. There is now a selected clone, 'Adiyam', which is much better in this respect, but any of the clones in cultivation should do well outside in dryer climates. They are tall plants, usually up to 60–100 cm (2–3 ft) in the garden, but even taller in 'Adiyam'. The blue-green leaves are in abundant whorls up the stem, and are attractive even when the plant fails to flower. Each stem should produce a spire of up to twenty nodding bells on long pedicels. The colour varies from greenish to deep blackish-purple in the best forms, including 'Adiyam'. When introduced in the '60s the greenish pale-stemmed forms were separated as *F. libanotica*, and the dark-stemmed dark-flowered plants as *F. persica*, but they are now 'lumped', and the less attractive greener forms are not often seen.

Although *Fritillaria imperialis* must be considered too large for inclusion here, its very close ally *F. raddeana* is irresistible. In justification one can say that it is usually more slender and not quite so tall, but it has the same glossy light green leaves in whorls up the stem and identical clusters of flowers beneath a ruff of thin upright bract-like leaves. Its most appealing feature is its colour, which is a beautiful soft pale yellow, enhanced by a tinge of green most marked towards the base. It is easily raised from seed, and seems to grow well in sun or shade, in a soil with plenty of humus.

Fritillaria pallidiflora is one of the finest species for the garden, and one of the latest to flower, flourishing in partial shade in rich 'woodland' soil. It is also one of the easiest to raise from seed, generally blooming within three years of sowing. It is 30–45 cm (12–18 in) high. It has attractive, very glaucous, broad blue-green leaves, the uppermost in a whorl above or around the one to four flowers. The wide bells are probably the largest of any species, up to 5 cm (2 in) long and 2.5 cm (1 in) wide, pale yellow with green at the base.

The other species which I am including here is the unusual *Fritillaria sewerzowii*, sometimes considered to be in a separate genus *Korolkowia*. Many years ago this was regularly exhibited at early spring shows as a very large species with 20 or 30 flowers to a stem and a height of up to 50 cm (20 in). It is still seen regularly at shows and in collections, but it never achieves these dimensions, usually being 20–30 cm (8–12 in) high with 4–8 flowers to a stem. The leaves are broad, lanceolate and very glaucous. The flowers appear in the axils of the upper leaves and are outward-facing rather than pendent, with reflexing segments. The colour is usually a deep greenish-yellow within, with deep maroon towards the base. The outside of the segments is mainly greyish-maroon, overlaying the green to a greater or lesser extent. It is usually grown under glass but it will succeed in the open, especially in a drier climate than that of Britain.

Two species of *Fritillaria* from the Himalayas are regularly in cultivation, *F. cirrhosa* and *F. roylei*. Like many Himalayan plants these are more easily grown in cool moist areas with a high summer humidity, having in fact almost the opposite requirements to the majority of species. They enjoy damp woodland conditions in shade, with abundant humus in the soil. *Fritillaria cirrhosa* grows to 30–45 cm (12–18 in) with whorls of green to greyish-green, very narrow leaves sparsely up the stem, the upper leaves extended into tendrils. The large pendent flowers, 2.5–3.5 cm (1–1½ in) long, are often solitary, especially in cultivation in less than ideal conditions, but may be up to four to a stem. Their colour varies considerably, and I have grown two markedly different forms which probably represent the extremes, one with bright green flowers minimally chequered with brownish-purple, the other a dull greenish-cream colour, so heavily overlaid with brownish-purple tessellation that the immediate impression is of a purple flower spotted with cream.

Fritillaria roylei is very similar in size and leaf arrangement but the whorls are more closely spaced and are always glaucous, with the upper lacking tendrils. The flowers are larger, up to 5 cm (2 in) long and, in the plants that I have grown and seen, are a uniform greenish-cream colour.

Fritillaria walujewii is a native of a drier area in Central Asia, and for that reason will probably prove easier to grow in many places than the two species last described. It has only recently appeared in cultivation but seems to be well established. It is similar in habit to *F. cirrhosa*, with very narrow leaves, which may be opposite rather than whorled and usually have tendrils above. The flowers, up to three to a stem, are 3–4 cm (1–1½ in) long, an attractive pinkish-purple colour with faint greenish tessellation.

Fritillaria thunbergii (*F. verticillata*) grows in Japan and China and is an outstanding easy garden plant for sun or partial shade. It has a reputation for not flowering freely, which I think is ill-deserved, but it may require a year or two to settle down, especially as it increases very freely by bulbil formation and these small bulbs take some time to reach maturity. It is one of the taller species, usually around 45 cm (18 in) with grey-green glossy leaves, some in whorls and some opposite, the uppermost often extended into tendrils. The nodding flowers are in a loose raceme of three to six cup-shaped bells, creamy white with faint green veining, most marked at the base and along the middle of each segment.

The only other Japanese species seen regularly in cultivation is the dainty *Fritillaria japonica* var. *koidzumiana*. This seems to require the conditions suggested for the Himalayan species but, because of its rarity, is usually grown in a pot. It is only 5–10 cm (2–4 in) high, with narrow leaves and one to three nodding widely open bells with reflexing segments, white with a faint brownish tessellation – a most beautiful little species.

Several new Chinese species are now being introduced but it will probaly be several years before they become commercially available. One other species forms a link with the next group, as it grows in north-east Asia and in north-west America. This is *Fritillaria camschatcensis*, one of the most striking of all species with nearly black flowers, which is quite easy to grow in moist shade in humus-rich soil, and it increases freely by forming many small bulbils. It is late-flow-

Fig. 28. Fritillaria affinis

ering and has broad, pale-green glossy lanceolate leaves in whorls. Usually it grows 20–40 cm (8–16 in) high and has one to six large nodding flowers to a stem. The flower colour is variable and pure yellowish-green forms are in cultivation, but normally it is a very dark chocolate purple.

American Fritillaria species

Although most of the commonly grown fritillaries for garden use are in the geographical Groups described above, the American species have a special fascination, varying greatly in flower shape and habit, often in brighter colours than the European and Asiatic species. The majority present a challenge to the enthusiast and they are generally plants for the alpine house or bulb-frame rather than for the open garden. They grow in a wide variety of habitats and can be grouped according to their preference in Nature for woodland, for clay soils, or for screes, a grouping which is helpful in considering their cultural requirements.

Woodland species: These species grow in and around woodland in cooler conditions than the others, but in many instances in soils which become dry in summer. Even in countries with a higher summer rainfall they are well worth attempting in semi-shade and humus-rich soil with good drainage. *Fritillaria camschatcensis* has already been described. It is a plant of damp woodland, with a the range which extends into Canada and as far south as the north-west United States. The easiest garden plants among the remaining woodland species are the forms of *F. affinis* (*F. lanceolata*). This is a very variable species both in colour of flowers and in size of plant. Typically it grows from 20 to 60 cm (8–24 in) high with whorls of narrow lanceolate blue-green leaves and up to 12 flowers to a stem. The flowers vary greatly in size and in colour. At one time most of the plants in cultivation had very small, widely open, cup-shaped flowers, usually green or yellowish with very heavy dark-purplish mottling, occasionally unmottled. During recent years some much better forms, which are probably tetraploid, have been introduced, mainly as a result of the work of Wayne Roderick. One excellent clone received the Award of Merit of the Royal Horticultural Society as *F. affinis* 'Wayne Roderick'. This has up to six large bells 2.5 cm (1 in) wide and similar in length, with wide segments only separate at their tips, dark brownish-purple with a very marked greyish 'bloom'. *F. affinis* var. *tristulis* is similar, with even larger very dark flowers with very square bases and minimal greenish chequering. All these plants are easily grown under glass and are also successful in the garden in 'woodland' conditions.

The spectacular *Fritillaria recurva* is perhaps the most coveted of all the species for its brilliant red colouring. Unfortunately it is not an easy plant to grow and

has become increasingly rare in cultivation recently, but it can be raised from seed quite readily. Several growers have been successful with it in the garden, in similar conditions to those favoured by *F. affinis,* as well as under glass. My experience is that its seedlings flower in five or six years, but in subsequent years they tend to form large numbers of 'rice-grain' bulbils rather than continue flowering. Deep planting is probably helpful in preventing this. *F. recurva* is very similar in habit to *F. affinis* with whorls of very narrow leaves, but the long flowers are almost tubular except at their tips which recurve strongly. The colour is usually a brilliant orange-red with some yellowish chequering, In var. *coccinea* the flowers are a deeper shade of red with little or no chequering, and var. *gentneri* is similar in colour.

Fritillaria micrantha is a delightful small-flowered species which is very similar to the smaller forms of *F. affinis* in its manner of growth, with a few whorls of narrow blue-green leaves up the stem and a cluster of three or more small flowers. In cultivation it is usually up to 20 cm (8 in) high, but it can be larger in the wild. The flowers are widely open bells with slightly recurving tips, very variable in colour. In plants that I have grown the flowers have been reddish-brown with a green tinge, especially down the centre of the segments, but they can be yellowish-green throughout, or brown with a well-marked green stripe. The bulbs increase freely by rice-grain bulblets.

Fritillaria viridia is rare in cultivation and seems to be more difficult to grow. It resembles *F. micrantha* except in the colour of its flowers, which are usually pale green throughout, with segments tending to incurve at the tips rather than reflexing. It generally bears more flowers to a stem, 6–12 or more, and these tend to face in one direction. Unlike *F. micrantha* it does not form rice-grains and this is probably the reason for its scarcity.

Fritillaria phaeanthera (*F. eastwoodiae*, *F. affinis gracilis*) is an interesting plant, and one of the most beautiful small species, thought to have originated as a hybrid between *F. recurva* and *F. micrantha*, and certainly growing where the two species overlap. It is very variable, but resembles *F. micrantha* in size and leaf arrangement. My plants have had 4–6 flowers to a stem, usually about 15 cm (6 in high), but it can be considerably taller. In the best clone the flowers are bell-shaped, opening less widely than those of *F. micrantha* but with strongly recurving tips to the segments, a pleasing shade of pale reddish-orange tinged with green at the base. In another clone the flowers are more conical and the colour greenish with a faint orange tinge.

F. atropurpurea should perhaps be mentioned here, although its habitat varies from woodland to scree. It is extremely widespread in nature and is most commonly found in the shade of low scrub. Despite a wide range of habitats it seems to be a surprisingly difficult species to grow, and is only rarely seen in collections. It resembles a small *F. affinis* in height, usually less than 15 cm (6 in), with a few widely open flowers which are generally brownish, heavily overlayed with green chequering, although this colour can vary between green and reddish-brown.

F. pinetorum is sometimes considered to be a subspecies of *F. atropurpurea*. It is very rare in cultivation and differs from the latter mainly in having outward-facing, or even upward-facing, rather than nodding, flowers

F. brandegei is another rarity, very striking in the appearance of its individual flowers. Like the other woodland species it has mainly whorled leaves but these are light green rather than blue-green. It is

very low-growing, at least in cultivation, with one or two flowers to a stem (more in the wild). The flowers have long narrow segments held out horizontally and recurving towards their tips, pale yellowish-green in colour, with a small purple blotch at the base and a remarkable boss of a deep brownish-purple style and stamens, on broad filaments of the same colour.

Grassland species: These are species which grow in heavy clay soils which dry out in summer. Despite these hard-to-imitate conditions in nature some of them prove reasonably easy under glass with normal treatment, and should prove amenable in the rock garden in areas with dry summers. They difffer fundamentally from the woodland species in having bulbs composed of a few scales without rice-grains, except in *F. pudica*, and in having leaves mainly basal with a few arranged alternately up the stem, rather than in whorls.

The easiest of these to grow is *Fritillaria biflora*, a variable species which is considered by some authorities to include the widely grown plant first named *F. rodericki*. *F. biflora* is usually 15–20 cm (6–8 in) high in cultivation although sometimes larger in nature. It has bright green glossy leaves, mainly in a basal rosette but with one or two up the lower part of the stem. There are frequently two flowers to a stem but there can be one to four. The flowers are bell-shaped flaring widely towards the tips of the segments, usually dark purplish-brown with a variable pale-green band down the centre of each segment, and with some green chequering, or sometimes green throughout. It increases by forming bulbils of reasonable size, rather than 'rice-grains'.

Fritillaria grayana (*F. rodericki*, *F. biflora* var. *ineziana*) has presented problems regarding its name since its first introduction as *F. rodericki*, and both the above alternatives are in favour with at least one botanist. For the poor gardener the problem has been solved by giving the plant in cultivation a clonal name of *F. biflora* 'Martha Roderick'. It is a more robust plant with up to six or sometimes more flowers to a 25 cm (10 in) stem. The flowers are characterized by having a greenish-white blotch over most of each segment.

Fritillaria agrestis is considered by some botanists to be a subspecies of *F. biflora* and only differs materially in its colour, which is creamy white, with green around the nectaries, and a few reddish spots within.

Fritillaria pluriflora is one of the loveliest of all fritillaries, with large clear-pink bells. Unfortunately it seems less easy than *F. biflora*, but good pots of it regularly appear at shows. It does not make any small bulbils, but it can be raised from seed. In cultivation it is usually 20–30 cm (8–12 in) high, with a cluster of pale-green leaves at the base and one or two narrower leaves up the stem. There can be up to eight flowers to a stem, large bells 2.5–3.5 cm (1–1½ in) long, outward-facing or pendent, opening wide as they mature but not reflexing at the tips. The colour is usually pale pink with a deeper band down the centre of each segment.

Fig. 29. Fritillaria pudica

Fritillaria striata is another extremely rare species, occasionally in cultivation. It is closely allied to *F. pluriflora* but differs in having white or very pale-pink flowers with segments recurving strongly at their tips.

Another outstanding species is *Fritillaria pudica*, which closely resembles some Turkish species, such as *F. carica*, in having pure yellow flowers, on stems 10–20 cm (4–8 in) high, but differing in the freedom with which it increases by formation of small bulbils. It seems that some forms are more vigorous and free-flowering than others and one particularly good clone, which is near the upper size limit, flowers regularly and increases freely. It has been named 'Richard Britten'. The narrow leaves are mainly clustered around the base, and the flowers, usually solitary but occasionally in pairs, are a very deep yellow, sometimes darkening to orange as they fade.

Fritillaria liliacea is a delightful white-flowered species which is not difficult to grow under glass and would survive outside in dry climates. It has mainly basal, broad, bluish-green leaves, with a few narrower stem leaves and solitary leaf-like bracts which overtop the flowers. The height is 20–30 cm (8–12 in) with a very stout stem bearing up to six flowers, creamy-white in colour with a central green stripe to each segment and green at the base. The flowers are widely cup-shaped with the segments tending to incurve at their tips.

Scree species: These are among the most delightful small species, native to scree soils and needing well-drained compost under glass, with a possibility of growing them in scree outside in low rainfall areas. *Fritillaria pudica* and the 'woodland' species *F. atropurpurea* described above could have been included here as they are found in a wide variety of habitats including gritty soils at high altitudes. The three remaining species to consider are *F. falcata*, *F. purdyi*, and *F. glauca*. The easiest and most widely grown of these is *F. purdyi*, which is now seen frequently as a comparatively robust plant with several flowers to a stem which may attain 15–20 cm (6–8 in). For many years the most widely grown form, which is still in cultivation, was a plant of only 7.5–10 cm (3–4 in) with a basal rosette of pale-green leaves, one or possibly two stem leaves, and one or occasionally two flowers. The broad cup-shaped flowers are greenish-white, heavily flecked all over with brownish-purple. In either form it is a beautiful plant for pan culture. *F. falcata* is one of the daintiest of all species, with a basal rosette of very glaucous blue-grey leaves, and stems only 5–7.5 cm (2–3 in) high, each with a solitary, widely open, upturned flower 2.5 cm (1 in) across, greenish-cream, very heavily speckled with reddish-purple. I grew it successfully for several years in a pot but it has now succumbed and is not often offered commercially.

Perhaps the most exquisite of all these scree species is *Fritillaria glauca*. In its most widely grown form the flowers are of a clear golden yellow, but they can be so heavily tessellated with reddish-brown that they appear brown. The leaves are extremely glaucous, placed alternately up the short stem, 7.5–10 cm (3–4 in) high in plants in cultivation. The flowers are usually solitary but may be up to three to a stem, broad pendent cups with very little overlap to the segments. It increases modestly by forming a few small bulbils and is not too difficult to grow under glass with a dry summer resting period.

TULIPA

Tulips have never been very popular with rock gardeners, when compared with other genera such as *Fritillaria* or *Narcissus*. There are several possible reasons for this: they have a reputation for doing badly in the open ground and requiring lifting and keeping dry every summer; many of them are too large to associate comfortably with alpine plants; and many of them are a little 'gaudy' for alpine enthusiasts' taste. There is some justification for the first reason, at least in wet areas, but where summers are dry most species can be grown outside and many will increase well with no further attention, the only restriction on the species suitable being the size of plant and the size and colour of individual flowers, which may be out of character in the average rock garden.

Where summers are likely to be wet the number of tulips which will grow well in the open may be limited; but it is larger than most gardeners realize if the bulbs are grown in full sun in soil with excellent drainage, to avoid rotting of the bulbs while they are dormant. Frost-hardiness is not generally a problem, as they are native to extremely cold areas.

It is not easy to divide the tulips into satisfactory groups botanically with any

45. *Fritillaria glauca*

relevance to gardeners. I propose to group them here according to their basic colour, and to concentrate on those which are available commercially and are small enough to associate with rock-garden plants, especially those which have grown well over a number of years in a garden in one of the drier areas of Britain. I will summarize some of the less common and larger species in a table. I have excluded the majority of the larger hybrids of *Tulipa kaufmanniana*, *T. greigii* etc.; although they are spectacular garden plants, both their size and their colours seem to me out of place on the rock garden, and full descriptions of them can be found in bulb catalogues.

Red species

There is a large number of red-flowered tulips ranging from dazzling giants, usually marked with a striking central black blotch, to dainty species only 15–20 cm (6–8 in) high. Of the smaller species, the best for the rock garden are probably *Tulipa linifolia* and its allies, and the group centred on *T. orphanidea*, together with a few species which are small but less easy to grow. *Tulipa linifolia* grows to about 20 cm (8 in) in the garden, with narrow grey-green leaves and brilliant scarlet flowers with a black central blotch. *T. maximowiczii* is very similar but the black blotch is absent or margined with white.

Tulipa orphanidea is an excellent rock garden plant of similar size to *T. linifolia* or occasionally a little larger, with less brightly coloured flowers, one to three to a stem. The base colour varies between orange and dull red, but the outside of the segments are a more subdued greenish or yellowish. *T. whitallii* is very similar but is generally more vigorous. *T. hageri* as introduced by Paul Furse was a very dainty

species, only 15 cm (6 in) high, pure red apart from a small black blotch, but the plant now in commerce is a larger plant closely resembling the description of *T. orphanidea*.

Tulipa montana (*T. wilsoniana*) is another species which seems to have been 'improved' by growers; it is no longer the small delicate species introduced by Paul Furse and others in the 1960s, which grew up to 20 cm (8 in) or less, and had narrow slightly undulate leaves, and pure-red flowers with no blotch. It was a difficult plant in the garden, and the forms now available, which differ in being larger in all their parts, are probably better garden plants.

Tulipa sprengeri is a unique tulip in that it flowers long after the others are over, when bulbs are almost forgotten. It is a little tall for the smaller rock grden, at 30–40 cm (12–16 in), with vivid scarlet flowers with a golden reverse to the petals, and with no blotch. Although it does not increase much vegetatively, it increases very freely by self-sown seedlings, and in many gardens these make a dramatic feature.

46. *Tulipa sprengeri*

Most of the remaining red tulips are over 25 cm (10 in) high with very large flowers, and are not therefore suitable for any but the largest rock garden. I have given further details of some of them in the table below.

Yellow and white species

Among these paler-flowered species are some of the best plants for the rock garden, which will grow and increase well even in areas with a considerable summer rainfall. *Tulipa batalinii* is one of the best of all dwarf tulips, growing only to about 15 cm (6 in), with grey-green mainly basal

Fig. 30. Tulipa batalinii

leaves with waved edges and large flowers up to 7.5 cm (3 in) wide as they open, a beautiful shade of cream with the centre a deeper yellow, and yellow anthers. It appears in catalogues under this name but is generally considered to be a yellow form of *T. linifolia*. A number of intermediate hybrids between the two species have been raised, and these are all excellent bulbs for the rock garden. They include 'Bronze Charm', a beautiful soft reddish orange, and 'Apricot Jewel', 'Red Jewel' and 'Yellow Jewel'. Apart from the colour variation they tend to be a little taller.

Another favourite for the rock garden is *Tulipa urumiensis*, with a rosette of narrow leaves which are greener and less undulate, and even shorter stems with large bright yellow flowers tinged with green on the outside, which open wide in the sun. It seems to increase reasonably freely, but not with quite the vigour of *T. batalinii*.

Tulipa biflora is the most widely available of a group of similar species which all do well in the open garden and which, in my experience, will increase very freely even in partial shade. *T. biflora* itself is usually about 15 cm (6 in) high, with a

pair of glossy, green, rather narrow leaves and one to three flowers to a stem. These are white within, with a very broad bright yellow blotch, and greyish-green with a tinge of purple on the outside of the segments. *T. turkestanica* is very similar but is probably a tetraploid, and is considerably more vigorous, with many flowers to a stem, the individual flowers identical to those of *T. biflora*. *T. polychroma* is probably identical to *T. biflora* although introductions of it 20 years ago seemed less easy to grow. *T. bifloriformis* is sometimes offered commercially. It differs from *T. turkestanica* in having brown anthers rather than yellow.

Tulipa sylvestris is one of the easiest of all species to grow and the only one with a preference for shady growing conditions. Under these conditions it increases very freely. Unfortunately it does not always flower freely, although a well-established clump seems to produce sufficient flowers to make it well worth growing in the shade of shrubs. It grows 20–30 cm (8–12 in) high and has two or three long narrow stem leaves. The flowers are usually solitary, deep yellow with greenish shading on the outside, 7–8 cm (3 in) wide when they are fully open.

T. tarda grows well in the garden and is freely obtainable. It makes a basal cluster of green leaves from which arise 15–20 cm (6–8 in) stems, each with several flowers which are white inside with a broad central dark-yellow blotch, and a bright green band down the outside of the segments, broader on the outer than the inner. The name *T. dasystemon* is often applied to *T. tarda*, but the true species is a smaller tulip with pure-yellow flowers with no blotch.

Tulipa clusiana (*T. aitchisonii*) and its allies are among the most attractive

species and can be grown in the open, but they do not increase as freely as those described above. *T. clusiana* has alternate grey-green leaves up the stem and long slender flowers, which are usually solitary, white, the exterior of the outer segments rose-pink with a white margin – a beautiful colour combination. *T. clusiana* var. *chrysantha* is similar except in colour, which is deep-yellow apart from the orange-red of the outer segments. *T. c.* var *stellata* is occasionally seen. It has white flowers similar to those of *T. clusiana* but has a yellow eye rather than the purple eye of the latter.

Tulipa kolpakowskiana is another attractive small species of similar colouring, with mainly basal green leaves and 15 cm (6 in) stems; the flowers are solitary, deep yellow, with some red suffusion on the outside of the outer segments. The true *T. kaufmanniana* has larger flowers of a similar deep yellow and red colour and broader undulate leaves, but is mainly used as a parent of many magnificent and popular large garden hybrids.

One other striking species which has been unexpectedly successful in the open is *Tulipa tschimganica*, which I grew from Russian seed; it has persisted for many years outside although without much vegetative increase. It is a little tall to be included here, usually 20–30 cm (8–12 in) high, with broad bluish-green leaves and very large deep-yellow flowers which are unusual in having a broad red band halfway up the inside of the segments, rather than a basal blotch, and further red on the outside of the outer segments.

There are three other excellent dwarf species which seem to do better under glass than in the garden, although they might be successful in drier areas. *Tulipa australis* (*T. sylvestris* ssp. *australis*) is a delightful little plant under 15 cm (6 in) high with small deep-yellow flowers with narrow segments shaded reddish-brown

47. *Tulipa* 'Bronze Charm'

on the outside. *T. cretica* is another favourite dwarf, usually about 15 cm (6 in) high with very dark green leaves and slender white or pale pink flowers, with the outer segments tinged on the exterior with reddish-purple, and the inner segments with a central narrow band of the same colour. This plant grew well in a sunny bed in my garden for several years but succumbed to a severe winter eventually. *Tulipa neustrevae* is a species which has only been exhibited recently at shows. It will be a great addition to the range of very small species, especially if it proves amenable in the garden. It is very dwarf, only about 10 cm (4 in) high, with bright green leaves and very dark yellow flowers marked on the outside with green.

Pink species

Two of the most satisfactory tulips in the garden are the pink-flowered species *Tulipa bakeri* and *T. aucheriana*, which

48. *Tulipa aucheriana*

produce an ever-improving display from year to year. The name *T. bakeri* has been in some doubt, as the plant bears a close resemblance to *T. saxatilis,* which also grows on Crete, but in a different habitat, *T. saxatilis* in rock crevices or scree, *T. bakeri* in meadows only on the Omalos Plain. However, it seems to me that there is an important difference from the gardener's point of view, in that *T. saxatilis* spreads widely by means of 'stolons', and often fails to flower, whereas *T. bakeri* flowers freely every year. The same description can be applied to both species, although *T. bakeri* is said to be darker in colour. They have broad glossy grey-green leaves and stems up to 25 cm (10 in) long bearing up to three flowers, but most often with only one. The large flowers are a good clear pink deepening towards the tips of the segments, with a large deep orange-yellow eye.

In contrast to the very large flowers of *Tulipa bakeri* or *T. saxatilis,* which make a splash of colour visible across the garden, *T. aucheriana* has smaller flowers on much shorter stems and gives a more restrained display. It is usually considered to be a variety of *T. humilis* but is very distinct in the garden. It has narrow channelled blue-green leaves, and stems usually 15 cm (6 in) high; the solitary (usually) flowers are similar in colour to *T. bakeri* but with

Fig. 31. Tulipa aucheriana

more pointed segments paler on the outside, with a cream-coloured eye, opening in the sun to a wide star shape.

Tulipa humilis itself is a little taller than *T. aucheriana* with larger flowers, deep pinkish-purple in colour with a yellow blotch. It is another good garden plant and has several interesting named varieties. Var. *pulchella* is similar to the type but has a deep-blue centre with a pale margin. Var. *violacea* has deep-violet purple flowers, and there is a rare but very beautiful white variety of it, var. *pallida* (*T.pulchella* var *coerulea-oculata*), which is pure white with a deep-blue central blotch. All these can be grown outside, especially in areas with dry summers, and they all make excellent pot plants for the cold greenhouse.

The table following lists some other species of tulip which are either uncommon in commerce or unsuitable for the average rock garden or raised bed because of their size. The majority can be grown in the garden, but they look better associated with larger perennials and shrubs or grown on their own in some form of 'bedding'.

OTHER TULIP SPECIES

SPECIES	AVERAGE HEIGHT	SEASON	COLOUR	COMMENTS
T. acuminata	35 cm (14 in)	late	red and yellow	long pointed flowers
T. albertii	30 cm (12 in)	mid	deep red edged yellow	
T. aleppensis	20 cm (8in)		deep red small black blotch edged yellow	
T. altaica	15 cm (6 in)	mid	deep yellow tinged reddish	
T. butkovii	20 cm (8 in)	mid	crimson	
T. carinata	20 cm (8 in)	late	red	
T. celsiana (*T. persica*)	15 cm (6 in)	late	yellow exterior bronze	
T. didieri	35 cm (14 in)	late	red	slender flower
T. eichleri (*T. undulatifolia*)	30 cm (12 in)	mid	orange-red, large black blotch	very undulant leaves
T. ferganica	20 cm (8 in)	mid	yellow, outside reddish and green	
T. fosteriana	20 cm (8 in)	early	scarlet with black eye	many varieties and hybrids
T. fulgens	40 cm (16 in)	late	red with yellow or white eye	
T. galatica	15 cm (6 in)	late	pale yellow, exterior greenish, green blotch	
T. greigii	35 cm (14 in)	mid	red with black eye with yellow margin	striped leaves, large flowers, many hybrids

OTHER TULIP SPECIES *(cont.)*				
SPECIES	AVERAGE HEIGHT	SEASON	COLOUR	COMMENTS
T. hissarica	10 cm (4 in)	mid	yellow, greyish reverse	
T. hoogiana	20 cm (8 in)	early	scarlet, black blotch	
T. ingens (T. julia)	35 cm (14 in)	mid	scarlet, black blotch	very large flowers
T. kurdica	20 cm (8 in)	mid	red, greenish-black blotch	
T. lanata	60 cm (24 in)	early	orange-red	very large flowers
T. marjolettii	25 cm (10 in)	late	cream bordered pink	
T. platystigma	40 cm (16 in)	late	pink flushed orange	
T. praestans	25 cm (10 in)	early	red	several flowers to a stem
T. shrenkii	15 cm (6 in)	mid	red, margined orange	colour variable
T. suaveolens (T. subpraestans)	30 cm (12 in)	mid	orange-red, small yellow eye	
T. tubergeniana	25 cm (10 in)	mid	red, black blotch	
T. vvedenskyi	30 cm (12 in)	mid	orange-red	height very variable

49. *Muscari chalusicum*

MUSCARI

The genus *Muscari* seems to evoke less enthusiasm and excitement than most other genera of small bulbous plants, but it contains a few excellent plants for the rock garden and its environs, as well as a few species capable of becoming a serious menace in any but the wildest gardens. I have had the misfortune to take on a garden planted many years ago with a muscari, probably identifiable as *Muscari racemosum*, which has become a serious and ineradicable weed in certain areas. On the other hand there are few better small bulbs than *Muscari (Pseudomuscari) chalusicum*.

The genus can be divided into four reasonably well-defined groups, two of them immediately obvious and two needing a closer inspection of the flowers. The typical Grape Hyacinths are universally recognizable, with their dense spikes of tiny bells in shades of blue, but close inspection reveals that they fall into the larger Botryanthus Group, in which the the bells are markedly consricted at the mouth, and the smaller Pseudomuscari Group with the bells open at the mouth. The popular *Muscari comosum* and its allies belong to the Leopoldia Group, taller plants with more widely spaced flowers, the uppermost sterile flowers facing upwards and forming a tuft which may be blue, the lower fertile flowers in shades of greenish-white or yellow. The final Group, the Muscarimias, contains only two species, more exotic plants which require cultivation under glass except in warm areas with dry summers.

Botryanthus Group

These are the most widely-grown Grape Hyacinths, which must be chosen with some care for a rock garden or anywhere where other small plants are grown. None of them present any difficulty. The following species are generally available. Except where stated they all have several long, channelled leaves.

Muscari armeniacum varies between 10 and 15 cm (4–6in) and typically has bright blue flowers with white tips (lobes). Several named varieties can be found, varying in the shade of blue, and including a good white. *M. aucheri* (*M. tubergenanum*) increases less freely. It has broader leaves and good bright-blue flowers with white tips and a cluster of very pale sterile flowers at the tip of the spike. *M. botryoides* is similar with almost globular light-blue flowers, and this species also has a useful white variety. *M. latifolium* is a rarer species with one or two broad leaves and a tall stem with a long spike of blackish-purple flowers with paler sterile flowers. *M. neglectum* (*M. racemosum*) is a species to avoid except perhaps in the wildest part of the garden. The flowers are deep blackish-

blue with white tips, and usually with paler sterile flowers at the tip.

Pseudomuscari Group

This group contains only two species commonly in cultivation, *Muscari azureum* (*Pseudomuscari azureum*) and *M. chalusicum* (*Pseudomuscari chalusicum*). The former is an appealing little species usually not more than 10 cm (4 in) high, with small sky-blue flowers which are not constricted at their mouths. There is also a good white form available in commerce. *M. chalusicum* is my favourite species of Grape Hyacinth with slightly larger sky-blue flowers. It increases moderately well but never gets out of hand.

Leopoldia Group

Only one species in this Group is generally available, *Muscari comosum*, together with its form 'Plumosum' ('Monstrosum'). This is very different in appearance from the common Grape Hyacinths. It is a taller plant, up to 30 cm (12 in) high, with several long, narrow basal leaves. The lower fertile flowers are brownish-green and are widely spaced on the stem with a dense cluster of deep-violet sterile flowers above them, the uppermost on long upright stalks. In the weird variety 'Plumosum' the flowers are all sterile and threadlike so that the whole inflorescence is a mass of purple threads. These are easy to grow in well-drained soil in full sun, and seem to increase more freely by self-seeding than by division of the bulbs.

Muscarimia Group

There are two interesting plants in this Group valued especially for their powerful perfume, but they present more problems in cultivation than the other species. In *Muscari macrocarpum* the bulbs are much larger than those of other Grape Hyacinths and have thick fleshy roots. It has several long, channelled leaves and a stem 10–17cm (4–7in) long. The long, tubular flowers are bright yellow with a brown edge, opening from bluish-green buds. *M. macrocarpum* is more tender than other species but it can be grown outside in warm climates if the soil is well-drained.

Muscari muscarimi, better known under its synonym *M. moschatum*, has similar requirements, and differs in being smaller and having white flowers faintly tinged with blue. *M. ambrosiacum* is sometimes offered in catalogues and is generally considered to ba a variety of *M. muscarimi* with bluer flowers.

BELLEVALIA

These are so closely allied to *Muscari* that they can be considered here. Although several species have been collected in the past, especially from Turkey, they have limited appeal to the gardener except for two species, *Bellevalia forniculata* and *B. pycnantha*. The remaining species resemble the Leopoldia Group in their individual flowers, generally in somewhat dingy shades of brown, green and purple, and they are rarely offered in catalogues.

Bellevalia pycnantha is a popular Grape Hyacinth with long, dense, conical flower spikes, which are very dark blue in colour with a greyish bloom. The individual flowers have a narrow yellow band around their mouths. This species seems quite easy to grow and certainly does not increase excessively like the darkest species of muscari. *B. forniculata* is a remarkable species, which provided one of the most memorable sights of a trip to Eastern Turkey, its brilliant sky-blue flowers turning one meadow into an azure carpet. Unfortunately it is not often seen in cultivation and seems to be less easy to grow than most muscaris.

CORYDALIS

The tuberous species of *Corydalis* are among the most fascinating of all 'bulbs', and have become increasingly popular with the introduction and reintroduction of many exciting new species from all over Europe and Asia. Most of them have attractive grey or grey-green compound leaves which at their simplest consist of three leaflets but are usually further subdivided, and in some species are finely dissected. Each flower has a bract beneath it, which is often conspicuous. The flowers have four petals, the upper and lower being much larger than the inner. The upper petal is extended into a long spur and the lower has a broad lip. The two inner petals are joined at their apices, around the style and stamens, and are often of a deeper colour different from the remainder of the flower.

The species are very diverse in their cultural requirements, some being easy plants for woodland, or for the rock garden, and others needing special care in the cold greenhouse. I have only included the strictly tuberous-rooted species, thus missing out such beauties as *Corydalis flexuosa*, *C. cashmeriana* and *C. nobilis*. I have subdivided them into the Sections described in a comprehensive article by Liden and Zetterlund in the *Bulletin of the Alpine Garden Society* (Vol. 56, p. 146), and I have omitted many species which are not readily available at present.

Section Corydalis

The species in this Section have tubers which are re-formed every year, alternate leaves on the flower stems, and a single scale leaf below the bottom leaf, which may be just below ground level. In general these are the easiest species to grow in the open garden, and they can be divided according to their basic cultural requirements into woodland and dry-land species. The former enjoy shady conditions with abundant humus in the soil and moisture at all times. The dry-land species need to be kept almost dry during their summer dormancy and therefore need to be grown under glass in wet areas. The more robust of them may grow satisfactorily in areas with occasional summer rainfall, for example in the drier parts of Britain, and are certainly suitable for any dry-summer areas elsewhere. Many of the species are as yet comparatively untried and as stocks are built up I suspect that more and more will be found to be amenable to garden conditions, especially in the rock garden with its good drainage.

In view of the rarity of most of the dry-land species of this Section and of the species in other Sections, the notes below concentrate on the best garden plants and the remaining species are summarized in tables (p. 000).

Woodland species: Although I have followed Liden and Zetterlund in this grouping and all the species will grow in the woodland conditions mentioned, my own experience suggests that *Corydalis solida* and its allies grow better in full sun, and *C. caucasica alba* does equally well in either situation. The easiest of the definite shade-lovers are *C. ambigua* and *C. bracteata*, with the possible addition of *C. angustifolia*.

Corydalis solida is one of the most vigorous and easily grown of all the tuberous species. It is very variable, the leaves blue-green, divided into many lobes, and the flower colour varying in shades from lilac to pink to an unusual shade of brick-red. The most common form from trade sources has flowers in shades of pale pinkish-purple, somewhat wishy-washy to some eyes but pleasing pastel shades to others. It increases rapidly by division of its tubers and by self-sowing. The colour can be a much deeper shade of deep reddish-purple, and this seems to apply

50. *Corydalis solida* 'George Baker'

to some plants acquired as *C. decipiens*, botanically a synonym of *C. solida*. The best colour forms are the plant which was given the cultivar name 'George Baker' with flowers of a clear brick-red colour, and some more recent introductions with clear pale-pink flowers. The best known of these introductions was originally being grown as 'ex-Munich Botanic Garden'; it has now been named, and has received an Award of Merit, as *C. solida* 'Beth Evans'. These beautiful plants have proved very easy to grow in a sunny place in well-drained soil, increasing well by splitting of the tubers. They do not set seed regularly and do not often come true if the seedlings are grown on. *C. solida* 'George Baker' was originally introduced as *C. transsylvanica* (*C. solida* ssp. *transsylvanica*), but this name is considered incorrect, although it is sometimes still applied to plants with brick-red flowers. There is a desirable pure-white form, *C. solida* ssp. *incisa* f. *alba*, which remains uncommon at present.

Corydalis caucasica and the more widely grown *C. caucasica alba* have proved as good as *C. solida* as garden plants, increasing rapidly by self-sown seed which is set in abundance. The tubers do not increase as freely as *C. solida* forms and it therefore seems to produce scattered clusters of a few leaves and flower stems rather than building up into substantial groups. The blue-flowered type plant is

51. *Corydalis caucasica* 'Alba'

52. *Corydalis ambigua*

not often seen, and the white is probably a better plant with sparkling white flowers with a hint of green. The name of this species is in some doubt and it seems probable that it should be referred to *Corydalis malkensis*.

Among the excellent blue-flowered species of *Corydalis* readily available, *Corydalis cashmeriana* has the beautiful pure blue colour that every grower wants, but it is not an easy plant except in cool humid areas; *Corydalis flexuosa* has almost the same colour and is very easy to grow and increase in any shady place with plenty of humus. However, neither of these has a true tuber and only *C. ambigua* fits our criteria. At its best the flower colour can be almost as good as that of

the two other species mentioned but it is important to obtain a clone of clear blue colour. An increasing number of somewhat dingy, bluish-coloured plants seems to be appearing recently.

For ease of cultivation *C. ambigua* seems to fall between *C. cashmeriana* and *C. flexuosa*. The former is almost impossible in dry areas without considerable irrigation, whereas *C. ambigua* will grow well in a shady position in well-drained but humus-rich soil even in the drier areas of Britain. It is a taller plant than *C. cashmeriana*, usually 15–20 cm (6–8 in) high, with much larger green leaflets and clear pale-blue flowers with white in the throat. *C. lineariloba* is occasionally obtainable. It closely resembles *C. ambigua* but has narrower and more deeply divided leaves.

Corydalis bracteata is an excellent yellow-flowered species that needs the same conditions as *C. ambigua* for success in the garden. It is similar in height, in its leaves, and in its comparatively large flowers, each subtended by a large bract with a deeply dissected margin; but the flowers are clear yellow with a very wide lower lip and deeper-yellow inner petals. *C.x allenii* is occasionally obtainable. It is thought to be a hybrid of *C. bracteata*, and it grows well in similar woodland conditions. It has grey-green leaves and yellow flowers 2 cm long with some purple coloration on the lip.

C. angustifolia is another very attractive white-flowered species which is said to grow well in woodland conditions. It is a recent addition to my own collection and has proved easy to grow in a pot in a well-drained compost kept just moist at all times. As it sets abundant seed, which germinates well, there will be scope for experimenting with it in the garden. It is a slender plant with very narrow leaflets. The flowers are white or may be cream, up to 3 cm long, with long slender spurs. The bracts are characteristically divided into three. *Corydalis alexeenkoana* is very similar to *C. angustifolia* but the flower is broader, about 2 cm long, with a thicker spur.

Dry garden species: This group includes some excellent plants for the bulb-frame or cold greenhouse, where the tubers can be kept dry during their dormant period in areas with a high summer rainfall. Where there is little or no rain during the summer they should thrive in the open garden, and it seems quite likely that with further experimentation others will be found to grow in a well-drained rock-garden, particlarly those which appear to be close to *Corydalis solida*.

Section Duplotuber

This differs from the previous Section in having two to four scale leaves below the bottom leaf, and only contains one species currently in cultivation. This is *Corydalis decumbens*, a small plant with very dissected leaves and a few small pinkish-purple flowers. It grows and increases well in woodland conditions.

Section Radix-Cava

The plants in this Section have perennial tubers, no scale leaves and two alternate leaves. The species are mainly European, and two of them at least are easy in woodland or lightly shaded conditions in the garden.

SECTION CORYDALIS DRY-LAND SPECIES

SPECIES	LEAVES	FLOWERS	COMMENTS
C. glaucescens	grey-green, pinnate, leaflets deeply divided	few-flowered raceme, flowers 2.5 cm long, pink or pale purple, broad lip	one of the most striking
C. integra	biternate with rounded lobes	flowers up to 20, 1.5-2.0 cm, pale purple, dark tips to inner petals	like C. solida but bracts entire
C. intermedia (C. fabacea)	biternate with rounded lobes	flowers few, 1–1.5 cm pale purple	like C. solida but bracts entire
C. nudicaulis	3 leaflets with narrow lobes	dense raceme of 2–8, 1.5–2 cm, pale purple	rare
C. paczoczii	biternate with narrow lobes	loose few-flowered raceme, up to 1 cm, pale purple fading at the lip	like C. solida, bracts divided
C. schanginii	grey-green much divided	loose raceme, long, up to 4 cm, slender, very pale pink, deep-purple tips	striking species.
C. schanginii ssp. ainii	grey-green much divided	yellow with a white spur and brown centre	
C. wendelboi	grey-green, biternate, deeply lobed	crowded curving raceme up to 2cm, pale purple, inner petals tipped deep purple	bracts dissected

Corydalis cava (*C. bulbosa, C. tuberosa*) is a common and easily gown plant. It has a pair of light-green leaves and and a dense raceme of 10–20 flowers, each up to 2.5 cm (1 in) long with a down-curving spur, usually purple in colour, but sometimes white. A most attractive named albino is sometimes offered in catalogues. The subspecies *marschalliana*, sometimes given specific status, has pale-yellow flowers, but is unfortunately uncommon.

Corydalis parnassica is a high alpine plant, generally grown under glass. It is shorter than the two species described previously; it has more glaucous leaves and a dense raceme of large flowers in a shade of palest violet, darker on the tips of the inner petals.

SECTION LEONTICOIDES

SPECIES	LEAVES	FLOWERS	COMMENTS
C. afghanica	grey-green, pinnate, leaflets many	few, white or very pale pink, up to 4 cm, spur long and curved	
C. aitchisonii	greyish, few leaflets on long stalks	yellow, maturing darker, 3–5 cm, very slender	
C. chionophila	grey-green, few leaflets	few, whitish with purple tips	
C. darwasica	pinnate, grey, much divided	few, whitish with maroon lip	
C. diphylla	grey-green, few narrow leaflets	few palest pink with deep . purple lips	variable in colour Close to *C. rutifolia*
C. firouzii	as *C. chionophila*	as *C. chionophila* but flowers pale yellow with pink shading with age	allied to *C. chionophila*
C. ledebouriana	grey-green, ternate	long loose raceme, pale pink with violet lip, 2 cm, thick pale spur	vigorous
C. macrocentra	grey-green, tall	stems branched, bracts toothed, 2–3 cm, otherwise close to *C. aitchisonii*	
C. popovii	grey-green ternate	loose raceme, very large, up to 5 cm (2 in), very pale pink with deep-purple lips	robust, one of the easiest
C. rutifolia	glaucous, very variable in division	one to few, vary pale pink with dark reddish-purple lips	several subspecies based on leaf divisions
C. sewerzowii	leaves more divided than *C. aitchisonii*	as *C. aitchisonii*	very close to *C. aitchisoni*

Section Leonticoides

This Section differs from Radix-Cava in having opposite leaves. From the gardener's point of view it contains some of the most beautiful species, but in Britain and other areas with a high summer rainfall the species need the protection of a frame or cold house to keep them dry in summer. They grow well in a well-drained compost, and can be increased by seed. The species all have similar requirements and their main features are summarized in the table opposite.

Fig. 32. Corydalis rutifolia

Section Dactylotuber

This Section contains species with branching tubers, but none of its members are in general cultivation.

ERYTHRONIUM

Of all the bulbous plants that flourish in shade, two genera stand out as providing the most exciting and rewarding plants, *Erythronium* and *Trillium*, and few of the species can fail to come up to the expectation of the gardener. Both genera need 'good' shady conditions – i.e. the soil should be acid, should have abundant humus incorporated and should be moist at all times – but, given these conditions, most of them will flourish and increase over the years. In a peat bed in my own garden several species of both genera have been established for over twenty years with no more attention than weeding and

an occasional top-dressing with leaf-mould.

The erythroniums are all hardy plants of exquisite beauty, having flowers with long recurving petals resembling those of the 'Turk's Cap' lilies and, in some species, with well-marked leaves. Their common name, 'Dog tooth Violet', derives from the shape of the bulbs, which are long and slightly curved like a dog's canine teeth. In my experience the commonest and most readily available species, *E. dens-canis*, is not the most satisfactory in the garden, its floriferousness and rate of increase being surpassed by *E. revolutum*, among the pink-flowered species, by *E. tuolumnense* among the pure yellow-flowered species, and by *E. oregonum* and *E. 'White Beauty'* among the near-white species. Recent experience suggests that some of the newer hybrids will also prove to be long-lived plants with a reasonable rate of increase. They will be described after the species.

In mid- to late spring, groups of *Erythronium revolutum* are among the most striking features of the garden. Their leaves are beautiful marked with brownish-purple and pale-green zig-zags, varying in intensity from plant to plant; the stems, up to 20 cm (8 in) high, bear solitary flowers or occasionally two or three, each up to 5 cm (2 in) across, deep

Fig. 33. Erythronium dens-canis

53. *Erythronium tuolumnense* with
E. *revoluta*

54. *Erythronium revolutum*

pink in colour with a small yellow centre and long, slender, recurving petals and a white style and cream stamens. They enjoy moist shade and will increase by seed and by division of the tubers. Var. *johnstonii* is a particularly good deep-pink variety.

E. *dens-canis* is the most popular species and the least expensive. It has mottled leaves which are more rounded, smaller, and less striking than those of E. *revoluta*. The flower stems are also shorter, the flowers solitary and a little smaller. Flower colour is variable from deep pink or pale purple to white, and the centre may be yellow, white, or brownish, the anthers bluish-purple. Several named varieties are in cultivation, including 'Franz Hals' with large pale-purple flowers; 'Lilac Wonder', rich lavender; 'Niveum' and 'Snowflake', both white; 'Pink Perfection', pale pink; 'Purple King', deep purple; and 'Rose Queen' deep pink. E. *japonicum* is a close ally of E. *dens-canis* with large violet-coloured flowers with a darker centre. E. *caucasicum* is also a close ally, but differs in having cream-coloured flowers.

E. *hendersonii* is a fine species which increases slowly in shady conditions. It is a little taller than E. *revolutum*, with several flowers to a stem, which are lavender in colour with a darker purple centre.

The best of the yellow species for the garden is *Erythronium tuolumnense*, a robust trouble-free plant which increases by splitting of the bulbs, and improves as the years go by. It has light-green unmottled leaves, and stems of similar height to E. *revolutum* carrying one or two, or occasionally three or four, flowers each. These are pure deep yellow throughout and have an unlobed stigma.

The two other pure yellow species present difficulties in the garden. E. *americanum* is reasonably easy to grow and increase, and it has perhaps the most beautiful leaves of the genus, mottled with reddish-brown, and very deep-yellow flowers with dark-brownish shading on the exterior, but these, alas, are only rarely produced. It is worth growing for the leaves and the occasional unexpected pleasure when it does flower. E. *grandiflorum* is much more difficult to grow, but it will sometimes settle down in good moist shady conditions, and it will then flower regularly. It can produce up to five flowers to a stem, and has unmottled leaves. The flowers differ from those of E. tuolumnense in having a trilobed stigma.

Several species have flowers which are predominantly white or cream, with or without a yellow centre, and they are not always easy to distinguish without a study of their floral parts, In the garden they are generally not difficult to grow in good conditions, but increase is usually slower than of those mentioned previously, by division or by seed. From experience of growing several of them in the same peat bed, it seems that Erythronium oregonum increases most freely, but I suspect that most of the increase is by self-sown seedlings; whereas E. californicum and E. albidum increase slowly into clumps by splitting of the bulbs. E. multiscapoideum supposedly forms stolons and increases by them, but so far I have not found it increasing quickly. E. helenae I have also found slow to form clumps. The differences between these very similar species are tabulated below.

There are several excellent hybrids. Some of them are of recent origin and not yet readily available but are showing great promise for the future. 'White Beauty' has been one of the most popular erythroniums for many years. Its origin seems to be obscure but it is closely related to E. oregonum and E. californicum, with mottled leaves and white, yellow-centred, flowers. It seems to be the most free-flowering and rapidly increasing of all the erythroniums I grow. 'Kondo', and the doubtfully distinguishable 'Pagoda', are also readily available. 'Kondo' is a tall vigorous plant with mottled leaves and several flowers to a stem, pale yellow with a brownish centre. Two others which are just appearing in the trade and seem to be free-flowering and reasonably free to increase are 'Jeanette Brickell' (white flowers), and 'Jeannine' (large yellow flowers with central brown markings).

TRILLIUM

This is another superb genus for good 'woodland' conditions in the garden. All

DIFFERENTIATING FEATURES OF WHITE-FLOWERED ERYTHRONIUMS				
SPECIES	LEAVES	FLOWER	STIGMA	ANTHERS
E. albidum	mottled, narrow at base	white, yellow centre, greyish exterior	three-lobed	yellow
E. albidum var. mesochoreum	plain	white, yellow centre, greyish exterior	three-lobed	yellow
E. californicum	mottled	cream, ring of brown marks in centre	three-lobed	white
E. citrinum	mottled	cream, swelling at base of petal	entire	white
E. helenae	mottled	cream, yellow centre	three-lobed	yellow
E. multiscapoideum	mottled	white, yellow centre	three-lobed	white
E. oregonum	mottled	creamy white, yellow centre	three-lobed	yellow on flattened filaments

the species have a whorl of three leaves, which may be mottled, at the end of a bare stem; and a solitary flower with three large and conspicuous petals and three insignificant green sepals. They benefit from a rich moist soil and thrive on abundant leaf-mould, or even on well-rotted ·compost or old manure, incorporated in the soil. Most species increase steadily to form large clumps if left undisturbed over the years, and they can be increased from seed, as described on page 31. The species fall into two main groups, those with sessile flowers and those with flowers on a definite stalk – the stalk may be erect, or may be nodding so that the flowers are below the leaves.

Sessile-flowered species

The two most common species in this group are Trillium sessile and T. cuneatum, which have been confused in the past and are probably still mixed from some trade sources; the former is the name most often offered, but the latter is the plant more often available. T. cuneatum is typically considerably taller, up to 30 cm (12 in) or a little more, large leaves mottled with paler green, and sessile deep-brownish-purple flowers up to 10 cm (4 in) long, with small green petals which may be flushed with purple. T. sessile is similar in colouring but a smaller plant rarely more than 20 cm (8 in) high, with flowers half the size of those of T. cuneatum.

Trillium luteum (T. sessile var. luteum) is very similar except in the colour of its flowers which are greenish-yellow. T. chloropetalum is an excellent, vigorous, easily grown species of similar habit, and the leaves are particularly well patterned in shades of green and brown. The flower colour varies but is most commonly greenish-yellow or greenish-white, which is a more effective colour in the garden than the sombre hues of T. cuneatum. An

uncommon variety is sometimes available with reddish-purple flowers. T. recurvatum is a less spectacular plant with stalked leaves and smaller reddish-purple flowers with strongly recurving sepals.

Two other American species with sessile flowers are occasionally offered in catalogues, T. viride and T. pusillum var. virginianum. The former is a tall plant with small green flowers. The latter is a much smaller plant, up to 20 cm (8 in) with white flowers 2.5 cm (1 in) long with undulate-margined petals.

Stalked species with erect flowers

This group contains many of the most striking garden plants of the genus, from the robust Trillium grandiflorum with its substantial pure white flowers, to the delightful miniatures T. nivale and T. rivale. They are generally easy to grow in the woodland conditions described previously, and any exceptions will be considered in the context of the separate species.

Trillium grandiflorum is a superb plant to brighten shady areas, and in good conditions will build up into a large clump. The height varies with growing conditions but is usually 20–40 cm (8–16 in). The large leaves are unmarked and the solitary flowers are carried on 5–8 cm (2–3 in) stems. The broad, pure-white, spreading petals are of similar length to the stems. The flowers often fade to pink as they age but there is an exquisite pure-pink variety in cultivation, unfortunately rare at present. There is also a popular double form, f. flore-pleno, with a beautiful arrangement of petals similar to that of a formal double camellia.

Trillium ovatum is similar to T. grandiflorum and is almost as good a garden plant. The leaves are more sharply· pointed at the apex and the flowers a little smaller, with the petals spreading widely from the base, whereas in T. grandiflorum they are erect in their lowest part. The

55. *Trillium grandiflorum* 'Roseum'

56. *Trillium erectum*

flowers are pure white and, as in *T. grandiflorum*, they frequently become pink with age.

Trillium erectum and its varieties are among the most attractive and easily grown species, making magnificent clumps if they are planted in well-prepared soil and left undisturbed. It usually grows to about 30 cm (12 in) in height but can be considerably taller in ideal conditions. The flowers are held singly on upright stems 5–8 cm (2–3 in) long and may face upwards or more frequently outwards, above the large unmottled leaves. The flowers typically are a deep reddish-purple in colour, but a white form is frequently grown, f. *albiflorum*, with a contrasting reddish-purple ovary. There is also a yellow form, f. *luteum*.

One of the most beautiful species is the dainty *Trillium undulatum*, only 10–20 cm (4–8 in) tall, with narrowly pointed stalked leaves and small white flowers with red at the base which stains the inner part of the petals with pink. Although this is one of the most desirable species it seems to be considerably more difficult to grow than most of the others, even in moist acid soil.

Trillium rivale is, at least to the small-plant enthusiast, one of the loveliest of all the species and not difficult to grow. However, its small size necessitates careful placing with other very small plants,

57. *Trillium rivale*

for example among the smallest ericaceous shrubs in a peat bed. It only attains about 5 cm (2 in) at flowering time, with stalked ovate unmarked leaves narrowing to a point, and flowers with basically white petals, up to 2.5 cm (1 in) long, variably spotted with pink at the base and sometimes halfway up the petals. An extreme form has been named 'Purple Heart', in which the spots are so close that the impression is of a deep-rose-purple centre.

Trillium nivale is similar in size but the flowers are pure white, the petals a little longer and broader with no spotting. It seems to be considerably more difficult to grow and increase than *T. rivale*, probably because it grows in more open situations on limestone in its habitat, and this should be borne in mind when choosing a postion for it in the garden.

Several Asiatic species are occasionally available in the trade, but are less spectacular than the American species. *T. kamschaticum* is one of the best of these with erect white flowers above unmottled leaves, the flowers about half the size of those of *T. ovatum*. *T. tschonoskii* is a similar but smaller plant with outward-facing flowers. The least conspicuous of those regularly on offer is *T. smallii*, similar in size to *T. tschonovskii* but with brownish-purple flowers

Stalked species with nodding flowers

The four species in cultivation in this group have pedicels which curve down and carry the flowers below the leaves, so that they are less conspicuous than in most other species; these are nevertheless attractive plants to grow, especially in a raised bed where their flowers are easier to see. The commonest of them is *Trillium cernuum*, a robust species, 30 cm (12 in) or more high with large unmarked leaves and nodding white or occasionally very pale-pink flowers, with reflexing petals and purple ovary and anthers.

T. vaseyi is another large species with broad unmarked leaves and nodding brownish-purple flowers beneath the leaves. *T. catesbaei* (*T. nervosum*, *T. stylosum*) is a smaller plant with more reflexed petals in shades of pink. *T. rugellii* is another uncommon American species occasionally available; it has large leaves and small white flowers with reflexing petals and purple anthers.

OTHER GENERA

The most important spring-flowering genera have now been considered but there remain a number of others containing only a few species, many of them valuable plants for the rock garden, which I will describe alphabetically. A few genera, for example *Calochortus*, have members flowering at this time but as the majority flower later, I will consider them together in the next chapter.

Bongardia

Bongardia chrysogonum is a surprising member of the Berberidaceae, with a large irregular tuber. It is hardy only in warm areas, but is a very easily grown plant under glass. It has such fine leaves that it is worth growing as a foliage plant. The basal leaves are long and pinnate, the leaflets greyish-green, with a toothed apex and a broad, reddish-purple, zig-zag band just above the base. From among the leaves arise loose sprays of small pure-yellow flowers, 1.5 cm across, usually to a height of about 20–30 cm (8–12 in).

Bulbocodium

Bulbocodium vernum is closely related to *Colchicum*, differing only in having three separate styles, rather than one divided into three at the tip. It has small rosy-purple flowers only just above ground level in mid- to late spring when the leaves are only beginning to form. The leaves lengthen later but are not too obtrusive for it to be suitable for the small rock garden.

Gagea

This is a rarely grown genus of small bulbous plants with umbels (usually) of quite attractive little yellow flowers. In my very limited experience of growing gageas they have proved short-lived in the garden, but they are more successful in a bulb-frame.

Gymnospermium

Only one species is readily available, *G. albertii* (*Leontice albertii*), which is another attractive member of the Berberidaceae, like *Bongardia*, with similar cultural requirements. It has dense clusters of deep-yellow flowers on reddish stems which are bent over when the flowers first open and then gradually straighten to a height of up to 30 cm (12 in). The leaves are then only just beginning to unfurl and are tinged with bronze. When fully open they have five leaflets and are pale green. The only other closely allied plant which is occasionally in cultivation is *Leontice leontopetalum*. It is considerably larger, with more divided leaves and more substantial heads of small yellow flowers with widely-spaced petals.

Gynandiris

Gynandiris sisyrinchium (*Iris sisyrinchium*) must be well known to travellers around the Mediterranean, where its pale-blue flowers are often so abundant that one may not be aware how fleeting they are, opening in the afternoon and dying at the end of the day. For this reason, and the fact that it needs a summer baking, it is rarely offered or grown, even under glass, but in dry summer areas where it can be enjoyed in the open garden, it is worth growing for typical iris flowers produced successively on stems varying greatly between 15 and 45 cm (6–18 in).

Hyacinthus, Hyacinthella, and Hyacinthoides

Hyacinthus and *Hyacinthoides*, apart from the wild form of *Hyancinthus orientalis* and *Hyacinthoides italica*, have little relevance in a book on bulbs for the rock garden, and *Hyacinthella* species are rarely seen.

Hyacinthus orientalis is the species from which the large hybrids were developed; it is surprisingly uncommon, considering that it is an attractive and dainty plant with very loose spikes of small blue flowers, bearing little resemblance to the fat 'hyacinths' of commerce. It seems quite persistent in well-drained soil in a sunny or partially shaded position.

The 'bluebells', whether the British *Hyacinthoides non-scripta* in its blue, pink, and white varieties, or the more robust 'Spanish Bluebell', *H. hispanica*, in similar colours, are useful plants for shady situations, but too vigorous to be in or near the rock garden. In fact most gardeners in cool climates consider the native Bluebells a menace, and not one that is easily controlled.

Hyacinthoides italica is better known as *Scilla italica*, and is one of the best late-spring-flowering species. It has linear leaves and dense spikes of good blue star-shaped flowers on 15 cm (6 in) stems. It seems to persist well in a sunny rock garden.

The hyacinthellas are a pleasant genus of rarely seen, small spring and early summer-flowering bulbs, which are offered in very few catalogues. They are suitable for well-drained soils in a sunny rock garden or are easily grown under glass. The species most likely to be available are *H. pallens* (*H. dalmatica*) with spikes of pale-blue flowers, *H. heldreichii* and *H. lineata* with very dark blue flowers, and *H. acutiloba* with mid-blue flowers.

Ipheion (Tristagma, Triteleia)

Although *Ipheion uniflorum* is the only species regularly grown, it can, with its various forms, play an important part in providing colour in the late spring in any reasonably well-drained soil. Its only fault is a tendency to over-leafiness, and perhaps to wishy-washiness in the type plant. It generally increases very well and may therefore over-power small plants in the rock garden.

Each bulb produces several long, narrow, slightly glaucous leaves during

58. *Ipheion uniflorum* 'Wisley Blue'

winter. The flowers, usually solitary, are carried well above the leaves on stems of varying height, generally about 15–20 cm (6–8 in) long. Typically the flowers are very pale blue with a darker line down the middle of each petal. 'Wisley Blue' is a strong-growing form with deeper blue flowers; 'Froyle Mill' is darker still with violet-blue flowers, but is less freely increasing. 'Rolf Fielder' is an excellent form; its well-rounded flowers have overlapping petals, a good clear blue and a white throat. I find that it does not persist well in the garden but it is an excellent pan plant.

Two white forms are available. *I. uniflorum album* resembles the type but has pure white flowers with a faint grey line down each petal, and it is much less vigorous as a garden plant. 'Alberto Castillo' is an excellent recent introduction with larger, more glaucous leaves and larger flowers of pristine white. In a brief experience of it, it has increased well and been undamaged by winter weather.

Leucojum

The only species not considered previously is *Leucojum aestivum*, which flowers later in spring and early summer. It resembles a large version of *L. vernum* with stems up to 60 cm (24 in) high carrying umbels of white, nodding, bell-shaped flowers with green tips. It is too tall for the rock garden but is an excellent plant for light woodland or in grass, especially on damp heavy soils. It varies in height and size of flower; and one of the biggest and best forms is 'Gravetye Giant'.

Ornithogalum

This is not a very popular genus in the garden although it contains a number of low-growing, spring-flowering species eminently suitable for the rock garden, as well as some very attractive taller species which flower later and will be considered in the next chapter. All the small species are very similar and instantly recognizable as ornithogalums, with short-stemmed clusters of star-shaped flowers, which are white with either green backs or a broad green band down the reverse of the petals. Their nomenclature is difficult and the reader is referred to more specialized literature for details (such as Brian Mathew's *The Smaller Bulbs*). Most of these smaller species seem to persist well and increase, with sun and good drainage. Among them are *O. balansae* (*O. oligophyllum*), with unusually large, green-backed flowers on 7.5 cm (3 in) stems, above broad leaves. *O. fimbriatum* is similar in height with narrow leaves and a broad cluster of smaller flowers. *O. lanceolatum* forms a rosette of very wide leaves, among which are clustered large, almost stemless, white flowers. *O. tenuifolius* is variable in height from 8 to 20 cm (3-8 in), with very narrow leaves and broad racemes of flowers. *O. sigmoideum* (*O. nanum, O. sibthorpii*) has narrow crocus-like leaves with a central white line, and stemless clusters of flowers nestling among the leaves.

Ornithogalum nutans deserves special mention. It is a taller species, usually

20–25 cm (8–10 in), with remarkable silvery-grey flowers with grey-green backs and recurving tips. It needs careful placing in a sunny or lightly shaded area, as it can increase rapidly and should not be associated with small plants.

Romulea (South African species)

The spring-flowering species of Romulea were described in the previous chapter, but there remain a few species from South Africa which are too tender for the garden in Britain, but can be grown outside in warmer areas and are excellent plants under glass where the cold is not sufficient to freeze the pots. These species are generally much more spectacular than those mentioned earlier, but they are rare in cultivation, only three being available with any frequency. Any species from the area are well worth trying, and seed is sometimes available from specialised lists.

Romulea sabulosa is a remarkable species with huge flowers 5–8 cm (2–3 in) in diameter, deep red with a black-and-yellow centre. Romulea hirta has large yellow flowers with deep-brownish markings around the centre. R. rosea is the commonest of these species. It is easily grown under glass and might seed too freely, like so many romuleas, in a warm climate. The flower colour is variable but the form usually seen has deep-pink flowers about 2.5 cm (1 in) long, with a yellow centre, on 15 cm (6 in) stems.

Scilla

Most of the scillas were described in the previous chapter, but there remain a few which flower in late spring and early summer. Scilla italica was described as Hyacinthoides italica. Scilla litardieri is one of the last to flower with narrow dark-green leaves, stems up to 20 cm (8 in) and up to 30 small mid-blue flowers in a dense spike. Scilla persica is a little taller with larger flowers in a much looser raceme – an excellent but uncommon species.

Scilla peruviana has very large bulbs, which seem to benefit from shallow planting in a warm sunny place. It forms a large rosette of somewhat untidy leaves in autumn, and a very robust conical spike of up to 50 or more flowers on long pedicels, each up to 2.5 cm (1 in) across. The colour varies but most commonly is a deep violet-blue. There is also a good white variety, 'Alba'.

Tecophilea

Tecophilea cyanocrocus has always been considered one of the most desirable of bulbous plants, for its astonishing blue colour, but it has never become common as it needs special care under glass. The bulbs will increase by division if they are being grown well, and it is not difficult to raise from seed, as long as the young plants are kept frost-free in the early stages. Opinions differ on the treatment it requires. One of the most successful growers considers that it should be given a thorough baking during its summer dormancy, but my own experience has been that it is better kept 'slightly moist' during this period. Evidently it will tolerate either treatment. The adult bulbs are hardy in an unheated house in Britain, but would need some heat in colder areas.

Three varieties are grown. The type plant has 15 cm (6 in) stems bearing solitary funnel-shaped flowers, which are an intense deep blue in colour. Var. 'Leichtlinii' has paler blue flowers with a white centre of variable width, which may be over more than half of the flower. Var. 'Violacea' is a deeper violet-blue. If more than one variety is grown from seed there seems to be considerable variation in the seedlings, both in the intensity of the blue and in the presence and size of a white eye.

CHAPTER 7

Bulbs for Summer

With the mass of colour which summer brings to the rock garden and elsewhere, bulbous plants become of less importance, but there are a considerable number which can add interest to sunny and shady areas, and to the alpine house or cold greenhouse. As in previous chapters I will consider the more important genera first: the alliums, various genera of aroids, brodiaeas and their allies, and *Calochortus*, *Oxalis*, and *Rhodohypoxis*.

ALLIUM

This is a very large genus containing species of all sizes and colours, of varying cultural requirements, but generally easy in the open garden, with more than its fair share of 'menaces'. The propensity for excessive increase of some of these should not be underestimated, and bulbiferous species which form small bulbs instead of, or as well as, flowers at the top of their stems, together with those which form a cluster of many small bulbils around the parent bulb, should be removed as soon as possible. Alliums are nearly all easily raised from seed and most will also increase by division of the bulbs.

Although not very popular with alpine enthusiasts the genus contains a number of excellent small species, which can be grown on the rock garden or near the front of a mixed border. The choice is wide and I will select some which have proved themselves in the garden without becoming too invasive, summarizing the main features of some other less common and less widely grown species in a table. I have omitted species which regularly attain over 30 cm (12 in) in height.

Two species are worth growing as foliage plants, for their very broad greenish-blue leaves, and they also have large umbels of flowers. In *Allium akaka* the umbels are up to 10 cm (4 in) across, of very pale-pink or whitish flowers on 15–20 cm (6–8 in) stems. In *A. karatviense* the umbels are even larger, usually pale-pink to purple, and the stems are smaller, so that the flower heads are only just above the leaves. Both species thrive in hot dry conditions, and *A. akaka* needs frame or cold-house treatment except in summer-dry climates.

There are several species with blue flowers which are good plants for the open garden in well-drained soil, but there may be some confusion over their names in catalogues. *Allium beesianum* is the most elegant of them, with drooping umbels of up to 10 cylindrical bright-blue bells 12–18 mm (½–¾ in) long, on 20–30 cm (8–12 in) long stems. Flowering in late summer, it is sometimes confused with the much commoner *A. cyaneum* or with *A. sikkimense*. The former is a shorter plant with a more slender stem and a denser umbel of more star-shaped flowers, with the stamens protruding from the mouth of the bell, whereas in *A. beesianum* they are shorter than the petals. It flowers around midsummer. *A. sikkimense* flowers in early summer with a looser umbel of up to 15 bell-shaped flowers, their stamens also hidden within, similar in height to *A. cyaneum.*

Allium caeruleum is a widely-grown taller plant suitable for planting among larger perennials and shrubs. The 20–60 cm (8–24 in) stems bear dense umbels up to 4 cm (1½ in) across, of cup-shaped flowers which are pale to mid-blue with a darker median stripe.

Pink to purple shades abound in the genus, and several of the species in these colours can make considerable impact on the summer garden, planted in groups among other plants: take care that they do not dwarf small alpines. *Allium amabile* (*A. mairei* var. *amabile*) is one of the most delightful small species from China, freely seeding to make clumps of grass-like leaves and small loose clusters of up to five narrow purplish-pink flowers on 10 cm (4 in) stems. Although correctly a variety of *A. mairei*, *A. amabile* of commerce has paler pink flowers. *A. cyathorum* var. *farreri* (*A. farreri*) is another Chinese species with similar requirements, enjoying reasonably moist soils and tolerant of partial shade. It is a variable plant but typically produces a one-sided umbel of deep-reddish-purple flowers, narrowly bell-shaped, on 15–25 cm (6–10 in) stems in early to mid-summer. It seeds freely so that you may be well advised to dead-head it if the increase becomes excessive.

The remaining species to be described in this colour range are native to Central Euope, Asia Minor or North America, and have somewhat different requirements, needing well drained soil and full sun; however they are reasonably easy in the garden except in very wet areas.

A. dichlamydeum is a delightful North American species which is growing well in the garden although it is usually recommended for the cold house. It has flattish heads of unusually large, deep-rose flowers on 15 cm (6 in) stems in mid-

summer. *A. murrayanum* presents nomenclatural problems, as the wild plant is thought to be identical with *A. acuminatum*; but the plant readily available under this name from trade sources is probably identical to, or a variety of, *A. unifolium*. It is an excellent species, flowering a little earlier than *A. dichlamydeum*, taller, and with even larger flowers in umbels of 10–20, clear pink fading to white in the centre. It needs similar conditions of excellent drainage and, like *A. dichlamydeum*, is easily raised from seed.

Allium insubricum is the plant widely offered as *A. narcissiflorum*, an uncommon species in cultivation. It is perhaps the most beautiful of all the alliums with a nodding cluster of 3–6 large pink cup-shaped flowers on 15–30 cm (6–12 in) stems. *A. narcissiflorum* differs in having more flowers to the umbel and more specifically in having seed heads which become erect, whereas those of *A. insubricum* continue to hang downwards.

Allium oreophilum (*A. ostrowskianum*) is a smaller member of this group with round umbels of small flowers, pinkish-purple with a darker stripe down the middle of each segment, on 5–10 cm (2–4 in) stems. A popular cultivar 'Zwanenburg' has flowers of a brighter reddish colour.

59. *Allium dichlamydeum*

In the pink-to-purple range are two other very popular species, which are extremely easy to grow; in fact deadheading may be needed to stop them seeding too abundantly. They are both a little too tall for the average rock garden but are splendid summer-flowering plants to group among shrubs or larger perennials. When in flower *Allium cernuum* varies in height between 15 and 50 cm (6–20 in), with dense drooping umbels of between 20 and 30 cup-shaped flowers, the stamens protruding from their mouths, the colour varying between pale-

OTHER ALLIUMS

NAME	HEIGHT	FLOWERING SEASON	FLOWERS	CULTIVATION ETC.
A. amplectens	10–40 cm (4–16 in)	spring–early summer	white or pale-pink globular heads	best with a summer rest
A. falcifolium	5–10 cm (2–4 in)	spring–early summer	deep rose in heads of 20–30	for a well-drained site, or bulb-frame, or alpine house
A. geyeri	10–50 cm (4–20 in)	summer	pale pink, small stars, in heads of 10-25	slightly tender
A. macranthum	20–45 cm (8–18 in)	summer	deep purple, in a loose umbel	easy
A. paradoxum var. normale	15-30 cm (6-12 in)	spring	white nodding bells	good in heavy soils
A. peninsulare	20-30 cm (8–12 in)	spring–early summer	deep rose, white at base, in wide umbel of 18–20	needs summer rest
A. scorodoprasum ssp. jajlae	25–80 cm (10–32 in)	summer	deep reddish-purple with a dark line outside	the subspecies does not make bulbils among the flowers
A. senescens	7–45 cm (3–18 in)	late summer	pale pink in round umbels	several similar ssps., all easy
A.s. ssp. glaucum (A. spirale)	7–15 cm (3–6 in)	late summer	as A. senescens, but dwarf	easy
A. stellerianum	10–30 cm (4–12 in)	summer	yellowish-white, few, in a globular head	needs good drainage
A. subhirsutum	8-30 cm (3–12 in)	spring–early summer	greenish-white in a loose hemispherical head	for a warm well-drained site
A. triquetrum	15–30 cm (6–12 in)	spring	white, green-striped, in a loose umbel	can become invasive in moist conditions
A. zebdanense	25–40 cm (10–16 in)	late spring	white with a green centre, large, starry	for a dry well-drained site

pink and deep purple. *A. carinatum* ssp. *pulchellum* (*A. pulchellum*) is usually 30–40 cm (12–16 in) high but dwarf forms can sometimes be obtained. The small bell-shaped flowers, constricted at the mouth with their anthers protruding prominently, are in loose, almost globular heads, the pedicels of the upper flowers being upright, those of the lower ones drooping. The flowers are usually deep rosy purple, but there is an excellent and equally prolific pure greenish-white variety. A mixture of the two has been a striking feature of my garden for several years.

Allium thunbergii, from Japan, has become more common recently. It is a beautiful dwarf species suitable for the rock garden or alpine house, especially valuable for its late flowering in autumn. The umbels of flowers on 10 cm (4 in) stems are similar in shape to those of *A. pulchellum* on a smaller scale, and may be very dark reddish-purple or pure white.

Among the yellow-flowered species, the two most common are *Allium flavum* and *A. moly*. *A. flavum* is an excellent plant for a well-drained sunny position; it usually grows to 10–30 cm (4–12 in), the smaller varieties sometimes offered as var. *nanum*. It has quite large loose umbels of bright yellow bells with protruding anthers, and either green leaves or very attractive glaucous blue leaves which enhance its beauty. It seems to be quite slow to increase vegetatively, but self-sows gently. *A. moly* on the other hand has a bad reputation for excessive increase, not deserved in all gardens. It is an attractive species with broad tulip-like leaves and 15–30 cm (6–12 in) stems bearing wide, loose, umbels of comparatively large, bright-yellow, star-shaped flowers.

Most of the white-flowered alliums are too tall for the rock garden but *A. neapolitanum* is usually around 30 cm (12 in) and asssociates well with larger rock plants or perennials. The pure-white starry flowers are borne on long pedicels in loose umbels of up to 30. In a warm spot this increases well from seed and bulbils, and could become a nuisance in a small rock garden. *A. callimischon* is a much smaller plant which flowers late in autumn, when it can be appreciated in spite of its small size and greyish-white colour. The subspecies *haematostictum* differs in having red spots within and in being a little smaller.

AROIDS

These seem to engender mixed feelings in gardeners, who are either fascinated by them or dislike them. They have certainly become more popular, and more readily available recently, mainly as a result of collections in the Middle East and the Himalaya and China. The greatest interest is in *Arisaema*, but I am also including *Arisarum*, and *Arum*, in this group.

Arisaema

These interesting plants have large flattened tubers, completely dormant during winter; they often start into growth very late in spring, with a cluster of striking leaves, from among which arise the flowers. These consist of a large hooded spathe, which is sometimes elongated into a long narrow pointed tip, surrounding the narrow cylidrical spadix, which may have a broad club-like tip, or may be elongated. The tiny flowers are at the lower end of the spadix, and are always hidden by the spathe. They are usually followed by a spike of brightly coloured berries.

The following are some of the species comparatively successful in the open garden, best planted in humus-rich moist soil in partial shade, tolerating more sun in moister situations. Some of them are relatively untried except under glass, where they are easily grown in rich but well-drained compost, with minimal frost protection. They have certainly survived a succession of mild winters, with temperatures down to 20°F (-7°C).

Arisaema candidissima is the best known and perhaps the most satisfactory in the garden of all the species, with its beautiful pink spathes striped longitudinally with white, and its 3-lobed leaves which grow quickly after flowering to become a striking feature in their own right. In my own garden it was planted at the edge of a peat bed shaded by a wall, which is not high enough to keep the sun off for a major part of the summer; here it has grown well for about fifteen years and increased gradually. Plenty of humus and reasonable moisture is evidently more important than shade, and this probably applies to other species also. Its only fault is that growth appears very late in spring or even early summer, and it is only too easy to plant something else on top of it inadvertently.

Arisaema consanguineum is another robust species, up to 1 m (3 ft) high, with remarkable leaves resembling a half-umbrella with radiating 'spokes' of long narrow leaflets. These overtop the spathe, which is green, sometimes tinged brownish, and faintly striped white, curving forward over the spadix and elongated into a very long slender point. A cluster of bright red fruits is produced in late summer. In contrast to this, *Arisaema flavum* does not grow to more than 30 cm (12 in) high, and has smaller flowers with a deep-yellow spathe, the long point of which is turned back on itself. It is said to be very hardy.

Arisaema griffithii has the most reptilian appearance of all the species, with a large three-lobed leaf on a stout stem overtopping the dark, purplish-brown spathe, which broadens out widely around the spadix, and is elongated into a tail which reaches the ground. Unfortunately this remarkable plant is only suitable for the cold greenhouse, except in very mild climates.

Arisaema jacquemontii has a quieter appeal with the leaves divided into several narrow leaflets, and the spathes rising just above them; their colour is the same shade of green but with white stripes, and their points elongated and curved upwards, with the tip of the green spadix protruding slightly from their mouths. Raised from seed collected in the Himalaya, it has proved an easy and floriferous species, which increases well in a shady part of my garden among shrubs.

Arisaema sikokianum is another very striking species, which seems to be reasonably hardy, although it does not increase very freely. It grows to 20–30 cm (8–12 in) high and has broad leaves with three to five lobes, usually below the

60. *Arisaema jacquemontii*

flowers. The spathe is blackish-purple, greenish within and striped faintly with white, with a long upturned point, and a pure white mouth, from which protrudes the white spadix with a white expanded tip.

Arisaema tortuosum is a widespread species in Eastern Asia, and is very variable. It typically has a stout spotted stem with a leaf composed of up to a dozen leaflets, and a pale-green spathe, sometimes suffused with purple, the point short and hooded-over slightly. The green spadix is exceptionally long and protrudes beyond the tip of the spathe and then curves upwards. It seems to be reasonably hardy in the garden.

Arisaema triphyllum, from North America, is very hardy, and an excellent plant for a shady place, as long as the soil is rich in humus. It has spotted stems and leaves with three quite narrow leaflets, from above which a green spathe arises, usually striped with white, and suffused to a greater or lesser degree with purple.

Several other species of *Arisaema* are occasionally available, and are on the border line of hardiness in the garden, but they present no problems in the cold house. *A. amurense* is probably hardy in mild gardens. It is a Japanese species with the spathe striped green and white, curving over the spadix, but with a short point. *A. costatum* is also reasonably hardy and is unusual in having an extremely long thin spadix, which reaches the ground, from the dark purple, white-striped spathe. *A. propinquum* has a spathe of similar colour, which curves over and then down to hide the long purple spadix. The same colour is seen in the spathe of the earlier-flowering *A. ringens*, but the spadix of this species is white. *A. serratum* is also early-flowering, but is a very variable plant, both in height and in flower colour, which may be green or purple, heavily striped with white. *A. speciosum* is a more tender species, which has large leaflets with reddish margins, and a purple spathe faintly striped with white and an elongated 'tail'. The spadix is purple and is also long and tail-like.

Arisarum

Only two species are commonly cultivated. *Arisarum proboscoideum*, the Mouse Plant, is extremely easy to grow in any shady place with adequate moisture, and may indeed be found to have increased excessively if it is moved and the tubers spread around. It forms a low carpet of arrow-shaped leaves, beneath which the long blackish spathes appear, with long tapering points looking exactly like the tails of mice disappearing into the leaves. *A. vulgare* is rarely grown, perhaps because it is more tender, flowering very early and requiring a warm sunny site with minimal moisture in summer if it is to be grown in the open. The leaves are frequently marbled with paler green, and the upright spathes, rising well above the leaves, are brownish with white stripes.

Arum

Most of the true arums are either too large or too freely increasing for the rock garden. *Arum creticum* is such a beautiful plant that I cannot resist including it, although, when growing well, it may be a little large for any but the biggest rock garden. Its large spathes appear in late spring among the plain-green arrow-shaped leaves. They may be white but are usually a good clear yellow, up to 20 cm (8 in) long, with the yellow spadix protruding from the mouth. It seems to be fully hardy.

BRODIAEA GROUP

The genus *Brodiaea* seems to have had a stormy past taxonomically, and although most of the species have been transferred by botanists to *Dichelostemma*, and *Triteleia*, with one or two in *Bloomeria*, many are still listed in catalogues under *Brodiaea*, so it may be helpful to consider them grouped together.

The main botanical features which separate the genera are the stamens, which may be six, as in *Triteleia*, and *Bloomeria*, or three with three staminodes, which do not produce pollen, as in *Brodiaea* and *Dichelostemma*. In *Brodiaea* the umbels are loose, and the leaves lack the distinct keel on the reverse, which is seen in *Dichelostemma*, in which the umbels are also more dense. In the group with six stamens, *Triteleia* and *Bloomeria* have keeled leaves, but may be separated on the presence of a cup at the base of the filament in *Bloomeria*, which is absent in *Triteleia*.

In spite of their nomenclatural problems the four genera contain some good plants which are easily grown in well-drained soil in a sunny spot, and flower when there are few other hardy bulbs contributing to the garden scene.

Brodiaea

The only true *Brodiaea* species that is commonly grown is *B. elegans*, which has large umbels, up to 15 cm (6 in) across, of deep-bluish-purple funnel-shaped flowers on stems up to 30 cm (12 in) or more high. *B. californica* is an even larger species with flowers of variable colour, usually pale to deep lavender, but occasionally pink. *B. coronaria* is uncommon in cultivation, but it is a smaller species more suitable for the rock garden, with a few long purple flowers in each umbel. *B. stellaris* and *B. terrestris* are even smaller, rarely more than 10 cm (4 in) high. The former is unusual in having star-shaped flowers, violet in colour, in a broad umbel. *B. terrestris* has a looser umbel of fewer flowers, which are usually paler in colour.

Bloomeria

Bloomeria crocea is an excellent yellow-flowered species, which is rare in cultivation, its place usually taken by the very similar *Triteleia ixioides*. It is generally about 20–30 cm (8–12 in) high, with a large umbel of deep-yellow starry flowers with a greenish line down the middle of each segment.

Triteleia

There are two yellow-flowered species which are very similar to *Bloomeria crocea* described above, *Triteleia crocea* (*Brodiaea crocea*), and *T. ixioides*. These differ from each other in the arrangement of the stamens, which are in two whorls of three in *T. crocea*. Those of *T. ixioides* are at the same level, and the filaments have two horn-like appendages at their tips. *T. ixioides* is the most commonly grown of the three, and seems to be easy and long-lived in the garden, although it does not increase freely by division. It is easily raised from seed.

There are two white-flowered species. *Triteleia hyacinthina* (*Brodiaea hyacinthina*) is an excellent, easy plant, though a little

61. *Triteleia ixioides*

tall for the rock garden. It can be 15–50 cm high (6–20 in) but in my experience is usually nearer to the latter. It has dense wide umbels of large white flowers with dark green centres on very stiff, narrow stems. It increases freely but without becoming a nuisance. The other white species, *T. peduncularis* is less freely available. It has very large loose umbels of white flowers, often faintly tinged with blue, on unusually long pedicels.

Of the blue-flowered species, the best known and most prolific is *Tritelia laxa* (*Brodiaea laxa*), which grows well and increases freely in full sun or partial shade, even in poor soil, producing large umbels of pale- to deep-blue funnel-shaped flowers around midsummer. The colour is very variable and it should be possible to select a clone with very dark flowers for propagation. *T. bridgesii* is very similar, but differs in the arrangement of stamens: they are at one level in *T. bridgesii*, and at two in *T. laxa*. The hybrid *Triteleia* x *tubergenii* (*T. laxa* x *T. peduncularis*) is very like *T. laxa*, and can be relied on to produce flowers of a good deep blue.

Dichelostemma

Separated from *Brodiaea* as described above, this genus contains two or three *Brodiaea*-like species, and the unique 'Californian Firecracker', *Dichelostemma idamaia*. This can be up to 30 cm (12 in) high with a loose umbel of pendent tubular flowers 2.5cm (1in long), which are deep crimson with green tips. It is a striking plant, but unfortunately it is only hardy in mild areas, or in a cold house.

The commonest of the blue-flowered species is *D. pulchellum* (*Brodiaea capitata*), with compact umbels of lilac-blue flowers with violet bracts. It is hardy in mild gardens, but is more suitable for the bulb-frame elsewhere. *D. multiflorum* and *D. congestum* are similar species with blue flowers in summer.

CALOCHORTUS

Of all the genera of bulbous plants for the rock garden and alpine house few are more fascinating than the beautiful *Calochortus* species. Although not many of them are available from trade sources, even in the USA, many are grown by amateur enthusiasts from seed, as described in Chapter 3, and I am therefore including a reasonable selection of those most likely to be available.

From the gardener's point of view most of the species fall into four groups: the Mariposas, which generally grow in open sites, and are tall species with very slender stems and very large, widely open or slightly cup-shaped flowers; the Globe Flowers, which have pendent globular flowers, and are often plants of light woodland; the Cat's Ears, which are smaller, and have cup-shaped flowers, usually with an abundance of hairs within, and are plants of woodland; and finally the 'Cyclobothra' group, which flower later and keep growing through the summer, with a winter dormancy.

Calochortus are generally grown in a bulb-frame or alpine-house, keeping them dry during their summer dormancy, and they are considered to be difficult or impossible to grow in the garden except in areas with a dry-summer climate. However, there is certainly scope for experiment, as Colonel C.H. Grey grew over 20 species in the south of England for many years, and in my own garden *Calochortus venustus* and *C. uniflorus* flourished for several years in a well-drained rock garden.

The Mariposa Group

These are the largest and most spectacular species, but in some ways are less satisfactory plants for the gardener than for the photographer. They generally have very slender stems and very large flowers, with the result that they tend to 'flop' unless they are supported. In their natural habitat they usually grow in low scrub which supports the stems, and this could be emulated in gardens in suitable climates.

One of the best of the Mariposas is *Calochortus clavatus*, because it has unusually rigid stems which support the large flowers well. These are deep yellow with a reddish-brown zigzag band halfway up the interior, a blotch of similar colour around the gland, and a mass of yellow hairs between. The other yellow-flowered species most commonly grown is *C. luteus*, which has more slender branching stems and bright yellow flowers with an orange gland surrounded by yellow hairs, and very variable markings, usually including various flecks of brown, and often a large or small blotch of the same colour.

Several species have a base colour of white or cream, and varying blotches and other markings within. *Calochortus venustus* is one of the easiest of these to grow. It is a very variable plant: it can be in shades of lilac or pink to deep reddish-brown, but is most often white or cream, with a conspicuous reddish-brown blotch above the rounded gland, which is also surrounded by reddish streaks. *C. vestae* is very similar, differing mainly in the shape of the gland, which is elongated horizontally. *C. bruneaunis* and *C. nuttallii* are also similar in colouring, but have smaller, more cup-shaped flowers, with yellow hairs in the centre, and a reddish or orange gland, and a band of dark reddish-brown above it. In *C. nuttallii* there is often a small dark brown blotch.

Calochortus superbus can have large flowers of similar colouring, but may be yellow or lavender. It has an inverted V-shaped gland. *C. gunnisonii* is one of the most striking species and, like *C. superbus*, can have white or deep-lavender flowers. In white-flowered forms I have seen in nature, the gland has been white, surrounded by green hairs, with a narrow dark-brown band outside them. In a beautiful lavender-flowered plant that I grew for many years, the hairs were orange and there was a pale-violet blotch at the base of each segment.

Other lavender-flowered species are *Calochortus splendens* and *C. macrocarpus*. The latter has very large, shallowly cup-shaped flowers of deep lavender colour with a greenish stripe down the centre of each segment and a purple band above the arrow-shaped gland. *C. splendens* is similar, but with a small circular gland, and it may be almost unmarked or have a basal purple blotch.

The fabulous *C. kennedyi* is a desert plant, with deep-scarlet flowers (occasionally yellow or orange), which is coveted by every grower. Seed is sometimes on offer, but it seems to be almost impossible to grow in areas without a hot dry summer, even under glass.

62. *Calochortus pulchellus*

The Globe flowers

These beautiful plants have several pendulous flowers to a stem, globular in shape and fringed with hairs. They flower earlier than the Mariposas, and usually make better pot or frame plants, as they have stems capable of supporting the flowers. *Calochortus albus* grows to about 20 cm (8 in), or sometimes taller, and has several pure white flowers. These may be faintly tinged with pink, or in var. *rubellus* may be uniformly deep pink. Some growers have succeeded in the open garden with *C. albus*.

Calochortus amabilis and C. pulchellus are similar in habit to C. albus, but the flowers and their hairs are deep yellow. In C. pulchellus the flowers are larger and there are hairs within the inner segments as well as fringing them. C. amoenus is perhaps the most exquisite of all the species, smaller-growing, with several globular flowers, their large inner segments deep rose, and the smaller pointed inner segments pale pinkish-grey.

The Cat's Ear group

Here I have included four species, two of them characterized by their abundant hairs inside the segments, which have given them their common name, and two by their small size and similar woodland habitat. They grow only to about 15 cm (6 in) or less, flower early, and make beautiful pan plants, quite easy to grow, requiring less 'drying off' in summer. The two typical Cat's Ears are the exquisite *Calochortus monophyllus*, and *C. coeruleus* (*C. maweanus*). *C. monophyllus* has shallowly cup-shaped flowers with narrow, pointed pale-yellow outer segments, and very broad deep-yellow inner segments, entirely covered inside with long yellow hairs, hidden among which is a small purple blotch above the gland. *C. coeruleus* is similar in habit but the flowers and the abundant hairs are white with a faint tinge

Fig. 34. *Calochortus monophyllus*

of palest violet, and there is a deeper violet area around the gland.

Calochortus nudus and C. uniflorus are similar in habit to the two described, but the flowers of C. nudus are small, pale lavender, or occasionally white, and almost hairless and unmarked. C. uniflorus is one of the easiest species to grow, even in the open garden. The flowers, several to a stem, are pale lavender with a darker blotch above the gland, and only a sprinkling of hairs.

The Cyclobothra group

These plants, which flower later and are winter-dormant, are most often represented by *Calochortus barbatus* (*Cyclobothra lutea*), an easy plant which will grow in the open in well-drained soil, or makes a good pan plant. It is usually about 20 cm (8 in) high, with several nodding cup-shaped flowers on branching stems. The flowers are variable, but those which I have grown have deep-yellow flowers with yellow hairs within, the small outer segments stained with green. *C. weeedyi* is occasionally grown. It is very different in habit from *C. barbatus*, having larger upright deep-yellow flowers. These have abundant yellow hairs within, and are uniformly flecked with small brown spots.

Fig. 35. Calochortus barbatus

RHODOHYPOXIS

These South African bulbs make up for their small size by flowering so freely and over such a long period that they can produce a colourful display, either as pot plants, or in the garden where winters are not too cold. They grow best in a humus-rich soil, and if this is well-drained and they can be kept reasonably dry in winter, they seem to be hardy to about -10°C (14°F), or even lower. Although some growers have been successful with them in the open garden in mild areas, they seem to do better generally in a frame, or in pots in a cold greenhouse, where they can be kept dry during winter.

Although originally only the pink-flowered *Rhodohypoxis baurii*, and its white-flowered variety *platypetala*, were introduced, a very large range of hybrids and selections is now available, together with two or three additional species. *R. baurii* has clusters of narrow, lanceolate, grey-green hairy leaves up to 10 cm (4 in) long, and deep-purplish-pink flowers up to 3 cm (1¼ in) across. Var. *platypetala* is usually a little more vigorous with slightly larger white flowers. The less common var. *confecta* has even larger white or pale-pink flowers.

Rhodohypoxis milloides is a more recent introduction, hardier and easily grown in the garden. It is a little taller than other species with deep-green, less hairy leaves and dark reddish-purple flowers, not always produced with the freedom of *R. baurii*.

A large number of cultivars appear in catalogues, and they are generally excellent vigorous plants with large flowers. Some of them closely resemble each other, and distinguishing between them is complicated by the fact that the colours vary with growing conditions, and especially with the weather, bright sunlight over a long period fading them considerably. I have described some of the most readily available and distinct in the table opposite.

An interesting hybrid between *Rhodohypoxis baurii* and *Hypoxis parvula* has recently become more readily available, and is an excellent small bulb for the alpine house. It has longer and broader leaves than *R. baurii*, and a taller flower stem; the flowers have a different appearance, because the inner segments are not turned in as they are in *Rhodohypoxis*, so that the stamens are visible. The flowers may be pink, but the the form usually seen is white with conspicuous yellow stamens. *Hypoxis parvula* itself is similar to the hybrid with leaves 1 cm (½ in) wide and up to 10 cm (4 in) long, and white flowers with greenish backs, and yellow stamens.

LILIES

It is a moot point whether lilies should be included in a book on bulbs for the rock garden, but there are several irresistible small shade-loving species, suitable for the peat bed or a shady pocket well-enriched with leaf-mould. They all grow much better in a damp climate with cool summers than in my own garden, in

RHODOHYPOXIS CULTIVARS

NAME	COLOUR	FLOWER DIAMETER	COMMENTS
'Albrighton'	purplish-red	3–3.5 cm (1¼–1½ in)	very similar to 'Douglas'
'Apple Blossom'	very pale pink with deeper centre	2.5 cm (1 in)	a good small cultivar
'Douglas'	purplish-red	3 cm (1¼ in)	very similar to 'Albrighton'
'Dawn'	white, flushed pink	3.5 cm (1½ in)	
'Eva Kate'	purplish-red	3 cm (1¼ in)	good vigorous cultivar
'Fred Broome'	deep pink, paler in the centre	3.5 cm (1½ in)	excellent vigorous cultivar
'Great Scott'	purplish-red	3 cm (1¼ in)	
'Harlequin'	white with pink margin and flush	3 cm (1¼ in)	
'Helen'	white tinged pink	3.5 cm (1½ in)	
'Margaret Rose'	pale pink, darker at margins	2.5 cm (1 in)	Good vigorous cultivar
'Perle'	deep pink	3 cm (1¼ in)	similar to 'Fred Broome' but smaller
'Pictus'	white with pink flush	3.5–4 cm (1½ in)	one of the best with very large flowers
'Ruth'	white tinged pink at margins	3–3.5 cm (1¼–1½ in)	paler than *Pictus*
'Stella'	deep pink	3–3.5 cm (1¼–1½ in)	similar to 'Fred Broome'
'Tetra Red'	purplish-red	3.5–4 cm (1½ in)	vigorous but variable
'Tetra White'	white with faint pink flush	4 cm (1½ in)	vigorous but variable

which many have eventually died of drought in the recent series of dry summers. Most of the sun-loving lilies are a little tall, and the enthusiast should consult specialist books for guidance on these.

The most exciting of the shade-lovers is *Lilium mackliniae*, a remarkable fairly recent introduction, which is very easily raised from seed, and thrives in moist shade in rich soil. Its height and number of flowers depends very much on growing conditions, from one or two flowers on 20 cm (8 in) leafy stems, to 10 on stems of 60 cm (2 ft), or more. The flowers are large broad pendent bells, the segments recurving a little at their tips, pale pink, or white faintly suffused with pinkish-violet, darker at the base and sometimes at the tips. It often appears to be short-lived, but this may be the effect of drought or of virus disease, to which it is particularly susceptible. Regular raising from seed is the answer.

Lilium nanum is a somewhat similar plant, equally beautiful but more difficult to grow, at least in dry areas. It is generally up to 30 cm (12 in) high, with solitary flowers, which are similar in size to those of *L. mackliniae*, but more funnel-shaped, the segments pale greyish-violet, green at the base and with a central pale-green line. Like *L. mackliniae* it will often flower within three years from seed, and enjoys similar growing conditions.

Lilium formosanum var. *pricei* is an easily grown, but short-lived, dwarf lily, small enough for the rock garden, which will flower within two years from seed, in a shady place with plenty of humus in the soil. It has trumpet flowers, remarkably large for the height of stem, which is rarely more than 30–40 cm (12–16 in). The flowers are white, with green in the throat, and a broad band of violet along the exterior of each of its strongly recurving segments.

Another most attractive lily for similar conditions is *Lilium duchartrei* which, in my own dry garden, has been small enough for the rock garden, spreading quite freely by stolons, producing one or two beautiful white 'Turks-cap' flowers with fully recurved segments, heavily spotted with violet towards the base, on 30–40 cm (12–16 in) stems. This describes the plant grown in far-from-ideal conditions, and in a cooler climate in rich soil it can attain twice the height and have up to 12 flowers to a stem. It then resembles *Lilium lankongense*, which is another glorious but taller lily with similar colouring.

OTHER GENERA

There is a number of other genera of summer-flowering bulbous plants, mainly from South Africa and South America, which are less hardy than those described previously, but can be grown in the garden in mild areas that experience only a few degrees of frost: these make excellent pan plants for the cold greenhouse with sufficient heat to maintain temperatures above -2°C (28°F) in colder climates. Among them are a few species which have proved hardy over a succession of mild winters, with occasional temperatures down to -8°C (21°F), and I suspect that with more trial in the garden the number found to be 'growable' in the open would increase.

African species

Eucomis

These are becoming increasingly popular, as more gardeners discover their hardiness, and their unusual appearance can add a touch of 'tropical' exuberance in late summer and autumn to the larger rock garden, patio pots, or to warm borders in full sun, in well-drained soil. The most widely grown and most colourful is *Eucomis comosa*, which has a large rosette of broad lanceolate leaves, which may be faintly or strongly tinged with purple, and thick upright purple-spotted stems with abundant white starry flowers up to 2.5 cm (1 in) across, sometimes tinged purple, and with a purple ovary prominent in the centre. Above the flowers is a further cluster of leaves, hence the common name of 'Pineapple Plant'. In good conditions with plenty of moisture in summer *E. comosa* can be too large for the rock garden, and two other species, *E. autumnale* and *E. zambesiaca*, may be more suitable. The former has broad wavy-edged leaves and stems to 30 cm (12 in), with greenish-white flowers; and *E. zambesiaca* has smaller leaves and similar flowers on a shorter spike, making it more suitable for smaller gardens.

Moraea

This fascinating genus of iridaceous plants from Africa barely comes within the scope of this book, as the only fully hardy species, *M. spathulata*, is too large for any but the biggest rock garden. Its tough leaves grow up to 1 m (3 ft) long, and the flower stems are of similar height, with a succession of large, deep-yellow iris-like flowers in summer. *M. stricta* should survive in an unheated house. It has one narrow basal leaf, and several flowers on a branching 10 cm (4 in) stem, lavender-blue with a yellow centre, each up to 2.5 cm (1 in) across. This is much more typical of the many species to be found in the wild, most of which have very beautiful flowers, often with blotches on the petals of a contrasting colour. Very few of them are in cultivation, although they are fairly easy to raise from seed. They have not been widely grown, and there is abundant scope for experiment by any enthusiast with a minimally heated greenhouse or a very mild climate.

Tulbaghia

This genus is not usually considered suitable for the garden, but experience suggests that they are considerably hardier than most catalogues and books suggest. The commonest, and probably hardiest species, *Tulbaghia violacea*, its pale variety *pallida*, and the very similar *T. cepacea* (which is sometimes included in *T. violacea*), have survived completely unscathed through four or five winters in my own garden, with temperatures falling to -8°C (20°F) on many occasions. They should be grown in a sheltered sunny bed in well-drained soil, and are suitable for the large rock garden, bearing in

mind that they form a considerable clump of long glaucous leaves which can overpower small neighbours. These three plants have attractive bluish-green leaves up to 30 cm (12 in) long and one-sided umbels of small, pale-violet flowers, with long tubes and open starry lobes, on stems 20–60 cm (8–24 in) long. The flowers first appear in early summer but usually continue intermittently until autumn. Var. *pallida* is similar but the flowers are white, faintly tinged with palest violet. There is a most attractive variegated form of *T. violacea*, with the leaves longitudinally striped white and blue-green, which seems equally hardy. *T. cepacea* is very similar to *T. violacea*, but a little shorter and with smaller flowers.

There are a few smaller species, more suitable for the rock garden or alpine house. *Tulbaghia natalense* has proved

63. *Moraea spathulata*

hardy for many years. It forms a cluster of linear green leaves up to 15 cm (6 in) long, and has clusters of small white long-tubed flowers with yellow centres on 15 cm (6 in) stems. A more recent introduction is *T. comminsii*, which has grey-green linear leaves and stems to 20 cm (8 in), bearing umbels of up to eight flowers with pale-purple tubes and white lobes, reflexing slightly at the tips. This is an excellent, very long-flowering plant for the unheated alpine house, but has not been adequately tried in the garden.

Anomatheca

This is a small genus of which one or two species are remarkably hardy, *A. laxa* being the most useful. It has suffered from name changes in the past, alternating between *Lapeyrousia* and *Anomatheca*, and between *cruenta* and *laxa*. It is a delightful little plant, usually 15–20 cm (6–8 in) high, with a flat fan of basal leaves and a wiry stem bearing several long-tubed flowers with lobes opening flat, deep pinkish-red with dark markings on the lower segments, opening successively over a long period, during mid- to late summer. There is an excellent pure-white form, which has been seeding about in the gravel plunge of

Fig. 36. *Anomatheca laxa*

my alpine house for years. In the open garden they are hardy to -5°C (23°F), or possibly lower, in a sunny place in well-drained soil. There is also a blue-flowered subspecies *azurea*, which I have not yet grown.

Anomatheca viridia is a spring-flowering species, a little taller, with small, deep-green, narrow-petalled flowers with a tinge of red in the throat. It increases freely and seems to be hardy in an unheated alpine house, but is perhaps more curious than beautiful.

Polyxena

This is another small South African genus, of which *Polyxena pygmaea* (*P. ensifolia*), has recently appeared in a few collections, and has proved hardy in an unheated house, certainly to -2°C, (27°F) in our recent mild winters. It flowers so late into autumn that in spite of its small size it is worth growing. It forms a basal cluster of 3–4 dark-green glossy incurved leaves, up to 10 cm (4 in) long, and usually has solitary flowers, on very short stems, up to 2.5 cm (1 in) wide, with recurving segments, which are white with a faint tinge of palest violet, and a median stripe of the same colour.

South American species

Habranthus

These are closely allied to *Zephyranthes*, discussed in Chapter 4 (page 47). They differ in having flowers with unequal stamens, held a little above the horizontal, whereas in *Zephyranthes* the flowers are upright with stamens of equal length. There are a few delightful species in this genus which are well worth trying in a warm border in well-drained soil. The commonest is *Habranthus tubispathus* (*H. andersonii*, *Zephyranthes andersonii*), most commonly known under one of its synonyms. It has flower stems from 10 to

20 cm (4–8 in), bearing solitary coppery-orange funnel-shaped flowers over a long period in summer and autumn, which rapidly develop seed capsules, from which plants can easily and quickly be raised. *H. texana* is very similar, but possibly a little smaller.

Habranthus martinezii is a species which I have found equally hardy and easy in a sheltered border. It is a beautiful plant with flowers similar to those of *H. tubispathus* but a delightful shade of pale pink, deepening towards the throat, and generally flowering later. *H. robustus* is even more striking with flowers that are deeper pink and much larger, at least 5 cm (2 in) long. I have not yet tested this in the garden, but it is said to be hardy outside in very mild areas.

Rhodophiala (Hippeastrum)

Plant-hunting trips to the Andes, notably by John Watson and companions in the 1970s and '80s, and in the last few years, have reawakened interest in South American bulbs, especially in the genus *Rhodophiala*, in which most of the smaller hippeastrums have now been placed. Experimentation with the earlier collections of these spectacular bulbs showed that some at least were very hardy, my own experience being that *R. advena*, then known as *Hippeastrum advenum*, was hardy in the rock garden during average winters to -10°C (14°F), although it eventually succumbed in the open to an exceptional winter as low as -18°C (0°F). They seem to set seed freely, and are easily raised from seed if it is sown in bottom heat and the plants kept growing without a drying-off period until they attain flowering size. Perhaps stocks can be built up sufficiently for all the species to be tried in the open, at least where temperatures do not fall much below -5°C (23°F). *R. advena* has narrow glossy leaves to 15 cm (6 in) long, and 1–4 typical trumpet-shaped flowers, borne horizontally, on stems to 20 cm (8 in). The flowers may be bright scarlet, yellow, or pink, the latter often with some yellow streaking, up to 5 cm (2 in) long, at or soon after mid-summer. *R. elwesii* is very similar, but usually has two flowers, which are yellow, sometimes with a red throat. *R. pratense* has been in cultivation for a long time, and is considered reasonably hardy. It is a more robust, taller plant with up to five ascending or horizontal deep-red flowers.

Other species which have been introduced recently are *R. andicola*, with solitary deep-violet, erect flowers on a 20 cm (8 in) scape, *R. bagnoldii* with several yellow flowers, mainly ascending on a 30 cm (12 in) scape, and *R. rhodolirion*, a taller plant with large solitary flowers, which may be deep-pink or white, with reddish veining. The Andes have become a popular destination for seed collectors, and many new rhodophialas and other exciting bulbs are likely to become available to gardeners over the next few years.

64. *Rhodophiala advena*

Bulbs with the Award of Garden Merit

The highest award made to plants for the garden is the Award of Garden Merit of the Royal Horticultural Society. It is given to plants that are readily available and of outstanding merit for general garden use, and includes some plants suitable for the alpine house. They are rated for hardiness: 1 for plants requiring heat; 2 for plants requiring an unheated greenhouse; 3 for plants hardy in some areas; and 4 for plants that are fully hardy in Britain. The table below includes the bulbous plants which have recently been confirmed as worthy of the award. All are H4 unless stated.

Allium beesianum
Allium caeruleum
Allium cernuum
Allium christophii
Allium cyaneum
Allium flavum
Allium karatviense
Allium moly
Allium insubricum (narcissiflorum)
Allium oreophilum 'Zwanenberg'
Allium pulchellum
Anemone blanda
Anemone blanda 'Atrocoerulea'
Anemone blanda 'Radar'
Anemone blanda var. rosea
Anemone blanda 'White Splendour'
Anemone nemorosa
Anemone nemorosa 'Allenii'
Anemone nemorosa 'Leeds Variety'
Anemone nemorosa 'Robinsoniana'
Anemone nemorosa 'Vestal'
Anemone ranunculoides
Chionodoxa gigantea
Chionodoxa luciliae hort. (C. forbesii)
Chionodoxa sardensis
Colchicum agrippinum
Colchicum 'Autumn Queen'
Colchicum byzantinum
Colchicum speciosum
Colchicum speciosum 'Album'
Corydalis cava
Corydalis malkensis (caucasica 'Alba')

Corydalis solida
Corydalis solida 'Beth Evans'
Corydalis solida 'George Baker'
Crocus angustifolius
Crocus banaticus
Crocus boryi H2/3
Crocus cartwrightianus H2/3
Crocus chrysanthus
Crocus chrysanthus 'Blue Pearl'
Crocus chrysanthus 'Cream Beauty'
Crocus chrysanthus 'E.A.Bowles'
Crocus chrysanthus 'Ladykiller'
Crocus chrysanthus 'Snow Bunting'
Crocus chrysanthus 'Zwanenberg Bronze'
Crocus corsicus
Crocus etruscus
Crocus flavus ssp. flavus
Crocus goulimyi
Crocus imperati
Crocus kotschyanus
Crocus malyi H2/4
Crocus medius
Crocus pulchellus
Crocus robertianus H2/3
Crocus sieberi
Crocus sieberi f. tricolor
Crocus sieberi 'Hubert Edelsten'
Crocus speciosus
Crocus × stellaris 'Golden Yellow' (Dutch Yellow)
Crocus tommasinianus
Crocus tournefortii
Cyclamen cilicium H2/4
Cyclamen coum

Cyclamen coum Pewter Group
Cyclamen hederifolium
Cyclamen libanoticum H2/4
Cyclamen mirabile H2/3
Cyclamen pseudibericum H2/3
Cyclamen purpurascens
Cyclamen repandum ssp. repandum
Cyclamen repandum ssp. peloponnesiacum H2/3
Cyclamen trochopteranthum H2/3
Erythronium dens-canis
Erythronium 'Pagoda'
Erythronium revolutum
Erythronium tuolumnense
Erythronium 'White Beauty'
Fritillaria acmopetala
Fritillaria meleagris
Fritillaria meleagris 'Alba'
Fritillaria michaelovskii
Fritillaria pallidiflora
Fritillaria pyrenaica
Galanthus 'Atkisii'
Galanthus caucasicus
Galanthus elwesii
Galanthus ikariae ssp. ikariae
Galanthus 'Magnet'
Galanthus nivalis
Galanthus nivalis 'Flore Pleno'
Galanthus plicatus (incl. ssp. byzantinus)
Galanthus reginae-olgae H2/4
Galanthus 'S. Arnott'
Ipheion uniflorum 'Froyle Mill'
Ipheion 'Rolf Fiedler' H2/3
Ipheion uniflorum 'Wisley Blue'
Leucojum autumnale

Leucojum nicaense H⅔
Leucojum vernum
Muscari armeniacum
Muscari azureum (Pseudomuscari azurea)
Muscari pseudomuscari (chalusicum)
Muscari tubergenianum
Narcissus cyclamineus

Narcissus 'Tete-a-Tete'
Rhodohypoxis baurii
Scilla bifolia
Scilla mischtschenkoana (tubergeniana)
Scilla sibirica
Tecophilea cyanocrocus H2
Tecophilea cyanocrocus 'Leichtlinii' H2

Trillium chloropetalum (T. sessile 'Rubrum' hort.)
Trillium erectum
Trillium grandiflorum
Trillium grandiflorum 'Florepleno'
Trillium luteum
Trillium rivale

APPENDIX 2

Societies and further reading

The specialist societies have excellent publications full of information about bulbous plants, and in most instances carrying advertisements of nurseries and seed collectors. The Botanical Society of South Africa at Kirstenbosch Botanic Garden provides an annual seed list, mainly devoted to native plants, as well as a regular publication, Veld & Flora.

Alpine Garden Society,
AGS Centre,
Avon Bank,
Pershore,
Worcs,
WR10 3JP,
UK.

Scottish Rock Garden Club,
Groom's Cottage,
Kirklands,
Ancrum,
Jedburgh
TD8 6UJ,
UK.

North American Rock Garden Society,
PO Box 67,
Millwood,
NY 10546,
USA

Botanical Society of South Africa,
Kirstenbosch,
Claremont 7735,
South Africa.

Further reading

Alpine Garden Society, *Encyclopaedia of Alpines* (1993). Includes small hardy bulbs.

Blanchard, John, *Narcissus* (1990). Alpine Garden Society.

Bryan, John, *Bulbs* (1989). Helm, now Batsford/Timber Press. Two volumes including information on tender and rare bulbs.

Davies, Dilys, *Alliums* (1992). Batsford.

Grey-Wilson, Christopher, *The Genus Cyclamen* (1988). Helm, now Batsford/Timber Press.

Grey-Wilson, Christopher and Mathew, Brian, *Bulbs* (1981).
Comprehensive on European Bulbs.

Harkness, *Seedlist Handbook* (1993). Batsford/Timber Press. A useful guide to plants available as seed.

Mathew, Brian, *The Smaller Bulbs* (1987). Batsford.

Mathew, Brian, *The Year-round Bulb Garden* (1980). Souvenir Press.

Mathew, Brian, *The Iris* (1989). Batsford.

Mathew, Brian, *The Crocus* (1982). Batsford.

Mathew, Brian and Baytop, Turhan, *The Bulbous Plants of Turkey* (1984). Batsford.

Phillips, Roger and Rix, Martyn, *Bulbs* (1989). Pan. Excellent illustrations.

Wells, James, *Modern Miniature Daffodils* (1989). Batsford.